Contents

Foreword

Victoria Street, London, contains two outstanding buildings. At one end is the Houses of Parliament and at the other end is Westminster Cathedral (fig. 1). The Houses of Parliament is the more familiar of the two. It was designed around 1835 and is a prominent example of Gothic Revival. Westminster Cathedral was built much later at the end of the century and is an example of the Byzantine Revival. The springs of the Gothic Revival are well known. They derive from a Romantic passion for the Middle Ages – a passion that inspired so many architects and builders in the nineteenth century – and they derive, too, from a more general preoccupation with the roots of British history. The motives for the Byzantine Revival are much less well known and often misunderstood. They were equally Romantic, equally fired by the desire to imaginatively recreate a set of ancient values, and equally involved with defining the present against the past. But they are much less British and much less linked to local building traditions. So, if we turn away from the encrusted surfaces and the pointed arches of the Palace of Westminster and walk for ten minutes down Victoria Street, Westminster Cathedral, the seat of the Roman Catholic Archbishop, appears on our left. The contrast with the buildings around Parliament Square could hardly be greater. Here we have oriental domes; here are smooth stone walls pierced with round-arched windows and crossed with horizontal layers of red and white. The models for Westminster Cathedral are much older than those that inspired the Houses of Parliament. They were drawn from the Byzantine churches of Ravenna, from the Doge's chapel of San Marco, Venice, and the great temple of Hagia Sophia in what used to be called Constantinople. They are also more exotic than the models for the Gothic Revival and their translation into the vocabulary of nineteenth-century culture – the Byzantine Revival – is the subject of this book.

Interest in Byzantium never took root in the West in quite the same way as the passion for Gothic, but the history of its rediscovery is colourful, enigmatic and paradoxical. During the nineteenth and early twentieth centuries many writers, painters, architects, churchmen, scholars and patrons turned to Byzantium for many reasons: in response to the current aesthetic and political climate, as the result of theological debates, and as the result of personal whim.

It is well known how in AD 330 the Emperor Constantine I, in an attempt to strengthen the Roman Empire, moved its centre from Rome to the ancient Greek colony of Byzantium on the European side of the Bosphorus, soon to be renamed Constantinople. Constantine's toleration of Christianity and his eventual position as the first Christian emperor established this as the religion which superseded all others. Upon the death of Emperor Theodosius I in 395, the empire was divided between his sons, and the abolition of the power of the last western emperor in Italy in 476 marked the demise of its western half. The eastern half continued as the Byzantine Empire, presided over by Constantinople. The Byzantines continued to think of themselves as Roman till the final fall of the empire, though by the sixth century their language was Greek, and their art and culture were a mixture of Greek and Roman traditions. Justinian (reigned 527–65), with his famous wife Theodora at his side, was one of the most vigorous of Byzantine rulers, and he expanded his territory by reconquests in the eastern Mediterranean, North Africa in the south and Italy in the west.

1 J.F. Bentley, Westminster Cathedral, London, 1895–1903

If the Byzantine historian Procopius of Caesarea is to be believed, Justinian's building programme was extensive, and he covered his enormous empire with monuments that became first the envy of and then the model for subsequent generations. New works in Athens, Trebizond and the spectacular mosaics of Ravenna were built in his reign, and Justinian's face together with that of his wife still arrests the visitor to San Vitale (fig. 2). Most prominent, of course, was the huge domed church of Hagia Sophia (fig. 15), which rapidly became one of the wonders of the world. Orthodox Christianity, unlike the more unified version of Roman Christianity, was persistently divided by heresies and differences that derived from local ethnic hostilities. The disunity of the Byzantine Empire was further increased by the threat of Arab invasions following the death of Muhammad in 632; and between 717 and 741 it was torn by the Iconoclastic Controversy, during which time various emperors tried to eliminate the veneration of icons. Leo III gave tempered support to the movement from 736 onwards, after which the destruction of works of art and persecution of the monastic clergy intensified. (After a series of reversals in official policy icons were definitively restored to their places of worship in 843.) The reign of Constantine VI (780–97) brought prosperity to the empire as a whole, and his work was much admired by his contemporary Charlemagne, who was crowned

2 Justinian with Bishop Maximian, clergy, courtiers and soldiers, c.546. Mosaic. San Vitale, Ravenna

Emperor of the Romans in 800. Charlemagne's Palatine Chapel at Aachen (Aix-la-Chapelle) was explicitly modelled on Justinian's church of San Vitale in Ravenna.

During this period, the Eastern Orthodox Church was strengthened by missions among the Russians, Bulgars and Slavs, thus taking the iconic tradition of Byzantine, as opposed to Catholic, art to these groups; and although the empire was pruned of some of its territory, the economy gained in strength. From 867 there was a general cultural resurgence under Basil I, but a return to internal civil disputes gave opportunities to enemies such as the Normans and the Seljuk Turks who began to exert a stranglehold on the empire. The Fourth Crusade, launched in 1202 and spearheaded by Venice, was a turning point in the history of Byzantium. The city was sacked in 1204 and its wealth carried off – much of it to Venice. The result was that by 1261, under the Palaeologan dynasty, Byzantium was little more than a city-state besieged on all sides. During this period Byzantine artists and builders travelled overseas, taking with them not only their expertise but also their special style of round-arched building. San Marco in Venice, for example, was built with Byzantine assistance and the Norman churches and palaces of Palermo, Monreale and Cefalù in Sicily were decorated with Byzantine help, but are assumed to have been constructed by local craftsmen in a richly eclectic mix of Islamic, Norman French and local styles and techniques. In the fourteenth century the Ottoman Turks became the principal enemy and they began their siege of Constantinople. This was a protracted affair because the city was in a nearly impregnable strategic position, but Constantinople, and with it the remnants of the Byzantine Empire, finally fell in 1453.

But why did Byzantium need reviving, since the basilicas of Rome, the mosaics of Ravenna and Venice and the church of Hagia Sophia all remained standing and were available for all to see? The answer to this is not easy to find, except to say that like the Middle Ages, ancient Greece and the culture of Egypt, the art and life of Byzantium went through a long period of neglect when it no longer appealed to the imagination. Some interest in Byzantium was maintained by Renaissance curiosity about ancient Greece, since it was in Constantinople that the Classical heritage had been largely preserved, and there were minor revivals, especially in Venice and Florence. But it was not until the middle of the seventeenth century that Byzantine studies really flourished. Scholars like Charles du Fresne and Giovanni Ciampini were passionate collectors of Byzantine archives and manuscripts, and under Louis XIII and Louis XIV the printing house of the Louvre began to publish a great series of works by the original historians of Byzantium.

Eighteenth-century rationalism reversed this trend, since there was almost nothing in the Byzantine world which appealed to the cool Neoclassicism of this period. Its religious scepticism despised the whole history of the Middle Ages, but special contempt was reserved for the conservative and religiously minded Byzantine Empire. Its history was merely 'a worthless collection of orations and miracles' (Voltaire), 'a tissue of rebellious insurrections and treachery' (Montesquieu), and for Gibbon its people represented a 'dead uniformity of abject vices'. Gibbon's account of Byzantine superstition and corruption in his *Decline and Fall of the Roman Empire* (1776–88) was particularly influential. It cast a long shadow over the nineteenth century and Gibbon's authority was a serious obstacle to any sympathetic understanding of Byzantine art, architecture or culture.

The reversal of Enlightenment views about Byzantium came at different times, in different places and for different reasons. Broadly, however, its causes were similar to those that lay behind the new interest in the Middle Ages some fifty years before. While architecture played a major role in both the Gothic and Byzantine Revivals, and continued to be of central importance to both, literature was much more important in the Gothic Revival. Both, however, were stimulated by the kind of nationalism that prompted exploration of the origins of local styles and cultures; both provided stylistic alternatives to prevailing orthodoxies; and both provided ways of defining the present in terms of the past. But one major difference was that Byzantium, with its Greek roots, its Roman imperial traditions and its Eastern affiliations, was more exotic and remote than the Gothic. Whereas the Gothic was 'Christian' through and through, Byzantium and Byzantine art were perceived as regressively primitive and childlike. Furthermore they carried associations with modern Greece, Russia and the Balkans, all of which were despised as uncultured and undeveloped by many people in the nineteenth century. Although Byzantium was the cradle of the most primitive and 'pure' forms of Christianity, it also carried within it the seeds of excess, decadence and depravity.

When the curious began to ask the question 'What kind of art and culture lay between the collapse of the Roman Empire and the flowering of the Middle Ages?', they encountered considerable uncertainty and much ignorance. Indeed, the idea of what exactly constituted Byzantine work was extremely vague. In the 1820s the Germans thought that early German painting derived from Byzantium and that many of the churches built by Charlemagne's Ottonian successors in the Rhineland were also Byzantine; the French used the term 'Byzantine' to describe what we would now call the Romanesque building of the southwest; and in Britain round-arched Saxon and Norman churches were collectively denominated 'Byzantine'. This tendency to call anything round-arched that was neither Roman nor Gothic 'Byzantine' led to great confusion, and it was only when a larger number of the buildings of Greece and Asia Minor as well as Constantinople were excavated, drawn and documented that a clearer picture of the divisions between Byzantine, Ottonian, Romanesque and Norman work emerged. The tentative revival of a round-arched style based on these forms, called simply *Rundbogenstil*, was championed in the writings of the architectural theorist Heinrich Hübsch and first took material form in buildings like Friedrich von Gärtner's Ludwigkirche in Munich, begun in 1829. *Rundbogenstil* was adopted by many Bavarian and Prussian architects in the second quarter of the nineteenth century not so much as an attempt at archaeological accuracy as an endeavour to echo something of the native German traditions of building. *Rundbogenstil* was neither Byzantine nor Romanesque but a generalized form of both, and its principal characteristic was that, in its unadorned simplicity, it was not Gothic. German experiments with round-arched building seemed very adventurous in the mid-nineteenth century when the Gothic Revival was the prevailing orthodoxy. Their influence spread across Europe and into America where, in the hands of such creative talents as H.H. Richardson, it appeared for a while that *Rundbogenstil* or Romanesque might become established as the principal style for the American people. Its simple dignity provided an attractive foil to the excesses of nineteenth-century Gothic and provided, too, a significant trigger for the development of a more focused interest in the domed structures of Byzantium. For the sake of clarity and brevity I have only summarized that important *Rundbogenstil* prelude to the Byzantine revival when Romanesque, Norman and the other styles were identified as 'Byzantine'.[1] The major part of my discussion instead concentrates on the way in which Byzantinism as developed in Constantinople, with its domical buildings, its stilted arches and often lavish deployment of marble and mosaic, all impinged upon the West.

In this purer form, the Byzantine Revival really begins only in the latter part of the nineteenth century. By the 1860s the taste for Gothic was becoming jaded and there was a demand for fresh sources of inspiration. Members of the international Arts and Crafts movement looked beyond Western Europe and came, as W.B. Yeats later put it, to the 'holy city of Byzantium'. Mosaic, with its permanence and its need for skilful application, appealed strongly to this group, as did the guild system of co-operation between architect and workman. Throughout Europe, however, the choice of neo-Byzantine murals and neo-Byzantine architecture was closely caught up with political and theological issues; in America theology played a less important role in the adoption of the Byzantine style, and one of its attractions was that it appeared less bound up with European history than some other possible stylistic choices.

Introduction

Perhaps the best-known tributes to Byzantium in modern literature occur in two poems by W.B. Yeats, 'Sailing to Byzantium' and 'Byzantium'. It is with Yeats that the story of the Byzantine Revival begins and ends since, albeit in a highly compressed way, these poems bring together many of myths that had grown up around Byzantium during the previous hundred years. 'Sailing to Byzantium' and 'Byzantium' were written four years apart. The first was begun in 1925 and completed in 1926, and the second dates from 1930. Yeats felt alienated in Ireland where, he claimed, 'all neglect / Monuments of unageing intellect.' Turning his back on his native land, he travelled eastwards: 'I have sailed the seas and come / To the holy city of Byzantium.' In the mythical Byzantium, tutored by the 'sages standing in God's holy fire', he hopes to find release from his sensual nature and be 'gathered / Into the artifice of eternity'. In travelling to Byzantium he also abandons Romantic aesthetic traditions, and finds a comforting anonymity in art forms whose connection with the turbulent sensuousness of nature is remote.

> Once out of nature I shall never take
> My bodily form from any natural thing,
> But such a form as Grecian goldsmiths make
> Of hammered gold and gold enamelling
> To keep a drowsy Emperor awake;
> Or set upon a golden bough to sing
> To lords and ladies of Byzantium
> Of what is past, or passing or to come.[1]

The sages 'standing in God's holy fire' have usually been ascribed to Ravenna, and the remarkable procession of saints that line the walls of Sant'Apollinare Nuovo (fig. 3). Yeats visited Ravenna in 1907 and a year later confessed that 'the Byzantine style … moves me because these tall emaciated angels and saints seem to have less relation to the world about us than to an abstract pattern of flowing lines, that suggest an imagination absorbed in the contemplation of Eternity.'[2] The sense of transcendence, a rising above the material world through the medium of Byzantine art that Yeats felt here in 1908, carried over into his Byzantine poems of the 1920s, and that experience in Ravenna aroused his curiosity sufficiently for him to read up on the history of the period.[3]

Yeats, of course, was neither Byzantinist nor art historian, but what makes his appropriation of the myth of Byzantium so powerful is its assimilation into his personal mythology, its incorporation into his interpretation of history, and its place in his understanding of the history of art. In 'Sailing to Byzantium' and 'Byzantium' Yeats employs the myth of Byzantium to explain something which was very modern. In other words, Yeats's Byzantinism is a form of neo-Byzantinism; it is the rereading of antiquity in contemporary terms. The trigger for this process was probably not Byzantine work at all, however, but something which was also a reinterpretation of Byzantium in modern terms.[4] At the end of 1923, at the age of fifty-eight, Yeats won the Nobel Prize for Literature. This was a considerable honour and gave him a significant position in the cultural Establishment of Europe. On 6 December he sailed eastwards with his wife to Stockholm to receive the prize, and was entertained in the recently completed Stadshus, or Town Hall, the work of the architect Ragnar Östberg. It

was, he wrote, 'the greatest work of Swedish art, and the most important building of modern Europe'. It was organized, he added, 'for an art … imaginative and amazing'.[5]

The approach to the Stadshus from Lake Mälaren is through a colonnade of Byzantine arches which lead into the basilica-like building. Yeats himself recognized the Byzantine influence, praised the unity of the arts in its design and decoration, and suggested that its artistic coherence 'carries the mind back to Byzantium'.[6] But it is in the so-called 'Golden Chamber' that this happens most vividly because, like a great Byzantine basilica, it glows and sparkles with wall mosaics. Designed by Einar Forseth in true Byzantine tradition, they are highly stylized and the scenes and figures are placed on a gold ground symbolic of a rarer and purer world than this. But the subjects of these mosaics are not Christian. Instead, they are drawn from Swedish national mythology, something which Yeats, with his passion for Irish mythology, clearly appreciated. Dominant in the Golden Chamber is a sense of civic pride, which reaches a climax in Forseth's mosaic on the north wall (fig. 4). The disposition of the incidents is similar to that of numerous apse mosaics in Rome, Ravenna, or Sicily.[6] Traditionally they are dominated by God the Father or Christ in Majesty, who in turn are surrounded by the apostles, the saints or the Fathers of the Church. Here a remarkable transliteration has taken place. In 1921 Forseth was in Sicily where he explored the mosaic work in the Cappella Palatina and in Monreale Cathedral. He then travelled along the coast to Cefalù, where in one of the side apses of the town's cathedral he saw the figure of St Peter placed on a throne (fig. 5). He sits amid cushions, and his sandalled feet rest on another cushion. In his left hand he holds a book, while his other hand is raised in blessing. Back in Stockholm Forseth has used St Peter as a model for his large mosaic. Now, however, the central

figure is female; she is 'Queen of the Mälaren' or Stockholm herself (fig. 4).
Like St Peter she sits on cushions, and she is dressed in a similar way down
to her sandalled feet. In one hand she bears a sceptre and in the other a
Byzantine crown. In her lap is a diminutive representation of the Stockholm
skyline and homage is being paid to her not by the figures of Scripture but
by objects drawn from the cultures of East and West. The West is
represented by (among other symbols) the Statue of Liberty and the Eiffel
Tower, whereas the East is represented by a decorated Indian elephant and
by Islamic minarets surrounding a building which is clearly Hagia Sophia.

The importance to Yeats of this visit to Stockholm in terms of his revived
interest in Byzantium is confirmed by the fact that the early drafts of 'Sailing
to Byzantium' contain allusions to the eastward boat journey to the
Swedish capital.[7] The trip also seems to have whetted his appetite to read
more about Byzantium, since he spent some of the Nobel prize money on
more books on the subject,[8] and it stimulated his interest in seeing the
Byzantine originals once again. So in November 1924 he went on a journey
to Sicily where, like Forseth, he visited the Cappella Palatina in Palermo and the cathedrals of Monreale and Cefalù. When
Yeats arrived at Capri on the return journey he recorded his experiences in Ravenna and Sicily in the form of a fantasized
journey back into history and to Constantinople. Stressing the central importance of Byzantium in the development of
Western culture, Yeats wrote in *A Vision*: 'I think if I could be given a month of Antiquity and leave to spend it where I
chose, I would spent it in Byzantium a little before Justinian opened St Sophia and closed the Academy of Plato.'[9] The
reason for his choice, he said, was that 'in early Byzantium … religious, aesthetic, and practical life were one, that
architect and artificer … spoke to the multitude and the few alike. The painter, the mosaic worker, the worker in gold and
silver, the illuminator of sacred books were almost impersonal.' This world is 'an incredible splendour like that which we
see pass under our closed eyelids'. It is the world of the ascetic and 'the dream of a somnambulist'.[10] Yeats's account of his
attachment to Byzantium is an amalgam of ancient and modern. Triggered by his trip to Sweden and the writings of the
Arts and Crafts ideals of Ragnar Östberg, he identified Byzantium with a utopian unity of the arts.

William Morris, whom Yeats greatly admired in his youth, proposed something very similar about the relationship
between Byzantine art and Byzantine society in a seminal paper called 'Gothic Architecture' back in 1889. At that time
Yeats was a regular visitor to Morris's house and he might also have met one of Morris's many disciples, W.B. Lethaby.
Under Morris's influence, Lethaby had written about Byzantine society in utopian terms in what was still in the 1920s a
classic monograph: *The Church of Sancta Sophia, Constantinople* (1894). Furthermore, the anonymity of Byzantine art
matched the modernist striving for a sense of authorial anonymity, and its ascetic incorporeality appealed to Yeats's desire
for sensual anaesthesia. 'Nobody,' he wrote in 1928, 'can stray into that little Byzantium chapel at Palermo, which

4 Einar Forseth, *Queen of the Mälaren*, 1923.
Mosaic. Golden Hall, Stadshus, Stockholm

suggested the chapel of the Grail to Wagner, without for an instant renouncing the body and all its works …'[11] Finally, Yeats's claims about the hallucinatory character of Byzantine art and its culture of self-conscious artificiality owe a great deal to the Symbolist reaction against realism and the reinterpretation of Byzantine art at the beginning of the twentieth century.

In other words, the importance that Yeats attaches to Byzantine art is an amalgam of first-hand experience of buildings and mosaic work, of personal symbolism, of the current assessments of Byzantium in the scholarly and art-historical literature, and of the reinterpretations of Byzantine forms in modern art. Yeats was also drawn to Byzantium as a retreat from personal crisis. Outwardly he was a central pillar of the Irish Establishment. A senator, a public figure in Ireland, and with the Nobel Prize to his credit, he was an author of international renown. Inwardly things were very different. He felt old and alienated. Still disturbed by powerful sexual desire in a body that was often subject to poor health, he felt the need to find a locus that would remove him from inner conflict. He discovered this in the fable of Byzantium, and we shall see that from the first Byzantium operated as a facilitating myth. Within the parameters of a history that was all but unknown, an art that was misunderstood, and a culture which would seem alternately authoritarian, romantic and decadent, Byzantium was often the imaginative refuge for those who for one reason or another felt themselves to be on the margins of the established attitudes and values of their own society. Of course not all collectors of Byzantine art, patrons of Byzantine architecture, designers of Byzantine buildings or practitioners of mosaic arts felt alienated. But because Byzantine culture itself was mysterious, little understood and came somewhere between the Orient and the West; because it had affinities with both Christian and Muslim cultures and was thought to have maintained something of the values of its Greek origins, yet participated in the Western tradition, it presented an exotic, un-European image to the world, and therefore tended to attract those who wished to express their unease with central Western values, whether those values were aesthetic, religious, sexual or political.

The remoteness of Byzantine culture was increased in the nineteenth century by contemporary politics. Throughout this period, the problem of how to deal with the consequences of the disintegration of the Ottoman Empire and to contain Russian influence in the Balkans – known as the 'Eastern Question' – preoccupied the Great Powers, whose interests and sentiments were often conflicting. Many turbulent struggles arose, such as the Greek War of Independence (1821–30), the Crimean War (1853–6) and the Russo-Turkish War (1877–8). British hostility to Turkey was running particularly high in the 1870s, and it was the strength of national feeling that precipitated William Morris into his first active involvement in politics. He became treasurer for the Eastern Question Association in 1876 and campaigned vigorously for peace. It was in 1878 that he first took an interest in Hagia Sophia, which in turn led to his fascination with Byzantine art and architecture. The more general effect of the unstable political situation was to make Constantinople a difficult city to visit, and that unease was increased by the unfriendliness of the Muslim authorities who, with some notable exceptions, did not welcome casual visitors to Hagia Sophia. As a result, for many Western Europeans Byzantine art and architecture were much more easily seen in Venice, Ravenna and Sicily, and many of the most articulate and outspoken champions of Byzantium had never visited Greece, Turkey and Constantinople.

5 St Peter, 1180s. Mosaic. Monreale Cathedral

I | Bavaria, Prussia and Austria

Yeats was what he called 'a last Romantic', and his interest in Byzantium was a late manifestation of something that had emerged among early Romantics in Germany about one hundred years earlier. The best-known figure in the cult for what was then considered Byzantine art is Goethe, but the most important actors in the drama were the brothers Sulpiz and Melchior Boisserée.

1 | Goethe and the Boisserée Brothers

The Boisserée brothers were born in Cologne in the mid-1780s, the sons of a wealthy merchant. As young men they developed a passion for medieval art under the tutelage of the writer Friedrich Schlegel, with whom they stayed in Paris between 1803 and 1804. In 1804 they returned with him to their home town, where the brothers started a two-fold project that was to revolutionize attitudes to German art and architectural history. On the one hand Melchior began to make an unprecedented collection of early German painting, while Sulpiz started to measure and draw medieval German buildings. The availability of old German religious art was in part the result of the physical dissolution of German ecclesiastical establishments. The French occupied Cologne and other parts of Germany between 1794 and 1815, and in the wake of the Revolution were strongly anticlerical. At first this meant that large numbers of German ecclesiastical art works were released on to the market, but it also led to a German sentimental reaction in favour of the Church and Church history which resulted in a more sympathetic attitude to medieval art. In addition it produced an upsurge of German nationalism which in its turn tended to associate the origins of Gothic with the Teutonic races of Northern Europe.

Early in their collecting career the Boisserée brothers made an astonishing purchase. In 1808 they bought a triptych of the *Adoration of the Magi* by Rogier van der Weyden (then thought to be by Van Eyck) from the monastery of St Columba (fig. 7). This painting gave them what they thought at the time was a significant insight into the history of German painting. It was, wrote Sulpiz, 'a fact of which nobody had so far had the slightest inkling, the fact that the earlier painting of Cologne before the van Eycks, no less than the contemporary Italian school, relied on an old tradition of Byzantine models and that it had emerged from the same foundations of that traditional art, although with distinct individual characteristics.'[1] In other words, they thought that northern European medieval art, and German art in particular, was a late flowering of Byzantine work.

The Boisserée brothers needed help with publicizing their activities, and in 1810 Sulpiz was introduced to Goethe, who was then arch-dictator of German taste. The point of contact between the young man of twenty seven and the sixty-year-old celebrity was the work that Sulpiz had been doing on Cologne Cathedral. He had prepared a series of careful drawings and was writing a history of the building, and Goethe, who in his youth had had a passion for Strasbourg Cathedral, received Sulpiz with cautious warmth. Goethe was hesitant on account of Sulpiz's connections with Friedrich Schlegel, whom he loathed. Furthermore, in his later years Goethe had become a passionate classicist, an 'old pagan' as Dorothea Schlegel called him, and was now deeply suspicious of the excesses of German neo-medieval Romanticism. Nevertheless, the first meeting went well and Sulpiz wrote to Goethe telling him about their picture collection. 'We possess,' he wrote, 'not merely remarkable works but paintings which are at least in their expression more noble and more beautiful than can be usually seen in works of the old masters.' He spoke of the delicacy of the later German works, and of the history of the earlier ones which, he said, 'resemble … the clumsy figures known from the Byzantine miniature paintings of the *Menologium* and other manuscripts.'[2]

6 (previous spread) Leo von Klenze, Allerheiligen-Hofkirche, Munich, 1826–37 (destroyed 1942). Watercolour by Franz Xaver Nachtmann, 1848, 41.6 x 31.1 cm (16½ x 12¼ in). Stadtmuseum, Munich

PHAIDON PRESS INC.

Fourteenth Floor

180 Varick Street

New York, NY 10014

PHAIDON PRESS LIMITED

Regent's Wharf

All Saints Street

London N1 9PA

Dear Reader, Books by Phaidon are recognised world-wide for their beauty, scholarship and elegance. We invite you to return this card with your name and e-mail address so that we can keep you informed of our new publications, special offers and events. Alternatively, visit us at **www.phaidon.com** to see our entire list of books, videos and stationery. Register on-line to be included on our regular e-newsletters.

Subjects in which I have a special interest

☐ Art ☐ Contemporary Art ☐ Architecture ☐ Design ☐ Photography

☐ Music ☐ Art Videos ☐ Fashion ☐ Decorative Arts ☐ *Please send me a complimentary catalogue*

	Mr/Miss/Ms	Initial	Surname

Name └─┴─┘

No./Street └─┴─┘

City └─┴─┘

Post code/Zip code └─┴─┴─┴─┴─┴─┴─┘ Country └─┴─┴─┴─┴─┴─┴─┴─┴─┴─┴─┴─┴─┴─┴─┴─┴─┴─┴─┘

E-mail └─┴─┘

This is not an order form. To order please contact Customer Services at the appropriate address overleaf.

Goethe's knowledge of Byzantine work (like that of most of his contemporaries) was very limited, extending very little beyond such rare texts as the one which Sulpiz mentions here – Cardinal Albani's 1727 edition of the *Menologium of Basil II* in the Vatican Library – and the small collection of late Russian icons he himself possessed. Consequently it was not until 1814 that the Boisserée brothers managed to persuade Goethe to come and see their collection, by which time they had moved to Heidelberg. Even then they had to wait another two years, until 1816, for Goethe to write a piece about the works in the journal *Kunst und Altertum*.

The article, entitled 'Heidelberg', is fascinating for its ambivalence towards Byzantine art. Goethe is caught between the then orthodox view that dismissed Byzantium as negligible, and the romantic enthusiasm which he had caught (somewhat reluctantly) from the Boisserées. During the Byzantine period, he said, the defined individualism of Christianity produced 'an archaic, stiff, mummy-like style'.[3] To be fair, he adds, since Byzantine art was a development out of Greek and Roman art it possessed 'great merits … of which we have been able to say little good'. Although the Byzantine School 'persisted in that strict and dry symmetry … nonetheless there are cases where

changes of posture in figures facing each other produce a certain grace.'[4] Goethe's uncertainty continues until he comes to account for the *St Veronica with the Sudarium* of the early fifteenth-century school of Cologne, now in the Alte Pinakothek, Munich (fig. 8). On the one hand he suggests the whole conception of the picture is 'traditional', yet on the other 'the grace and softness with which the saint is painted, and with which the children are represented, obliges us to place the execution of the picture in that lower-Rhenish period.'[5] For Goethe, Byzantium is made acceptable or tempered by being Greek in its early phases and German in its later ones, but the reader comes away from his 'Heidelberg' essay with the sense that even for this classicist there is a real power, energy and a strange attraction latent within Byzantine art.

The pattern of Byzantine influence that the Boisserée brothers thought they detected in German painting they also transferred to the history of German architecture. Together with Friedrich Schlegel they developed the idea that early Rhenish churches were characterized by traces of Hellenism which came to them through Byzantium. This older period, Schlegel wrote in 1806, 'one might call Grecianizing [gräzisierend] on account of some similarity with Constantinian-Byzantine Christian architecture.' Meanwhile in 1810 Sulpiz Boisserée identified the Romanesque architecture of the Rhine as 'neugriechisch' or 'néo-Grec' which became for him synonymous with 'Byzantine'.[6] Although Sulpiz Boisserée was fully aware that the churches of the Rhine were not exclusively Byzantine, the vocabulary which he invented stressed their debt to Greece and to Rome. And by the time that Schlegel came to write

7 Rogier van der Weyden, *Adoration of the Magi* (central panel of the Columba Triptych), 1455. Oil on wood, 138 × 153 cm (54½ × 60¼ in). Alte Pinakothek, Munich

8 Master of St Veronica, *St Veronica with the Sudarium*, *c*.1420. Oil on wood, 78 × 48 cm (30¼ × 19 in). Alte Pinakothek, Munich

his *Philosophy of History* (published in 1828) it had become for him an established fact that 'the style of the Byzantine churches was the first and principal model for … Gothic architecture', and that what he called the 'fantastic singularity' of Byzantine architecture breathed 'the true spirit of the German Middle Ages'.[7] Thus both men were convinced of a continuity between the German Middle Ages, the early Christian period and antiquity. It was in this way that early Romantic interest in Byzantium began.

It was stimulated and consolidated, however, by royal patronage and particularly by the important figure of Ludwig I of Bavaria (r.1825–48). In the early years of the nineteenth century the Bavarian Wittelsbach family, by attracting some of the foremost artists and architects to live and work in the city, were slowly fashioning Munich and its surroundings into one of the most artistically innovative centres of Europe. Ludwig in particular attracted the German Nazarene painters back from Rome, invested in collections of early medieval German painting, and helped to develop a new architectural style that was partly Byzantine and partly Romanesque.

2 | Ludwig I of Bavaria

In 1825 Ludwig I of Bavaria came to the throne at the age of thirty-eight. A contemporary portrait of him by J.K. Stieler shows him informally dressed, confident and romantic. In his active and energetic life, 'politics, art, and patronage took up approximately equal shares,' as his biographer Heinz Gollwitzer puts it.[8] He might have added 'women' to that list, since from an early age Ludwig's passion for women equalled his love of the arts and politics. Ludwig can be credited with the first attempt to build a neo-Byzantine building in Europe. His little Allerheiligen-Hofkirche or Court Church of All Saints, begun in 1826, exerted an influence and created an interest among European builders out of all proportion to its size or its place in Ludwig's ambitious architectural programme (fig. 6). Ludwig's taste in architecture was eclectic, and he built in a wide variety of styles. The Ludwigstrasse alone contains the neo-Roman Siegestor, the Romanesque Ludwigskirche, and the Renaissance Feldherren Halle. Ludwig has been remembered mainly for his versions of classical antiquity, and it was his principal architect, Leo von Klenze, who put such a strong neoclassical stamp on Ludwig's Bavaria. Klenze was a committed Romantic Classicist, the designer of the Glyptothek (1816–30), the austerely antique Walhalla at Regensburg (1830–42) and the Greek Propyläen (1854). Yet it was Klenze who was the architect of the Romano-Byzantine Allerheiligen-Hofkirche.

From an early age Ludwig had collected pictures and sculpture. He had been interested equally in ancient and modern art, at home and abroad, and surrounded himself with artists. He cultivated them socially and intellectually, and he encouraged the teaching of art in Bavaria. Although not himself a practising artist, he used architecture as his principal means of self-expression, impressing his personal stamp on the city in this very public way. For this purpose he collected architects, of whom Leo von Klenze was the most prominent; it was Klenze whom he first employed when he was Crown Prince in 1816, and who became his lifelong companion. But they were joined by others, notably Friedrich von

Gärtner, who began work for him in 1826 and who developed the Romanesque arm of Ludwig's architectural plans. Ludwig was determined to make Munich the most beautiful city in Europe, the 'Athens on the Isar', and he would do this through art. His ambitions were hugely expensive, however, and he met with powerful opposition from many of his ministers who accused him of bankrupting the country to satisfy a personal obsession.

Connoisseur, collector and Maecenas, Ludwig lived through his senses, and although there is no necessary connection between an artistic passion and a strong sexual drive, in Ludwig's case the two seemed to be intimately connected. Ludwig's sexual appetite was voracious. He became involved with women in every major city in Europe and, in spite of his marriage to the Princess Theresa in 1810, his affairs in Munich were public knowledge. His taste in women was as eclectic as his taste in architecture and he embraced females whose class extended from aristocrat to dancing girl.[9] These women ranged from the Marchesa Florenzi, whom he met in Rome at the age of eighteen and with whom he kept up constant communication for twenty-six years, to the notorious Lola Montez. She was an actress and dancer but her influence over Ludwig, and consequently over the politics of Munich, was such that it precipitated his abdication in 1848.

Reckless unconventionality also marked Ludwig's first encounter with Byzantine architecture, which took place in Sicily in 1817. According to his principal biographer, 'etiquette was banished' as Ludwig and his travelling companions roamed the island incognito on horses and mules. 'The sun … and the many monuments delighted the Crown Prince, no less than "the beautiful eyes of the Sicilian women".'[11] On Christmas Eve he attended mass in the Cappella Palatina in Palermo (fig. 9). The light of the candles reflecting from the richly encrusted mosaics captivated his imagination, and he told one of his companions, the doctor Emile Ringseis: 'I will build myself a private chapel like it.'[10]

This was an important moment in Ludwig's personal development. Not only was he was moved by early Christian architecture and design, but he began to devise the idea of a collective German consciousness built upon the culture of the arts. This notion of aesthetic culture was reinforced by his meeting with Christian Bunsen in Rome in the early months of the following year. At the young age of twenty-five, Bunsen had been appointed to assist the famous scholar and diplomat Barthold Niebuhr as secretary to the Prussian Legation to the Vatican, and was at the heart of a thriving German community in Rome.[12] Much was made of the visiting Crown Prince of Bavaria. Dinner parties and festivities were arranged in his honour and they were attended by well-known German artists. Ludwig was particularly impressed by the work of the Nazarenes, who combined a meditative late-medieval style with something that was peculiarly German. He struck up a relationship with two of them, Peter Cornelius and Julius Schnorr von Carolsfeld, whom he later invited to Munich. Although Bunsen was impressed by Ludwig's intense amiability, sociability and knowledge of the arts, he did not like the Crown Prince. Bunsen was a serious Protestant theologian, and his work on early Christian basilicas was an adjunct to his religious beliefs; Ludwig was a courtly Catholic who, in Bunsen's eyes, failed to prioritize his values as future king and leader of his people. Both men felt strongly and positively about German unity but, as a Prussian, Bunsen saw in Ludwig a man who would place Bavarian interests before larger

national concerns. Nevertheless, Ludwig's meetings with Bunsen confirmed him in his enthusiasm for early Christian architecture. Bunsen was captivated by the basilicas of Rome, and in 1823 his innovative study entitled *The Christian Basilicas of Rome*[13] began to appear. His enthusiasm was infectious and, immediately after encountering him, Ludwig wrote to Klenze from Rome about a planned, though ultimately unexecuted, Apostelkirche: 'I came to the conclusion,' he said, 'not to make the Apostelkirche similar to a pagan temple. The spirit of Christianity is different, and to fit with it the church must be basilica-like.'[14]

In the winter of 1823–4 Ludwig's Byzantine project was developed further. He was in Italy to see his mistress, the Marchesa Florenzi, and spent the New Year once again in Palermo. At the same time, accompanied by Klenze, he examined the local architecture, and for a second time was delighted by the Cappella Palatina. Ludwig was a maverick figure in Bavaria. He was obstinate, self-willed and dismissive of conformism, and his later insistence on a Byzantine style for the court church is paralleled by his refusal to heed warnings about his emotional entanglements. Disquiet about his sexual behaviour encouraged his friend Ringseis to write bluntly to him in Sicily, saying that people 'cannot believe that anyone who is really religious could offend against religion on such an important point'.[15] Outraged by his openness, Ludwig dismissed the doctor for his pains.

Thus, for many psychological and political reasons, Ludwig was determined upon a Byzantine style for his own court chapel. Klenze clearly hated the idea and he struggled with Ludwig through the planning and the early building stages. He tried to steer him away from the eccentricities of Byzantine style but Ludwig was determined. So Klenze tried another tack, recommending the simpler style of San Marco in Venice rather than the more exuberant Normano-Byzantine of twelfth-century Palermo. In this Klenze had his way, and also managed to confine the Byzantine impulse to the interior. The two shallow domes inside the chapel reflect those in the narthex of San Marco, and were carefully concealed under a steep roof, the exterior design being pure Romanesque and consequently far more Germanic in appearance (fig.10). The interior, however, remained richly neo-Byzantine. The designs were commissioned from the painter Heinrich Hess. Ludwig wanted mosaic, and instructed him to model his drawings on the interiors of the oldest basilicas. Hess had had plenty of opportunity to study these mosaics since his move to Rome in 1821 to join the Nazarenes. Although younger and less well-known than Peter Cornelius, Friedrich Overbeck and Franz Pforr, who had established the principles of the Brotherhood in around 1811, Hess had nevertheless caught the attention of Ludwig, who in 1824 commissioned from him an 'early Renaissance' portrait of his mistress, the Marchesa Florenzi. Ludwig then sent letters to mosaicists in Rome, Vienna and Venice requesting estimates, but ultimately Klenze succeeded in vetoing the idea on the grounds of expense. Undoubtedly Klenze, who had studied under J.N.L. Durand and Charles Percier in Paris, would in any case have found mosaic repellently primitive and quite unsuitable for a royal chapel. An 1848 painting of the interior (now destroyed; see fig. 6) shows the Hofkirche resembling the small Cappella Palatina in

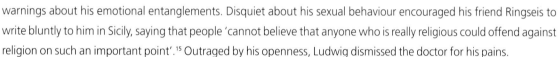

9 (opposite) Sanctuary mosaics, Cappella Palatina, Palermo, 1142–3

10 (above) Leo von Klenze, Allerheiligen-Hofkirche, Munich, 1826–37 (destroyed 1942)

some of its detail but more broadly modelled on the scheme of San Marco. The nave is a simple hall-like structure roofed with its two domes. It is flanked by a colonnade of six round arches on each side with an open gallery above, and terminates in an apse. Hess's frescoes were placed on a gold ground reminiscent of the sumptuous interior of San Marco, although the monumental, gracefully posed figures of God, Christ, the Evangelists and the prophets appear to modern eyes to have stronger affinities with High Renaissance work than figures from Byzantine mosaic. But to the first visitors to the church this scheme must have appeared revolutionary, romantic, and quite extraordinary.

Hess's scheme for the chapel was based on biblical history. The first dome contained incidents from the Old Testament, the second dome incidents from the New, and the apse the Acts of the Apostles and the Trinity. Here, God the Father presides over the Holy Ghost as a dove who, in turn, hovers above a full-frontal standing figure of Christ with arms outstretched in blessing. Beneath him sits the enthroned Virgin surrounded by Moses, Elijah, Peter and Paul – two figures from the Old and two from the New Testament.

The unusual architecture and decoration produced some powerful responses. Dante Gabriel Rossetti's friend Ann Mary Howitt, an art student in Munich in 1850, was amazed by the Hofkirche. 'I had no conception how sublimely beautiful is this chapel,' she wrote soon after her arrival.[16] It is built, she said, 'in the Byzantine style; the circular arches, the three domed roofs [she includes the apse], the niches, the three altars, are all one glow of gold, of rich draperies, of angelic forms and faces, of rainbow-tinted wings, of mystical flowers and symbols.'[17]

Less gushing and one of the most influential, if not the first, account of Hess's work came from Hippolyte Fortoul, who was to play a crucial role in naturalizing the Byzantine style in France (see below, p. 71). In his extensive critique of modern German art, *Concerning German Art* (1841–2),[18] Fortoul saw the archaizing elements in Hess's work as explicitly Byzantine in origin. His decorations, according to Fortoul, are 'austere' and 'naïve', but also expressive of 'deep feeling', 'conviction' and 'masculine energy'.[19] Fortoul's enthusiasm for Hess's work in the Hofkirche, 'the most precious jewel of Munich',[20] derived from the importance that Fortoul attached to the originating place of Byzantine art in the history of the Western imagination. 'Byzantinism', he claimed, 'is the dream which rocked European art in its infancy.'[21]

Not everyone approved of this new Byzantinizing tendency in German art. The important French functionary Frédérique Mercey, for example, took Fortoul to task and denounced Hess's Byzantine tendencies. In neo-Byzantine work, he says, 'the bizarre replaces grace, fantasy the rule, abundance, correctness.' In this trend, 'roughness takes the place of strength and the spirit of true genius.' It is, he adds, 'the style of a period of decadence',[22] and one which had been encouraged by Fortoul and his 'blind mania for archaism'.[23]

In Ludwig's mind, however, archaism and modernism were intimately connected, and he actively promoted the study of Bavarian history and myth in a conservative religious context. In 1831 he encouraged the setting up of the

Gesellschaft für Deutsche Altertumskunde (Society for the Study of German Antiquities), whose brief was to study German medieval culture. At about the same time he offered university chairs to Catholic philosophers and theologians such as Friedrich Schelling, Johann Görres and Franz Baader, who in turn attracted to Munich some of the most outstanding intellectuals in the Church. In 1832 the chief representatives of the French Ultramontane party, a conservative Catholic group that asserted papal authority in Church matters over the interference of king and state, travelled to Bavaria.

Throughout this period art, too, had been playing a major role in Ludwig's self-conscious programme of archaism. Upon his accession in 1825, he had brought to Munich representatives of the most modern developments in German painting, the Nazarenes, and now he turned his attention to the collection of ancient German art. The pictures amassed by the Wittelsbach dynasty had already grown too numerous for their home in the Residenz, and Ludwig was determined to give Munich a gallery unequalled in Europe. In 1826 he laid the foundation stone of just such an institution – the Alte Pinakothek. There were no very early works among the existing paintings, so in 1826 he approached the Boisserée brothers with an offer to purchase their collection. Discussions were protracted partly because Ludwig met opposition from his ministers and partly because another buyer – King Wilhelm V of Württemberg – was also negotiating with the brothers. The Munich parliament argued against the collection on financial and pedagogic grounds. In their view it contained no Italian masters and could, therefore, provide no reliable models for contemporary artists. Peter Cornelius, who was the king's principal art adviser, took Ludwig's side and the two of them ensured that in 1827 the paintings entered the royal collection. The sale catalogue had proudly announced them as 'Byzantinisch-Nieder-Rheinische Schule vom Ende des 13ten bis zum Anfang des 15ten Jahrhunderts' ('Lower-Rhine Byzantine School from the end of the 13th century until the beginning of the 15th century') and they included both the rich and detailed Rogier van der Weyden *Nativity* (see fig. 7), which must have looked stiff, mannered and ancient to early nineteenth-century Germans, and the *St Veronica with the Sudarium* by which Goethe had been so moved (see fig. 8). In her reminiscences, Ann Mary Howitt summed up Ludwig's programme in forming this collection. 'Strange old pictures they are, with their gold grounds, revealing the fact that German as well as Italian art springs from Byzantine origin, and that Germany has had her Cimabues and Giottos.'[24] As for pedagogy, Ludwig was satisfied that this newly acquired group of German works would provide early examples for study by those artists, including Hess, who were working to decorate the new churches that were going up in Munich.

Unfortunately Ludwig fell out with Cornelius in around 1840, and at the invitation of Ludwig's brother-in-law, Friedrich Wilhelm IV, the artist moved to Berlin. Friedrich Wilhelm came to the Prussian throne in 1840, and although he shared a number of Ludwig's passions, including a love of Italy and distaste for France, in temperament he was very different from his brother-in-law. Where Ludwig was an aesthetic Catholic, Friedrich was a committed Protestant; where Ludwig was something of a libertine, Friedrich was a Puritan; and where Ludwig wished to establish Munich as an eclectic art capital of Europe, Friedrich was committed to establishing a state modelled on early Christianity. It was to Friedrich Wilhelm that Bunsen had dedicated his book on the basilicas of Rome.

3 | Friedrich Wilhelm IV of Prussia

Like the Roman emperor Constantine, who for Friedrich was something of a role model, the Prussian monarch was attempting to rebuild an empire ruined by invaders (the French in Friedrich's case), and like Constantine, too, he was attempting to build that new monarchical state out of a fervent belief in the political efficacy of Christianity. Friedrich wished to see himself as the 'primate of Protestantism'[25] and historical precedent played an important part in shaping that ambition. Both he and his brother Karl had access to books on medieval and Byzantine history from the library of Frederick the Great. These included Charles du Fresne's *History of the Empire of Constantinople* (1668), M. Cousin's *History of Constantinople* (1685) and Charles le Beau's *History of the Byzantine Empire* (1765–83).[26] The two boys were encouraged in this interest by their tutor Johann Peter Friedrich Ancillon, well known for his own philosophical and historical works. Prince Karl went on to develop an academic knowledge of this early period of Church history and formed an extensive collection of mainly Veneto-Byzantine objects,[27] while his brother Friedrich, who focused on architecture, tended to be more freely imaginative in his interpretation of history.

Friedrich Wilhelm's enthusiasm for basilican architecture was fuelled by the Gutesohn–Knapp engravings in Bunsen's *Christian Basilicas of Rome*. He met Bunsen in 1827, so by the time of his first trip to Italy in 1828 he was enormously receptive to this style of building and particularly fascinated by the way in which the early Church had adopted the Roman formula for liturgical use. Bunsen had made regular visits to Friedrich's father, Friedrich Wilhelm III, in Berlin, but it was with the Crown Prince that he developed a close and intimate friendship based upon common attitudes and values. The two men were of the same generation, and they shared a love of Italy and the early Church. They were both committed to the reform of the Evangelical Church in Prussia and were dedicated to the idea of developing a society whose strong religious values would counteract the destructive forces of republicanism and Jacobinism.

Returning from Rome via Ravenna and Venice, Friedrich Wilhelm determined to bring Byzantium to Prussia, but it was not until he came to the throne that he was able to put his ambitions fully into operation. These were to revitalize the Prussian Church and to encourage a return, as his biographer David Barclay puts it, 'to the values and the "apostolic" character of the *Urkirche*'.[28] Friedrich Wilhelm saw himself as the head of a new non-materialist Christian state – divinely appointed, but not absolutist. This state was to be dignified through its associations with antiquity and sanctified by tradition. Many of these values he attached to the Byzantine basilican style and he adopted architecture as the most prominent symbol of his political and social goals. In Karl Friedrich Schinkel, his principal architect, he found a sympathetic interpreter of his ambitions. Only a year after the accession, however, Schinkel died, leaving his pupil Ludwig Persius in the role of architect to the king; he, too, was rapidly succeeded by Friedrich August Stüler on his premature death in 1845.

Although Schinkel's intervention in Friedrich Wilhelm's monarchical building programme was brief, his posthumous influence was considerable. Schinkel had been brought up in the neoclassical tradition of David Gilly, Professor of Architecture, and Aloys Hirt, who taught archaeology, both at the Berlin Academy of Arts. In 1803–4, at the age of twenty-three, he visited Italy for the first time where he was much moved not only by the classical buildings with which he was familiar but also by the basilicas and medieval structures. He noticed the special qualities of what he called 'byzantinisch' style, and planned to write a work that illustrated the monuments built in this manner as a possible pattern for a modern form. Careful studies in his notebooks of the eleventh-century basilica at Aquileia, of SS Giovanni e Paolo in Rome, early Renaissance buildings in Bologna and the Normano-Arabic churches of Sicily are a testimony to a kind of private fascination for early building on his part. In the period 1813 to 1830 Schinkel is best known for his unmatched Greek Revival buildings in Berlin, but the churches that he built in those years ranged across a number of styles and include several prominent examples of Gothic Revival work. Wilhelm Friedrich (then Crown Prince) insisted that the Friedrich-Werdersche-Kirche (1821–30) should conform to the medieval design of surrounding churches; others, such as Paulskirche (1832–3) and Elisabethkirche (1830–5) were strongly classical, though the Nazarethkirche (1832–3) is strongly reminiscent of Romanesque work. It was not until 1835, however, with his St-Johannes-Kirche, Alt-Moabit (fig. 11), that Schinkel produced a fully fledged exercise in the historicism of this very early period. Here the alternate dark and light strips of colour rather like Italian marble incrustations, and the apse with blind arcading all derive from his youthful studies of SS Giovanni e Paolo in Rome. Schinkel's return to his earlier interest in Byzantine and Romanesque building was precipitated by his close association with Friedrich Wilhelm. The difference between them was that Friedrich's involvement with this style was predominantly ideological, whereas Schinkel's (as with many of his architectural colleagues) was structural and aesthetic. Like many contemporary theorists in both Germany and France, Schinkel believed that the great strength of the Romano-Byzantine mode was its potential for development in a modern context. But it was under the direction of Schinkel's pupil Persius that neo-Byzantine work in northern Germany came to its full flowering. In 1841, Persius began his Heilandskirche at Sacrow (fig. 13). Friedrich Wilhelm's own rather classically oriented design formed the basis, but Persius modified a rather complex structure of arcades and tower buildings to produce a tall, simple Roman basilica with an externally arcaded apse and a free-standing campanile derived from Sta Maria in Cosmedin in Rome.

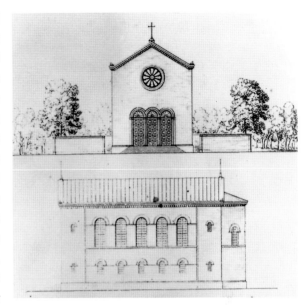

Persius's Friedenskirche (fig. 14) in Potsdam followed soon after (from 1843), and this was explicitly modelled on the basilica of San Clemente in Rome. Like the slightly earlier Heilandskirche it is placed within a picturesque landscape, though the brickwork has been covered with stucco to resemble stone. Several years before, in 1834, Friedrich Wilhelm had obtained a mosaic from San Cipriano, Murano, which was in the process of being demolished (fig. 12). The *Christos Pantocrator*, or Christ in Judgement, took its place in the apse of Persius's church – a self-conscious emblem, as David Barclay puts it, of the king's 'vision of monarchy, the essence of the Prussian state, and of himself as *Primas* of German Protestantism'.[29] As another scholar, Gerd-H. Zuchold, suggests: 'The king's church was supposed to symbolize the state's very essence, while the Murano mosaic itself evoked Friedrich Wilhelm's notion of his own ordination through the grace of God.'[30]

11 Karl Friedrich Schinkel, drawing for St-Johannes-Kirche, Alt-Moabit, Berlin, 1835

Although Friedrich's interests tended to Romanesque and basilican rather than Byzantine, he made one extremely significant contribution to the Byzantine Revival in Europe. It took the form of a publication illustrating the greatest Byzantine church in the world – Hagia Sophia in Constantinople. In 1847, Friedrich Wilhelm commissioned the architect Wilhelm Salzenberg to go to Constantinople to make a visual record of the church. The result was *Ancient Christian Architecture in Constantinople* (1854; see fig. 19).[31] This sumptuous collection of detailed drawings of the architecture and mosaics opened people's eyes to the splendour of Byzantine art in the Eastern Empire, and it remained a standard reference work for the rest of the century.

Hagia Sophia was built by the Emperor Justinian between 532 and 537 and was the third church dedicated to 'The Holy Wisdom' to have stood upon the site (fig. 15). The first, built by Emperor Constantius in 360, and the second, by Emperor Theodosius II in 415, were both destroyed in fires started during rioting. The most recent building was erected by an act of imaginative daring. A huge dome was placed on a square base, its thrust carried by four great arches (fig. 17). Beneath the dome to the north and the south are semicircular tympana, supported by two-storey arcades. To the east and west the area below the great arches is created by semidomes, the lower part of which opens out into yet smaller semidomes (fig. 16). The effect on the observer on the floor is one of vastness, lightness and mysteriousness. The structural logic is incomprehensible as dome merges into dome, and dome into niche. The great dome, which became established as a standard feature of Byzantine architecture, was mythologized to represent the arch of heaven itself, and the church interior not simply a microcosm, but a literal glimpse of heaven and divine order. Hagia Sophia had been the cathedral church of Constantinople for more than a thousand years when in 1453 it was taken by the Turks and turned into a mosque. In the succeeding centuries it was difficult to visit. Complicated systems or permits were in place to inhibit the curious, and in the first half of the nineteenth century the turbulent political climate discouraged visits to Constantinople.

12 (opposite) The Pantocrator. 13th-century mosaic from San Cipriano, Murano, installed in the Friedenskirche, Potsdam

13 (left) Ludwig Persius, Heilandskirche, Sacrow, 1841–3

14 (right) Ludwig Persius, Friedenskirche, Potsdam, 1843–8

The story of the restoration of Hagia Sophia begins with the young Sultan Abdülmecid. The fabric of the building had been neglected and was in a very dilapidated state when in 1846 the Sultan decided to intervene. No substantial restoration had been done since the repairs of 1573 and none has taken place on this scale since. Earthquake tremors had caused superficial damage to the building, but many of the cracks and holes in the walls and domes had been generated by the slow processes of erosion and decay. A strange pair were commissioned to take on the task, the brothers Gaspare and Giuseppe Fossati – strange because they had no special training in the restoration of ancient buildings. But nonetheless they had made substantial careers for themselves in Constantinople. They came originally from Ticino in Switzerland, had studied architecture at the Brera Academy of Milan and were brought up in the austere neoclassical tradition of the period. Gaspare was more highly qualified than Giuseppe, who played a secondary role to his brother. In 1833 Gaspare had gone to St Petersburg to find work. Ever since its foundation by Peter the Great, St Petersburg had been a fruitful source of employment for Italian architects, Luigi Rusca and Carlo Rossi among them, and the Fossati qualified as native

Italians. By 1836 Gaspare had made himself a substantial reputation and in December of that year he was issued with a Russian passport to travel to Constantinople with a view to designing the Russian embassy there. The opening up of Constantinople to the West, the attempted liberalization of Turkish culture and the increasing volume of sea trade between Constantinople and Western Europe brought rich rewards to the Fossati brothers, whose competence in the neoclassical mode was much in demand. They became, Cyril Mango tells us, 'the busiest and most sought-after architects of Constantinople'.[32] The exact process by which the Fossati were appointed to the restoration of Hagia Sophia is not known. A contemporary commentator, Albert de Beaumont, speaks of the Sultan waiting until the more conservative Muslims departed for Mecca before entrusting such a delicate task to the hands of foreign employees, but in May 1847 the Fossati brothers threw themselves into the project with enormous energy. They proved their credentials with a spectacular beginning. Many of the columns in the gallery were leaning dangerously as the result of subsidence and settling. The brothers righted these by moving them into a vertical position and locating them on new bases.

Other dramatic events took place in quick succession, but the most spectacular moment of the restoration had not been planned. This was the uncovering and cleaning of the mosaics whose full extent was barely known in 1847. When Hagia Sophia became a mosque in 1453 all the emblems and decorative elements that related to Christianity were painted over. It was while working on the vaults of the north aisle that Gaspare Fossati first came across them. He cleaned off the whitewash, placed a veil over them and invited the Sultan to inspect the work. As he stood before the mosaic, the veil was dropped and the Sultan was amazed by what he saw. The huge area of gold particularly arrested his attention and, assuming that Fossati had put it in place during the restoration, he exclaimed: ' Wretched man, you have ruined me!' When it was explained to him the gold had long been in place, the Sultan could hardly believe that his predecessors had concealed such beautiful ornaments.[33] Fossati himself later published a set of highly atmospheric lithographs recording his work in Hagia Sophia under the title *Aya Sofia as Recently Restored* (London, 1852). The fifth of these (fig. 18) shows the north aisle with the Sultan about to have the mosaics revealed to him. The original caption read: 'It was here that S.M. the Sultan admired the mosaics for the first time.'[34] Behind the diminutive figure of the Sultan and his assistant is a man carrying a portfolio, presumably Gaspare Fossati himself.

An order from the Sultan to uncover the other mosaics added considerably to the Fossati brothers' brief. The non-figurative ones were exposed, restored and strengthened where necessary. The figural designs continued to be uncovered right up to the moment of the ceremonial inauguration, but they did not remain so for long. In order not to offend the religious customs of the Turks they soon disappeared beneath a coat of white paint, although the Sultan gave instructions that the new covering should be such that it could easily be removed in the future. Meanwhile the mosaics were diligently recorded by Fossati with the intention of publishing a comprehensive account at a later date (this ambition was never fulfilled, possibly through lack of funds). Fossati appealed to the Russian emperor for a subvention to record in the most detailed way 'the sacred church of

St Sophia, whence Christianity appeared in the great Russian Empire',[35] but his appeal was refused; and when finally he published his *Aya Sofia* it bore no dedication to Tsar Nicholas I but carried, instead, the emblem of Abdülmecid. These drawings, which certainly communicate the scale and magnificence of Hagia Sophia, show views both inside and outside the church. In accordance with Muslim tradition, however, they contain no record of the mosaics, no Christian symbolism, and the whole Christo-Byzantine ethos of the church is absent.

This gap was filled by Wilhelm Salzenberg, who in 1847 spent five months in Constantinople. When he arrived he found the church full of scaffolding, which enabled him to climb up and make a close inspection of the mosaics. But he did not get on with the brothers, with whom he may have been commissioned in conscious rivalry. Friction developed over who had the principal right to publish material from the newly uncovered mosaics, and even though Gaspare Fossati was offered grudging thanks in the introduction to Salzenberg's *Ancient Christian Architecture*, the pair never saw eye to eye.[36] In spite of their personal differences, however, the publications of these two men played a crucial role in the Byzantine Revival in Europe and served to

18 Gaspare Fossati, plate from *Aya Sofia as Recently Restored*, 1852, showing the north aisle

determine the responses of subsequent generations to Hagia Sophia. Fossati's illustrations are imaginative, hugely atmospheric and convey a sense of the building's mysteriousness. Salzenberg's work impresses by its sheer scale. The volume is enormous, the architectural drawings gigantic, and the lithographs pulsate with colour. For example, Plate 27 shows a mosaic of Christ and the prostrate figure of an emperor, flanked by the Virgin Mary and an angel in two roundels, in the narthex of the church (fig. 19). The smoothing of the mosaic effect, the realistic representation of the hands and the soft modelling of the skin are all more suggestive of Nazarene painting than Byzantine mosaic, but to Salzenberg's contemporaries the engravings must have appeared powerful in their primitive magnificence.

19 Wilhelm Salzenberg, plate from *Ancient Christian Architecture in Constantinople*, 1854, showing a mosaic from the narthex of Hagia Sophia

4 | Ludwig II of Bavaria and Richard Wagner

Meanwhile, back in Bavaria, Ludwig I continued with his building programme. But time was against him and in 1848, as Europe was torn by revolutions and Hagia Sophia was still being restored, he was forced to abdicate in favour of his son. Although he lived until 1868, his scandalous involvement with Lola Montez, his huge spending on the improvement of Munich and his resistance to democratic reforms all forced him from the throne. Maximilian was crowned king and reigned for sixteen years. In 1864 he was taken ill and died. His son, Ludwig I's grandson, was only nineteen years old at the time, and on ascending the throne inherited much more than a name from his grandfather. Like Ludwig I, Ludwig II was a passionate builder; he, too, was possessed of an extreme romantic temperament, and had serious problems reconciling his sexual inclinations with his political and religious leadership. Most significant from our point of view is that both Ludwigs were equally attracted to the dignity, power and majesty of Byzantium.

Apart from Ludwig II's ascending the throne, 1864 also witnessed the death of Leo von Klenze. Klenze had continued to work for Ludwig I on a much reduced scale, and his last, unfinished building was a memorial chapel to the Stourdza princes in Baden-Baden (fig. 20). This simple octagonal building, fronted with a small portico, has a strongly Byzantine interior which well suited the Orthodox faith of its Romanian patrons. It was completed after Klenze's death by his brother-in-law Georg Dollmann, and decorated by Wilhelm Hauschild. Unimportant in itself, the chapel provides an interesting material link between the two Ludwigs, since it was Dollmann and Hauschild who were principally responsible for materializing in stone and sculpture Ludwig II's Byzantine fantasies.

All nineteenth-century historicism contains within it an element of fantasy. Ludwig I saw himself as a Maecenas, the instigator of far-reaching artistic projects, and Wilhelm Friedrich modelled himself on Constantine presiding over a Christian empire. Their building programmes reified their desire to link themselves to ancient traditions, and each historical style had its own vocabulary of symbolic significance. Ludwig II took this further than any other patron or ruler of the nineteenth century. In his case the relative positions of fantasy and reality became displaced to the extent that his primary activity was developing the first in order to flee from the second. He was enabled by his privileged position, his access to money and his huge influence. He was propelled by unrealizable homosexual desire – desire that was irreconcilable with his position as head of state. But he was also driven by guilt and anxiety, which became so stressful that they threatened his sanity and may have precipitated his suicide. His building projects were intimately related to his sense of personal identity and his need to lose himself in a past where he was glorified, sanctified and empowered. Sometimes it was the past of Louis XIV, his namesake, whom he fervently admired; sometimes it was the knights of the Middle Ages with their chivalric codes of honour; frequently, however, it was the world of Byzantium where sanctity, Christianity and monarchy went hand in hand. In this idealized world the monarch was removed from the petty demands of state and army, from the need to negotiate with bourgeois councillors or philistine generals. Above all the past provided a sanctuary from late nineteenth-century moral codes that anathematized his homosexuality. His grandfather had encountered severe problems with Church and State over his promiscuous

20 Leo von Klenze, design for the
Stourdza Chapel, Baden-Baden, 1863
Staatliche Graphische Sammlung, Munich

propensities; Ludwig II's dilemmas were infinitely more acute. Lola Montez had brought down Ludwig I; Richard Wagner was given the title 'Lolotte' by the Munich press for his unconventional, close and sentimental relationship with the king. Although Wagner was not the only man in Ludwig's life, it was the composer who fired most strongly Ludwig's fantasies about history, monarchy and sexuality.

The only Byzantine project which Ludwig fully realized was the extraordinary Throne Room in Schloss Neuschwanstein outside Munich, but many others were planned. As early as 1868 he asked the stage designer for the Court Theatre, Christian Jank, to produce a number of highly romanticized castle sketches and had the architect Eduard Riedel translate them into the first plans for the building of Schloss Neuschwanstein. In the following year, 1869, he asked Georg Dollmann to design a huge Byzantine palace in the Graswang Valley, near Schloss Linderhof, complete with gold-ground mosaics in the apse of the chapel (fig. 21). Ludwig had been enormously impressed by Joseph von Hammer's book *Constantinople and the Bosphorus* of 1822,[37] in which the author provided very detailed descriptions of the Seraglio and the Sultan's palace. The king sent Dollmann a copy with instructions that he should study it carefully and design likewise. He also marked up another, much more recent book for Dollmann – Johann Heinrich Krause's *Byzantines of the Middle Ages* of 1869.[38] Furthermore, Labarte's *The Imperial Palace of Constantinople* had been published in 1861.[39] The large secular basilica at the heart of Ludwig's project contained triclinia and consistory rooms based on the accounts of the palace in Constantinople found in these publications. The open layout of the buildings, linked by arcaded walks and enclosing formal parterres and a fountain, strongly evokes the plan of Versailles or the more recent Villa Berg in Stuttgart (built between 1845 and 1853). Copies of Versailles by groups nostalgic for the absolute monarchy of the seventeenth century were common in Europe. What is significant about Dollmann's design is that it was planned in a Byzantine mode.

21 Georg Dollmann, design for a Byzantine-style palace, 1869–70. Watercolour, 41.1 x 70 cm (16¼ x 27½ in). Ludwig II-Museum, Schloss Herrenchiemsee

Ludwig's fascination with Byzantium was encouraged by his belief in the close connection between Byzantine architecture and the mythical castle of Montsalvat, resting place of the Holy Grail. Montsalvat he knew from his childhood education in northern legends, but it received a huge mystical charge from his attendance at a performance of Wagner's Lohengrin in 1861, when he was fifteen.

> In a far-off land, inaccessible to your steps,
> There is a castle by the name of Montsalvat;
> A light-filled temple stands within it,
> More beautiful than anything on earth;
> Therein is a Vessel of wondrous blessing
> That is watched over as a sacred relic:
> The purest of men might guard it,
> It was brought down by a host of angels …[40]

So sings Lohengrin, the son of Parsifal, as he leaves his bride Elsa to return once again to the land of the Grail. Ludwig's meeting with Wagner in 1864 and the subsequent passionate, if turbulent, friendship served to fuel fantasies on both sides. The young nineteen-year-old king worshipped Wagner as a genius of the highest order to whom he had been sent as support and salvation; for Wagner, Ludwig's combination of riches and royalty made an irresistible appeal to one who had endured privation, poverty and disdain. The two men shared a belief in the virtues of masculinity and idealized militarism; they were both extremely anxious about their own sexuality and had a particular problem with female sexuality.

Ludwig also shared Wagner's enthusiasm for Wolfram von Eschenbach's twelfth-century legend *Parzival*, and when, in 1865, Wagner sent the king a prose draft of an opera based on the story, Wagner's mistress Cosima recorded in her diary: 'What a wonderful thing – the King is passionately keen to hear about Parzifal.'[41] In August of the same year, Wagner identified Ludwig with the Grail King in an entry in his own diary, and thereafter Ludwig joined Wagner in seeing himself as a figure who would regenerate the spiritually barren wasteland of Germany through his patronage and support of the arts.[42] Wagner's opera *Parsifal* also has strong Byzantine connections. His sources placed the Grail legend in the late Byzantine period, and in the designs which he supervised for the first performances of the work (see fig. 29) the Grail Hall draws upon Byzantine motifs. Ludwig, too, linked this thirteenth-century story with Byzantine Europe and Byzantine architecture, and his Imperial Palace in the Graswang Valley included a first-floor Throne Room and bedroom influenced by his readings in the Grail legend. Dollmann produced several designs, each rectangular in shape and ending with a semicircle on one short side and roofed with two domes. A watercolour by Eduard Ille, dated 1877 (fig. 22), almost certainly relating to this project, shows a Grail Hall powerfully influenced by the mid-nineteenth-century restoration of Hagia Sophia and the illustrations by Fossati and Salzenberg. Ille has moved the mosaic of the prostrate emperor before the throne of Christ from the narthex of Hagia Sophia into the central dome of the Hall. He has also substituted the figure of Titurel, the original keeper of the Grail, for that of the emperor, and has introduced

here and in the furthest apse the figure of the pure and innocent 'Lamb of God' supporting the cross. Ille has also erected a dais under the second dome where an altar displays the green and glowing Grail. On 23 May 1869 Ludwig noted in his diary: ' … read about the Temple of the Holy Grail', and on 22 June: 'Montsalvat'.[43]

Ludwig's admiration for the great theocracies of Byzantium and their architectural remains was being strengthened by his study of Krause's *Byzantines of the Middle Ages*, in which the author speaks of the grandeur and magnificence of the Byzantine emperors. At the same time Wagner, too, was making use of a source that drew upon the Byzantine past. He had first read *Lohengrin*, the final part of the *Parzival* epic that deals with the Grail legend, in 1845. Now that he was preparing his own version of the story, he reread the *Lohengrin* poem in an 1813 edition prepared by Johann Görres. Görres was a romantic philosopher who strongly promoted ideas about German myth and legend.[44] Neo-Byzantinism and German nationalism came together in the revival of medieval texts about the Grail, evidenced by Görres's introduction in which he suggests that one of the sources for Monsalvat in Wolfram von Eschenbach's twelfth-century fragment *Titurel* was in fact Hagia Sophia.[45] In Wolfram's poem the ritual of the Grail Hall is described in detail, but not the room itself. Architectural details were much more explicit in another work, entitled *The Younger Titurel*, written between 1270 and 1274 by the Bavarian Albrecht, in which the Hall is described as a Byzantine building or in the 'altdeutschen Stil'.[46] According to Albrecht it had four arms in the shape of a Greek cross, with each of the chapels covered by a dome. Among the versions of Ludwig's Throne Room that were being developed, Eduard Ille produced a design for a Grail Hall (frontispiece) in which he has borrowed two angel guardians of the Grail from Albrecht's version of the legend and depicted them hovering above an image of Hagia Sophia – complete with its minarets!

In parallel with the Byzantine designs for Graswang, Ludwig was maturing his ideas for Neuschwanstein. The size and design of the Throne Room changed a number of times in the decade that followed the original inspiration of 1868, but by 1876 Ludwig had decided that it would be based on his grandfather's Allerheiligen-Hofkirche. He told Ille that 'the Court Church of All Saints in Munich is to serve as a model … The domed vault is to represent the Heavens, strewn with golden stars, the blue of the sky is to be as bright as possible. All types of marble which the architect Salzenberg lists in describing the Church of St Sophia in Constantinople are envisaged for use in this Throne Room. At the rear of the room there is a great niche, where the throne will be placed on a high marble background. Separated by palms, will be painted six kings that have been canonized, including Christ, giving His blessing, as King of Heaven, beneath Him Mary and John the Baptist. The chair of the throne is covered by a canopy which rests on columns, similar to the altar in St Sophia's Church. Materials to be very rich.'[47]

The building of Neuschwanstein began in 1869. Around the neighbourhood of Hohenschwangau, where Ludwig had spent much of his childhood, there had at one time been four castles. The most spectacular had been Vorderhohenschwangau, whose ruins were perched high on an outcrop of rock. The architect Eduard Riedel and the stage designer Christian Jank drew up the first plans for the new building on this site. Unlike the Imperial Palace at Graswang, built on the open plain, Neuschwanstein was remote and inaccessible. The design was also placed in progressively remote periods of history. Jank's original piece of stage scenery was pure Gothic; his second design, of July 1868, was Romanesque, and much of the castle was finally built in this style. At the heart of the building, however, even more remote, was the Byzantine Throne Room.

The divinity of kingship was central to Ludwig's thinking. One of Wagner's first gifts to Ludwig was an essay *On State and Religion*, written in 1864, which in its tone and content unites many of Ludwig's lifelong obsessions about the relationship between the monarch and his people, and the nature of the role of the king. It is romantic, idealistic and conservative. 'In the person of the king', Wagner wrote, 'the State attains its true ideal.'[48] The king's lifelong struggle is towards the universal goals of justice and humanity, and his means to achieving these goals is religion, for 'religion alone can bear the king to the stricter dignity of manhood.' In Wagner's terminology 'religion' is close to 'mysticism'; it involves an order of perception and inspiration above and beyond the commonplace. 'For *this* is the essence of true religion,' he explains, 'that, away from the cheating show of the daytime world, it shines in the night of man's inmost heart, with a light quite other than the world-sun's light, and visible nowhere save from out that depth.' One of these modes of higher perception is provided by art, for in art 'there will return to him the invincible dream-picture of the holiest revelation.' [49] Ludwig's way of coping with a temperament entirely unsuited to day-to-day political activity, and ill-equipped to deal with affairs of state, was to adopt alternative royal personae through the medium of spectacle, theatre, music and art. His diaries show how, in addition to his unease with his role as monarch, he was tormented by his homosexuality and a sense of guilt and impurity. The staging of alternative identities seems to have been essential to his existence, and the Throne Room in Neuschwanstein was a vehicle for Ludwig's image of himself as an absolute monarch. In this way it provided him with the perfect arena for one of his personae: a thirteenth-century Byzantine King of the Holy Grail.

Ludwig was meticulous about the details of Neuschwanstein. Although the outward appearance retains something of a Disneyland Gothic quality (fig. 23), the labyrinthine interior is composed of narrow round-arched Romanesque halls and corridors in which space is densely filled by short, stocky, powerful columns resting on substantial bases. When one enters the Throne Room, the interior space opens out into a blaze of light and gold as the single-storeyed pattern established elsewhere in the castle expands unexpectedly into an area occupying two storeys (fig. 24). Ludwig announced this new plan in 1878, and in 1880 decided that it would be a 'Byzantine hall'.[50] The effect of this decision was that large portions of the castle that had already been built had to be reshaped. Dollmann pointed out that 'as a result the western part of the Great Hall must be completely restructured, the windows on the third and fourth floors

23 Christian Jank, Eduard Riedel and others, Neuschwanstein, from 1868

must be changed … Almost all the smoke flues will be unserviceable.'[51] But time, trouble and cost were never an issue with Ludwig. In many other places in Europe the Byzantine Revival was very much a co-operative Arts and Crafts venture. In Britain, Austria and Sweden, for example, the Byzantine model was one where patron, architect and craftsmen endeavoured to work in harmony. Here at Neuschwanstein, however, architectural work proceeded by royal fiat; all instructions were issued by the king. One of the greatest problems which arose out of this autocratic method was his decision to place the large domed Throne Room on the third and fourth floors of the castle. The ceiling of the second floor had to be reinforced by enormous H-shaped girders that accepted much of the downward thrust, but it was still impossible on such a tall and precarious site to buttress the outward pressure of the dome. An engineer called Moradelli came up with a brilliant solution: a steel-wire vault was constructed from which the dome was hung, and the iron web was supported on the surrounding walls.

On the outer wall of the castle the fenestration fails to record the presence of the Throne Room inside, and the windows remain the same shape and the same distance apart as they appear elsewhere. As in the case of the Allerheiligen-Hofkirche, the dome at Neuschwanstein is obscured from outside. It is as if the Throne Room were a secret presence in the castle, a presence representing those hidden aspects of Ludwig's identity that he did not wish to parade publicly. A preliminary watercolour by Dollmann of 1878–80, showing heavy Romanesque arches, a basilican 'nave' under two domes, and a very restricted (and, it is interesting to note, exclusively ecclesiastical) scheme of decoration (fig. 26), is closer in style to Lombard churches than to the Byzantine basilica. But by 1883 the two-domed pattern based upon the Hofkirche had been changed to a single domed space. The reason was a symbolic one. Ludwig pointed out: 'For a king the room may only have one dome.'[52] The spatial effect is remarkable: the feeling of progression down a nave has disappeared, and instead the interior space is carved out by the sweeping combination of dome and apse. Romanesque dignity has given way to Byzantine jouissance as the eye leaps up and around the richly decorated walls that give a sense of the inside of a jewel-box. All the decoration of the Throne Room is laid upon a gold ground which reaches from floor to dome, and even here the deep blue of the overarching firmament is pierced by gold stars. The circular dome is answered by the mosaic floor, echoing the relationship between sky and earth. This floor, designed by the Italian Anton Detoma, was not laid until 1885 (fig. 27), but its beasts and birds – possibly derived from the Byzantine mosaics in Roger II's royal palace in Palermo – complement the blue of the sky and provide an intermediate space for the deeds of man. Along the side walls the gold is punctuated by two rows of arcading. The upper row consists of columns covered with scagliola to resemble the deep blue of lapiz lazuli, while the lower imitates the royal purple of porphyry. A flight of dazzling white steps of Carrara marble, flanked by gilded banisters, leads from the floor up into the apse (fig. 25).

Like the architectural plans, the programme for the interior decorations underwent several revisions.[53] Originally they were based upon the story of Parzival – the sobriquet which Ludwig happily accepted from Wagner – and in the early planning stages the Throne Room was to be lavishly decorated with scenes from this legend. In 1869, Ludwig's literary adviser, Hyazinth Holland, had suggested themes such as 'Parzival Enters the Castle of the Grail' and 'Kundry Tells

Bavaria, Prussia and Austria Ludwig II of Bavaria and Richard Wagner

25 Eduard Ille and Georg Dollmann, Throne Room, Neuschwanstein, 1885–6

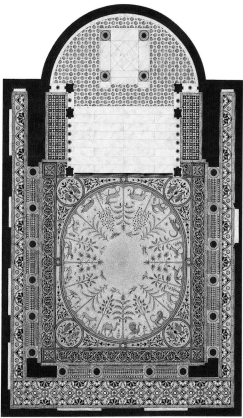

Parzival that he is the Chosen King of the Grail'. Even as late as 1880, Georg Dollmann was still submitting Grail proposals including 'Titurel Begins Building the Temple for the Sacred Cup'.

Wagner was also preoccupied with the legend and in 1877 began in earnest on his opera *Parsifal*. In November of that year he sent proofs of part of the libretto to his secret mistress, Judith Gautier, the daughter of the well-known critic Théophile Gautier. Wagner and Cosima had met and befriended Judith in the early 1870s, but in around 1876 Wagner had become sexually involved with her. The *Parsifal* proofs were accompanied by a note from the composer which read: 'I feel myself to be loved and I love. At last I am writing the music for Parsifal.'[54] He was then sixty-four and she was thirty-two. Wagner, however, was troubled by guilt about this relationship and when, in 1878, Cosima discovered that the affair had been going on for two years, she issued an ultimatum to her husband. He had no choice and in the same year broke with the young woman. Such problems of sensual desire are central to *Parsifal*; it is fundamentally concerned with the sense of guilt induced by desire and with the renunciation of women. Like the Grail King – embodied in the character of Amfortas, who suffers a sexual wound as the result of his involvement with the *femme fatale* Kundry – some part of Wagner was acting out his own inability to reconcile his behaviour with conventional proprieties.

26 (left) Georg Dollman, study for the Throne Room, Neuschwanstein, 1878. Watercolour, 65.5 x 49.8 cm (25¼ x 19½ in). Ludwig II-Museum, Schloss Herrenchiemsee

27 (right) Anton Detoma, study for the floor mosaic in the Throne Room, Neuschwanstein, 1883. Coloured pen and ink drawing by Julius Hofmann, 63.4 x 38.5 cm (25 x 15¼ in). Ludwig II-Museum, Schloss Herrenchiemsee

Although Ludwig came to ideas of renunciation from a different standpoint he, too, was constantly guarding himself against what he saw as the destructive power of sensuality. Early in his friendship with Wagner, and in the face of clear evidence to the contrary, he shut his mind to the possibility of Wagner's adulterous relationship with Cosima, who at that time was married to Hans von Bulöw. The physical manifestations of sexuality held great terror for him. At home he condemned the behaviour of young people and the way in which 'sensuality is mingled with their attraction towards the opposite sex';[55] abroad he regarded Paris as the 'throne of sensuality' and a 'modern Sodom and Gomorrah'.[56] His personal life was racked with guilt about physical contact and he kept a secret diary in which he was forever fighting a battle with the tyranny of the senses in coded hysterical terms: 'Remember, Remember From Henceforth never! … (Also from kisses strictly to abstain, I swear it in the name of the King of Kings).'[57] In *Parsifal* the hero's quest for purity and his renunciation of women is central to his qualification as the future Grail King and saviour of the Grail Kingdom. In the arms of Kundry he cries out in terms which resemble Ludwig's diary entries: 'The longing, the terrible longing which seizes and grips all my senses! O torment of love! How everything trembles, quakes and quivers in sinful desire! … My dull gaze is fixed on the sacred vessel; the holy blood flows … Redeemer, Saviour! Lord of grace! How can I, a sinner, purge my guilt?'[58] Ludwig did not attend the first performance of *Parsifal* in 1882, and Wagner never entered the Byzantine 'temple' which Ludwig had prepared to receive him, yet it is clear that the two men shared almost identical views about leadership and renunciation.

At Neuschwanstein the original scheme for the decoration of the castle was changed. Although the legend of Parzival was to be found everywhere else, it was excluded from the Throne Room. The Singer's Hall, decorated by A. Speiss with incidents from Wolfram von Eschenbach's narrative, became the place designed for the contemplation of the Grail mysteries. The Throne Room, which has so many connections with the early designs for the Grail Hall at Graswang, was stripped of its associations with Parzival and came more and more closely to resemble a Christian basilica. Wilhelm Hauschild was responsible for most of the paintings in the Throne Room, scenes that largely celebrate virtuous masculinity.[59] The room is dominated by the apse, whose decoration derives not from Hess's work in the Allerheiligen-Hofkirche, but from the apse which he painted for Georg Friedrich Ziebland's St Bonifaz in Munich (now destroyed; fig. 28). The image of Christ as Supreme Lawgiver and King of Kings unites two iconographic types. A hieratic, full-frontal Christ raises one hand in blessing while the other holds the book of Alpha and Omega, and he is encircled by seraphim and symbols of the four Evangelists – elements from an early medieval configuration known as the Majestas Domini. Likewise the present group of Christ accompanied by the Virgin on the left and St John the Baptist on the right echoes the Byzantine image of the Dëesis. Beneath, as at St Bonifaz, six canonized kings stand between stylized palms that signify spiritual triumph. These kings mediated between the King of Kings above and the King of Bavaria who would have sat below. In the Grail Hall the steps near the apse led up to the Grail itself; at the Allerheiligen-Hofkirche this position was occupied by the altar. Ludwig's Throne Room draws very strongly on his grandfather's attempt to find an image of divine sanction for temporal rule, and to this end the royal dais is situated directly beneath the enthroned Christ. The throne would have been placed on this dais, beneath a baldacchino which Julius Hofmann modelled on an altar by Arnolfo di Cambio in San Paolo fuori le Mura in Rome. The dais has remained forever empty, because before Ludwig could take his place on this throne he disappeared beneath the waters of the Starnberger Lake.

Although the Throne Room at Neuschwanstein was the only Byzantine project of Ludwig's to materialize, he initiated many others which existed in less tangible form. The proximity of Ludwig's version of Byzantium to theatre is pointed up by the fact that he turned first to stage designers rather than architects for ideas. Angelo Quaglio, who worked both with the architect Ziebland and on the staging of some of Wagner's operas, provided inspiration for parts of Neuschwanstein, and when Victorien Sardou's play *Theodora* came to Munich in 1885 he created a domed set for the scenes in Constantinople. Christian Jank, who had provided the first drawings for the outside of Neuschwanstein, offered Wagner a design for the Grail Hall in *Parsifal* in the early 1880s. Wagner turned it down in favour of a model created by a little-known Russian artist, Paul von Joukowsky.[60] 'Our utmost diligence', said Wagner about the stage set, 'was spent on giving the height of solemn dignity to the ideal temple of the Grail, whose model could only be taken from the noblest monuments of Christian architecture.'[61] Since *Parsifal* was finished in Palermo, W.B. Yeats, as we have seen (see above, p. 13), firmly believed that the Cappella Palatina had played an important part in Wagner's inspiration. In fact, Joukowsky's set was a Byzantinized version of the thirteenth-century cathedral of Siena, which moved Wagner to tears on a visit in 1880.[62] In the original legend the poet describes a circular temple or church, miraculously built by Titurel to contain the Grail. And S. Baring Gould described the set at Bayreuth as 'a circular space surrounded by a colonnade with radiating cloisters, and surmounted by a dome. In the centre is a sort of table or square altar clothed in red sammet; behind this is the couch for the wounded King.'[63] A contemporary illustration of the staging (fig. 29) shows an altar standing beneath an octagonal domed structure loosely modelled on San Vitale in Ravenna. The dome is supported by clusters of four columns crowned by lightly decorated cushion capitals. A clerestory runs around the eight sides and there is an ambulatory at ground level. The dome is lighted by an oculus which throws light on to the Grail from above.

28 (left) Heinrich Hess, apse mural, 1845. St Bonifaz, Munich (destroyed 1942)

29 (right) Max Brückner, study of Paul von Joukowsky's set for *Parsifal*, 1882. Oil on canvas, 51.5 × 65.5 cm (20¼ × 25¼ in). Richard Wagner Museum, Bayreuth

5 | Austria

Ludwig II died in 1886 and Neuschwanstein was completed a year later. It was never again used as a royal residence and was opened to the public within months of the king's death. With Ludwig's passing the spirit of Byzantium faded in Bavaria; in nearby Austria, however, it was alive and well. Its roots there go back to the 1830s when the decline of Neoclassicism prompted the director of the Viennese Academy of Fine Arts, Pietro Nobile, to explore alternatives. One of his pupils, Ludwig Förster, who in 1836 had founded the famous architectural journal *Allgemeine Bauzeitung*, began to experiment with the *Rundbogenstil* which, as we have seen (above, p. 8), was being developed by Heinrich Hübsch and Friedrich von Gärtner in Munich. The southern sensibility of both Bavarians and Austrians found the strong *Rundbogenstil* perhaps more appealing than the pointed northern Gothic, and in Vienna two of the outstanding monuments in this style were Förster's Synagogue (1853–8), and Eduard van der Nüll's design for an Arsenal on the outskirts of Vienna (1849–56). This huge complex contained Karl Rösner's delicately impressive Romano-Byzantine chapel (1854–6), and a strong 'Byzantine' statement in the form of the Arsenal Museum by Theophilus Hansen (1852; figs. 30, 31). In 1846 Hansen had become a member of the Viennese Academy where, though maintaining an eclectic practice, he enthusiastically taught Byzantine architectural history, eventually succeeding Van der Nüll to the professorial chair in 1868. He was a Dane, and together with his brother Christian had travelled in Greece between 1838 and 1846, establishing what might be called a vernacular neo-Byzantinism. As well as contributing many neoclassical buildings to Athens, Theophilus designed the city's Romano-Byzantine cathedral (1842–62) and a neo-Byzantine eye hospital (1840–4). The brothers imported this style back to their native Denmark. Theophilus's Municipal Hospital chapel at Bredgrade (1859–63), for example, is a round-arched domed building in yellow brick (now weathered grey) with little or no external decoration, but with a richly ornate ceiling beneath the dome (fig. 32). Brick particularly appealed to him, and he experimented with varieties of *Rundbogenstil* designs in his Chapel of the Invalids in Lvov (1855) and his Evangelist Cemetery Chapel in Vienna (1857; fig. 33).

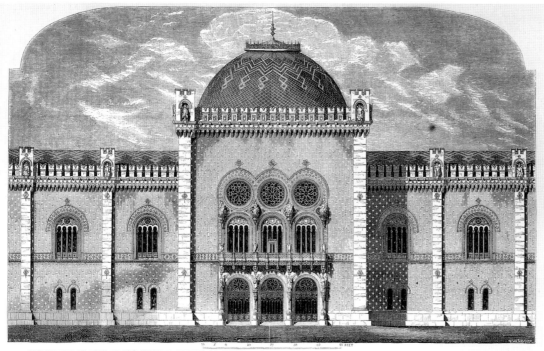

THE MUSEUM OF ARMS IN THE IMPERIAL ARSENAL IN VIENNA. CENTRAL PORTION OF PRINCIPAL FRONT.——HERR THEOPHILOS HANSEN, ARCHITECT.

30 (left) Theophilus Hansen, Arsenal Museum, Vienna, 1852. Engraving in *The Builder*, 22 September 1866
31 (above) Theophilus Hansen, 'Hall of Fame', Arsenal Museum, Vienna, 1852

32 (left) Theophilus Hansen, chapel of the Municipal
  Hospital at Bredgrade, 1859–63, interior
33 (right) Theophilus Hansen, Evangelist Cemetery
  Chapel, Vienna, 1857–8

One of van der Nüll's pupils was Austria's most prominent proto-modernist, Otto Wagner. Although he is well known for his anti-historicism, many of Wagner's buildings are in fact a subtle reworking of ancient idioms in modern modes. One of these, St Leopold am Steinhof in Vienna (1905–7), has strong Byzantine associations (fig. 35).[64] Wagner had already experimented with Oriental space in a synagogue for Budapest (1870–2), but the church at Steinhof, in its severe combination of flat decoration on a cube shape covered by a large dome, looks back to Hansen's Arsenal Museum and further back to an elemental version of Hagia Sophia. Outside, the church is formed from a cube, a cylinder and a hemisphere; inside, although 'Byzantine' mosaic is deployed extensively, all religious half-light has been expelled in favour of clear, hygienic, light-filled spaces (fig. 34). Wagner's notebooks make it clear that Byzantium was very much on his mind during the initial stages of the design, with pages of carefully constructed geometric motifs entitled 'Byzantinische Kreuersystem' and other sketches showing variations on proportions derived from Hagia Sophia.[65] The mosaics by Remigius Geyling and the stained glass by Kolo Moser combine, as Henry Russell Hitchcock suggests, 'to rival the most sumptuous domestic ensembles produced by the Wiener Werkstätte'.[66] The Werkstätte had been founded by Moser and Wagner's pupil Josef Hoffmann in 1903 with the aim of producing high-quality goods using industrial means. At this time the workshop was also providing tesserae and designs for an important Byzantine-influenced interior at the Palais Stoclet (1905–11), the culmination of which was Klimt's mosaic decoration in the dining room (see below, p. 51).

Otto Wagner hugely admired Klimt and his important part in the Vienna Secession in the 1890s, although Wagner himself did not join the movement until 1899. In France, Gustave Moreau and then the Symbolists had developed a movement in reaction to the materialism and naturalism of the period. In Austria, the Secession was prompted by similar motives. In 1900 Klimt showed his unfinished painting *Philosophy* at the seventh Secession exhibition. It was intended for the Great Hall in the University of Vienna but its symbolism and its frank treatment of the body caused considerable outrage. It was followed by *Medicine* (1901), and *Jurisprudence* (1903–7; fig. 36), which was also shown unfinished at the Secession exhibitions. *Jurisprudence* in particular marks Klimt's search for a new exotic or syncretic style, and when his friend the critic Ludwig Hevesi saw it on the walls of his studio in November 1903, he immediately detected one of the sources of this new work. 'Only four days previously,' remarked Hevesi, 'I had come back from Sicily. I was still intoxicated with the golden world of the mosaics, gleaming and glittering … It came back to me as I stood there in front of Klimt's picture with its shining gold.'[67] Klimt had never been to Palermo, but he had been to Venice and Ravenna. On his first visit, in early May 1903, he was accompanied by the artist Maximilian Lenz, who recorded that the mosaics of Ravenna made a 'tremendous, decisive impression' on Klimt.[68] On the second trip in early December, Klimt sent a card to his mistress, Emilie Flöge, in which he reported seeing mosaics of 'unprecedented splendour'.[69]

Klimt introduced the rich effect of the mosaic technique into a number of paintings, but most outstandingly in a portrait of Adele Bloch-Bauer (1907; fig. 37). The work is truly iconic in that the figure of the 26-year-old woman is caught and frozen

35 (above) Otto Wagner, St Leopold am Steinhof, Vienna, 1905–7
34 (opposite) Remigius Geyling, altar mosaics, 1907. St Leopold am Steinhof, Vienna

36 (left) Gustav Klimt, *Jurisprudence*, 1903–.
Oil on canvas, 430 × 300 cm (169½ × 118¼ in) (destroyed)
37 (right) Gustav Klimt, *Portrait of Adele Bloch-Bauer*,
1907. Oil and gold leaf on canvas, 138 × 138 cm
(54½ × 54½ in). Österreichische Galerie, Vienna

in its encasing mass of gold. There is something painfully artificial about the treatment of the exposed parts of the body. The face, with its soulful eyes, painted lips and thick black hair, looks like a mask which is slightly displaced from the neck upon which it should rest. The triangular decoration across the breast resembles the marble inlay around the apse of San Donato, Murano, and elsewhere the intense decorative detail operates to obscure rather than to establish the boundaries between clothing, chair and background. According to one review, the woman resembled an 'idol in a golden shrine', and when another said that the picture was 'more brass than Bloch' (a play on the words 'Blech', meaning brass, and Bloch, the surname) there was the suggestion that the sitter was a prisoner of her own enormous wealth.[70]

It is ironic that Klimt chose the most incorporeal of styles in which to couch one of his most powerful corporeal themes – salvation through physical coition. Images of sexual union occur in his *Beethoven Frieze* of 1902, which culminates in 'Diesen Kuss der ganzen Welt' or 'A kiss for all the world', and in the mosaic for the Stoclet frieze entitled *Fulfilment* (1905–9). The Palais Stoclet was commissioned in 1904 by the rich Belgian businessman Adolphe Stoclet, and its centrepiece is the dining room. The mosaic is a triumph of the marmoreal in a house which is itself petrified. Above the sideboard Klimt's frieze runs in two 7-metre (23-foot) sections. Plans in tempera, water colour, gilt and silver were prepared by the artist to be translated into white marble inlaid with copper and silver plate, corals, semiprecious stones, gold mosaic, enamel and coloured faience.[71] Although the Stoclet frieze displays the clear influence of other cultures whose art was stylized or primarily decorative, it remains an example of imaginatively rich Byzantinism. The Tree of Life, which forms the decorative background to the main sections of the frieze, is a characteristically Byzantine motif found prominently in the church of San Clemente, Rome. Adele Bloch-Bauer, on whose portrait Klimt was then working, appears as *Expectation*, her head turned to one side and her pose inherited from Egyptian dancers. The triangular Byzantine motif has expanded to fill the whole of her dress, from which extend her long nervous hands and her decorated head. On the opposite wall *Fulfilment* (fig. 38) takes the form of the visual absorption of the female into the male, while his penetration of her is represented by the strong black squares on his huge cloak immersed in a sea of female rounds and swirls. Apart from a section of her face and the back of one hand, the female is almost invisible, swallowed up in the all-embracing form of the male.

A similar treatment was used by Klimt in *The Kiss* (1907–8; fig. 39), where the female now kneels to receive the large black rectangles of the male into her swirling fluvial ambience. The architect Adolf Loos disliked Klimt's erotic treatment of ornament. 'All art,' said Loos, 'is erotic. The first work of art, the first exuberant gesture of the first artists drawing on a wall, was erotic. A horizontal line was a woman lying down, a vertical line was a man penetrating her … But he who in our age is driven by some inner compulsion to cover walls in erotic symbols, in obscene graffiti, he is a criminal or delinquent … Ornament is no longer an expression of our civilization.'[72] Of course one of the principal reasons for the popularity of *The Kiss* is its erotic power, and part of that power derives from Klimt's use of mosaic form. The regular, sharp, mineral quality of the shapes applied in abundance here and in the other images of physical embrace serves to point up the soft vulnerability of the small pieces of exposed flesh which peep out as faces, shoulders, arms and legs. Klimt was a master of the serpentine line. Elsewhere, his highly erotic studies of women are executed with a technical skill and power that

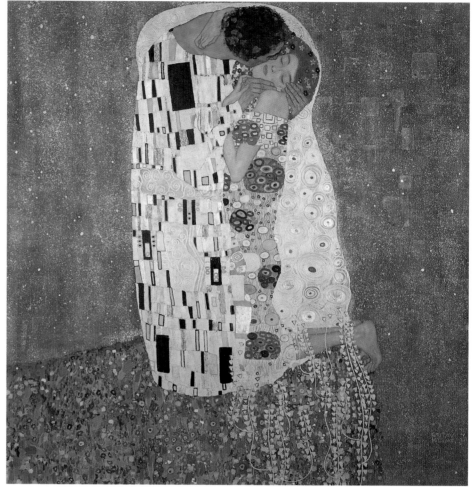

38 (left) Gustav Klimt, *Fulfilment*, preparatory study for
the Stoclet Frieze, *c*.1905–9. Tempera, watercolour,
gold and silver leaf on paper, 195 × 120 cm (76¾ × 47¼ in).
Palais Stoclet, Brussels

39 (right) Gustav Klimt, *The Kiss*, 1907–8. Oil on canvas,
180 × 180 cm (71 × 71 in). Österreichische Galerie,
Vienna

display a total command over the illusionistic aspects of mimesis. In these Symbolist versions of sexual encounter, illusion is banished to the fleshly margins; Byzantium introduces a kind of asceticism, preventing the forces of corporeal desire from taking over. If the erotic is held in check by the stiff armour of mosaic, it is done so only precariously. The lovers in *The Kiss* may be enjoying each other in a flower-filled meadow, but it is one which seems to be located on the edge of a cliff. In fact, the girl seems to be gripping the edge with her turned-in toes. Their position is an unusual one, and their symbolic status is equally special. The iconic treatment of the pair suggests sainthood and martyrdom, and like Byzantine saints they are located on a gold ground. Their haloes, however, have been melted by their passion and are beginning to flow towards the earth.

With Klimt, Byzantine iconography has been entirely secularized: instead of the gold ground suggesting heavenly bliss, it suggests sexual bliss; instead of visual isolation as a mark of asceticism, spiritual purity and superiority, the visual isolation of the lovers suggests symbiotic involvement apart from the world. Yet, conversely, Klimt's eroticization of Byzantium introduces a sense of control and containment. Like Ludwig I, Ludwig II and Wagner, Klimt was a man for whom sensual experience was important. Yet like them, too, his relationship with women (even allowing for the attitudes of his period) was imperious, dismissive and fearful. He seems to have found intimacy difficult, even threatening. Byzantine mosaic offered him a way of containing that threat and, although *The Kiss* has become an icon of eroticism, like Klimt's other visions of intimacy in a similar style, that intimacy is kept carefully confined within strict boundaries as the hieratic lovers are locked in their remote, golden world. Thus in *The Kiss*, Klimt has transformed the images, the symbols and the techniques of Byzantium, remodelling them and reusing them in a language that was readily understood by the citizens of the city of Sigmund Freud.

The transformation of Byzantium in nineteenth-century Germany and Austria was considerable. It is a long way from Ludwig I's little Byzantine Allerheiligen-Hofkirche to Wagner's Am Steinhof, or from the Boisserée brothers' collection of early German art to the erotic icons of Klimt. However varied the forms that it took, the Byzantine style provided for these patrons, architects and artists a mode which was unconventional. It facilitated the expression of ideas, attitudes and values which were less easily articulated through the more acceptable or dominant channels. The choice of Byzantine was determined by a number of contingent factors often operating simultaneously. In Germany and Austria the choice was often very personal; in France it was more political, as we shall see.

2 | France The revival of interest in Byzantium was developed in France in three different ways. The first was through the exploration of Byzantine sites in Greece, Turkey and beyond by French archaeologists and historians; the second was a fashion for Byzantine architecture which sprang out of the belief that there existed a native tradition of Byzantine work in France; and the third was a renewed interest in the decoration of churches in a Byzantine style.

Although Byzantine Revival buildings are not widespread in France, two of the most important are located at opposite ends of the country and between them span the period of the nineteenth century. The first, the cathedral of Sainte-Marie-Majeure, is situated in Marseilles on the Mediterranean basin, and has its stylistic roots in an early nineteenth-century Romantic architectural tradition. The second, the basilica of the Sacré-Coeur, which towers over Paris on the hill of Montmartre, is the product of an attempted Catholic Revival and was not finished until well into the twentieth century. Both of these churches were built in troubled times, both of them grew out of the passionate religious convictions of their respective patrons, and both record the turbulent relationship between the French Church and State in the nineteenth century.

The decoration of these and other churches in France was a vexed issue. In the early years of the century, artists and patrons of conservative temperament favoured conventional forms, whereas Byzantine (and Romano-Byzantine) style was adopted by architects of a radical disposition. In the second half of the nineteenth century, and under the powerful influence of Hippolyte Flandrin, neo-Byzantine church decoration was used in the service of liberal egalitarianism; but after the Franco-Prussian War (1870–1) the mosaic revival became a useful vehicle for the expression of ideas of national and religious stability. Byzantine art and the myth of Byzantium also had a secular appeal in the latter part of the nineteenth century since painters and writers of the French Decadence were strongly attracted to their material extravagance, excess and mysteriousness.

We have seen how Bavaria discovered Byzantium through the particular passions of Ludwig I. We have also seen the way in which Ludwig incorporated the then rather eccentric interests of the Boisserée brothers into the mainstream of modern art by purchasing their collection of medieval German paintings and placing them in the royal collection in Munich. The Boisserée brothers in fact also provide a link between France and Germany since Sulpiz Boisserée was a familiar figure in both Munich and Paris. In the mid-1820s Sulpiz was known in the French capital as a lecturer and writer on art and architecture, and was well known, too, for promulgating the idea that medieval Rhenish churches were *byzantin-roman*. But this fascination for the Byzantine origins of northern European architecture was naturalized in France not by Sulpiz Boisserée but by Ludovic Vitet. Vitet was famous as a novelist and as the editor of the widely read liberal journal *Le Globe*. Under the July Monarchy his passion for ancient architecture led to his appointment as first Inspector General of Historic Monuments, and his interest in early medieval work stemmed from a trip he made in 1829 to the Rhine, where he met the Boisserée brothers. Their enthusiasm was infectious and they took him around the churches of Sinzig and Maria Laach in a visit that he was to remember all his life. His journalism and his government post gave him considerable power over French taste, and he effectively brought the 'new' German attitudes to the attention of the French. Vitet adopted the passion and the terminology of the Boisserée brothers, translating their word 'neugriechisch' (neo-Greek) into the French 'néo-grec' or 'Byzantin', and describing it as a style burgeoning with 'youth and life'. 'Towards the second century', he wrote in a widely-read article of 1830, the emergent Byzantine style began 'to play like a shy child … Then, growing each day, little by little gained its independence: free, bold, original, it stepped out at last under Justinian, when in the designs of Isidoros, Sancta Sophia rose up in Constantinople.'[1]

40 (previous spread) Interior of the Sacré-Coeur, Paris, showing apse mosaic by Luc-Olivier Merson and Marcel Magne, 1923

1 | Rewriting French Architectural History

The inspiration of Byzantium was translated into modern terms by a group of radical architects, among whom were Henri Labrouste, Félix Duban, Louis Duc and Léon Vaudoyer. In the late 1820s they pursued their early training along conventional academic neoclassical lines, but developed unconventional or radical interpretations of classical buildings. In their different ways each of them reacted against the idealist approach to classicism and the notion that classical proportion and ornament could be translated wholesale into modern France. Instead they read ancient building in relativist terms, based upon the idea that architectural style had been persistently and subtly shifted to conform to special purposes. They abandoned the notion of a close correspondence between a hierarchy of historical periods and their expression in building, and developed instead theories about the importance of flux and change and a belief in the need to adapt ancient styles for modern use.

Many of these young architects had been impressed by the ideas of Claude Henri Saint-Simon, the founder of French socialism – ideas which indirectly opened the way for the rehabilitation of Byzantine art in historical terms. Saint-Simonian theory perceived historical processes in terms of a number of cycles that alternated between 'organic' periods and 'critical' periods. Organic periods were sustained by religious faith in conjunction with stable social organizations. Critical periods were times of change, disjunction and instability. Saint-Simon's great organic periods were those of Greek antiquity extending to the time of Pericles, and the age of Christianity up to the fifteenth century. This meant that the favoured architectural models were the Greek temple and the Gothic cathedral, since they were produced in times of cohesion. Byzantine architecture, although Christian in its associations, was more closely related to a period of transitional instability and therefore also close (so the young architects of the 1820s argued) to modern life and modern culture. The expansion and development of French historical studies also fed into the increased interest in Byzantium. The writer and statesman François Guizot appears in this context. Not only did he give Vitet the job of Inspector General when he came to power in 1830, Guizot was also by then well known for his *General History of Civilization in Europe*[2] which, like many contemporary histories, took the view that periods of transition were more interesting and creative than periods of stability. Augustin Thierry, in his *Narratives of the Merovingian Era* (1840),[3] focused on one such period and, in outlining the roots of modern France in the early Middle Ages, encouraged general interest in France's medieval 'néo-grec' or Byzantine-influenced architectural heritage.

There was also a certain amount of national rivalry about the supposed Byzantine origins of European culture. The German idea of a link between 'Byzantine' Rhenish churches and early Christian architecture was challenged by the French, who claimed that France, too, had its Byzantine monuments. Prosper Merimée, who succeeded Vitet as Inspector of Historical Monuments, suggested that French Gothic was deeply indebted to Byzantine models, and cited the evidence of 'Byzantine' elements in St-Maurice d'Angers, St-Gilles-du-Gard and even the lower portions of St Germain-des-Prés in Paris.[4] Furthermore, there was a growing number of more specialist texts, such as Arcisse de Caumont's *Course of Monumental Antiquities* (1830–41) or Armand Mallay's *Essay on the Romanesque and*

Romano-Byzantine Churches in the Département of Puy-de-Dôme (1838),[5] that promoted the idea of a France with the remains of Byzantine culture. Vitet's advice to modern architects, however, was not to simply copy. Instead he suggested that the Byzantine style offered a mine for architectural exploration, and like his German predecessors he felt that Byzantium was a sounder basis for future development than Gothic which, though beautiful, was complete, and had no potential for further development.

Alexandre Laborde's influential *Monuments of France* marks the change which took place in French sensibility about pre-Gothic architecture. The first edition, which appeared in 1816, had little space for the 'degenerate architecture' between late classical and the flowering of Gothic in the twelfth century. The second edition of 1836 is quite different: in this he devoted the whole first section of the book to some thirty-three French monuments in the 'Byzantine or Romanesque style'.[6] This interest in the Eastern influence on European architecture grew in the 1830s and 1840s. Léon Vaudoyer, a practising architect, and the architectural writer Albert Lenoir, began a long-running series for the readers of the *Magasin pittoresque* entitled 'Studies of French Architecture'. In 1839 they reached what had earlier been called the *'style Latin'*, which spanned the fifth to the late twelfth centuries. 'In the East,' they wrote, 'Christian monuments of this period … were called *Byzantine*; in southern Italy they were named *Sarrazin*, in the north *Lombard*, and in England, *Norman* or *Saxon*.'[7] In its early phase the *'style Latin'* was inherited from Roman architecture and had resulted in buildings like St-Trophîme in Arles. Later in the eighth century Byzantine influence, possibly coming via the Rhine, introduced the dome into France in churches in the Auvergne, Périgueux and Souillac.

It was the 'discovery' of St-Front in Périgueux, however, that confirmed the French in their belief about Eastern influence in France. Vaudoyer and Lenoir do not mention St-Front, yet it was to have a profound effect on French views about their own architectural history. St-Front (fig. 41) is an abbey church of 1120–50 dedicated to the follower of Saint Peter and first bishop of Périgueux. After many years of archaeological labour on the church, the archaeologist and historian Félix Verneilh published a study entitled *Byzantine Architecture in France*,[8] which appeared in 1851. As its title signifies, its claims were far-reaching. Verneilh suggested that France had a hidden tradition of Byzantine architecture which could be traced from the domed churches of Le Puy, Avignon, Souillac, Solignac and above all Périgueux back to Constantinople. The key building was St-Front, by then in an advanced state of decay, whose magnificent domes had long been hidden under a sloping tiled roof.[9] The similarity in plan between St-Front, San Marco in Venice and even Hagia Sophia was exploited to the full by Verneilh, and a restoration campaign was set in train. The architect chosen for the task was Paul Abadie, who had already stripped the domed cathedral of St-Pierre at Angoulême of its later additions and was later to be the designer of Sacré-Coeur in Paris. The debate surrounding St-Front centred on whether French architecture drew directly on Byzantium, as Verneilh argued, or whether this early influence was mediated through the Romanesque building tradition of Northern Italy. Vitet was well disposed to the Byzantine argument, but felt that Verneilh had overstated his case. In a substantial and largely sympathetic contribution to the *Journal des savants* in 1853 he took issue with some of the details of Verneilh's argument, but added his substantial weight to the idea of an Eastern influence on early French architecture.[10] The greatest authority behind the idea of French Byzantine, however, was Eugène Viollet-le-Duc. In the section 'L'architecture' in his *Comprehensive Dictionary of French Architecture* (1854–68), he praised Verneilh as 'one of our most distinguished archaeologists'[11] and devoted a large section to identifying the sources of Eastern influence in France. Using material from Verneilh's book, he suggested that trade between the

Mediterranean and the East, influences from Rhenish building in Germany, and the presence of Venetian colonies in Limoges in around 988 all served to introduce Byzantine planning and Byzantine detail into the architecture of the domed churches of Aquitaine and the Midi. Most important, he said, is St-Front, 'distinguished not only by the way in which it was laid out – which had no analogue in France – but was perhaps the original of all the churches possessing domes on pendentives in Périgord and the Angoumois.' But, Viollet continued in unequivocal mood, 'we believe that the domed churches in the Auvergne and the Lyonnais, like those of the cathedral of Le Puy, for example, were influenced by the East, or, rather, by the Adriatic, in a direct fashion, through Venetian commerce.'[12]

The restoration of St-Front by Paul Abadie took place in the wake of this enthusiasm. In modern terms this was not so much a restoration as a rebuilding, and recent historians have bemoaned the loss of evidence for the history of domed churches in France.[13] Coloured decoration was considered for the interior but abandoned because in his preliminary report on the building in 1851, Abadie suggested that the first architects had intended such decoration. Like San Marco, he said, 'it should have been covered with paintings,' but the idea was never taken up.[14] However, the work on St-Front and other buildings in southwestern France encouraged a belief in a native Byzantine tradition, which in its turn provided, as we shall see later, a basis not only for the design of the cathedral in Marseilles, but also for the famous shape of Sacré-Coeur in Paris.

2 | Byzantine Art and the Church

Ingres's *Christ Giving the Keys to St Peter* (1817–20; fig. 42) is at first sight a homage to Raphael's famous tapestry cartoon of the same subject in the Vatican. The strong, elegantly organized line which runs from the upraised right hand of Christ down through his left hand to the key in the hand of St Peter, and on down to the left foot of the saint, reflects the similar elegant grouping of Raphael's version. But a preliminary drawing done by Ingres in 1815 shows that there may have been another source of inspiration. This sheet in the Louvre shows the figure of Christ drawn in a severely full-frontal way, static and deliberately immobile. As Michael Driskel has shown, the hieratic stiffness of the pose derives precisely from an illustration of a mosaic in the basilica of SS Cosma e Damiano (fig. 43) in a seventeenth-century text – Ciampini's *Vetera Monumenta* (1699).[15] The correspondence between Christ's left-hand gesture in both the drawing and the illustration, the disposition of his robe, wrapped around the waist and folded at the neck, and the single-thonged sandals all suggest that it was early Christian mosaic art to which Ingres turned for his theme. The stimulus for this iconic style remains something of a mystery. The strongly royalist leanings of the Comte de Blacas, who had commissioned the picture for Santa Trinità dei Monti in Rome, and his belief in the divinity of kings meant that Ingres's choice would have been favourably received. Stylistically it may have been prompted by a group of artists associated with David's studio who had an interest in 'primitive' art, or it may have been inspired by the work of the Nazarenes who had been exploring the possibilities of the use of early Italian imagery since 1809. The secretary to the French Ambassador in Rome, Artaud de Montor, was certainly a pioneering figure in the appreciation of the 'primitives'. In his book *Considerations about the State of Painting in Italy* of 1808 he expressed admiration for the 'gravity, dignity, and even beauty achieved' by the Byzantines, even though 'their means were so slender'. De Montor also directed his readers' attention to the 'the noble simplicity of the Greek style of Constantinople' as it appeared in the engravings of Ciampini.[16] Ingres seems to have taken up de Montor's suggestion, though, as Driskel observes, his attraction to the mosaic form may have been as much

42 (left) Jean-Auguste-Dominique Ingres,
Christ Giving the Keys to St Peter, 1817–20.
Oil on canvas, 280 x 217 cm (110¼ x 85½ in).
Musée Ingres, Montauban

43 (right) Giovanni Ciampini, plate from the *Vetera Monumenta*, 1699, showing a mosaic from the basilica of SS Cosma e Damiano, Rome

political as aesthetic. The calm, static, monumental quality of these mosaic images may have been connected in Ingres's mind with his own authoritarianism, his distaste for democracy and his respect, like that of the Comte de Blacas, for papal authority. Of these things we cannot be certain, but in the first half of the nineteenth century the hieratic mode was certainly developed by those whose tendencies were conservative and authoritarian.

Among these were the painters Victor Orsel and François Picot. Following his early training in Lyons, Orsel went to Paris in 1817 and thence to Rome where he made friendships with the Nazarene painters, especially Friedrich Overbeck. He assiduously studied the mosaics in the basilicas and, like Artaud de Montor, was determined to retrace the path that art had taken on its way from its primitive Christian forms to the work of Raphael. But Orsel was also fired by a zeal for moral reform, and when his painting *Good and Evil* (fig. 44)[17] was shown in 1833 it met with considerable popular success. In this work the new aesthetic is employed in the service of conservative ideology. Orsel was himself profoundly conservative: like Ingres he had complete faith in monarchy and social hierarchy; he stressed the importance of paternalistic rule in the family as a model for society at large; and he even opposed the growing railway system as potentially socially disruptive. We can see something of this in *Good and Evil*, with its hieratic figure of Christ sitting upright on his throne, impersonally and impartially judging the deeds of good women who had devoted themselves to family life and matrimony, and the deeds of bad women who had abandoned themselves to the selfish or the erotic life. He developed this highly didactic principle further in a huge commission which he was offered three years later for the Paris church of Notre-Dame-de-Lorette, a project which lasted from 1836 until his death in 1850.

Notre-Dame-de-Lorette marks an important point in French ecclesiastical decoration. Throughout the eighteenth and early nineteenth centuries pictures tended to be painted in oil on canvas and brought from the studio to hang in suitable places in church buildings. Hippolyte Lebas, the architect of Notre-Dame-de-Lorette, decided instead to invite artists into the church to paint their works *in situ* on the newly built walls, so that they would fit precisely with the architectural design. The paintings under the aisle domes of Notre-Dame – Victor Orsel's Chapel of the Virgin (fig. 45), Alphonse Périn's Chapel of the Eucharist (1836–52) and Adolphe Roger's Chapel of Baptism – were created in this way. The artists also used the wax medium of encaustic, a move that in itself was a form of avant-garde archaism. These hieratic paintings by Roger, Orsel and Périn are above all symbolic, each of them reflecting aspects of contemporary Ultramontane dogma. Roger firmly believed that the simplicity of the hieratic style, based on formulas fixed by long religious tradition, was an ideal pedagogical tool. The simpler the form, the more simply the message is conveyed, but the political tendency of this group is best seen in François Picot's apse mosaic of the *Coronation of the Virgin* (fig. 46). In the basilican manner this, too, is clearly created for the space it occupies, and with his figures enthroned and isolated against a gold ground he is clearly operating in a Byzantine register. Charles de Montalembert, one of the leading Ultramontane

44 Victor Orsel, *Good and Evil*, 1833. Oil on canvas, 307 x 205 cm (121 x 80¼ in). Musée des Beaux-Arts, Lyons

45 (above) Victor Orsel, decoration of the
   Chapel of the Virgin, *c*.1836.
   Notre-Dame-de-Lorette, Paris

46 (below) François Picot, *Coronation of the Virgin*,
   c.1836. Mural. Notre-Dame-de-Lorette, Paris

figures of this period, was impressed by what he saw in this new style. Although he disliked the architecture of Notre-Dame-de-Lorette and the 'coqueterie' of many other paintings in the church that employed a historical and narrative method, he responded positively to the symbolism and the monumental dignity of the work of Orsel, Roger, Picot and Périn, which, he claimed, represented 'a new epoch for religious art'.[18] In contrast the critic Théophile Gautier, who had little time for art in the service of dogma, accurately perceived the socio-theological tendency of these murals. Writing in 1854, he suggested that the painters had employed the hieratic mode because they were 'persuaded that the more the forms in art are primitive, the more they approach the rigidity of dogma'.[19]

Orsel and Roger continued to labour at their decoration of Notre-Dame, whereas Picot, who was much swifter in finishing his apse mural, was soon employed on another project, that of St-Vincent-de-Paul a short distance away. This was a much more powerful and forbidding exercise in the Byzantine mode, and the impetus behind it was probably not Picot's but that of the architect, Jakob-Ignaz Hittorff. St-Vincent-de-Paul is far more reminiscent of an

early Christian basilica than Notre-Dame-de-Lorette, yet Hittorff, like Lebas, had grown up in the neoclassical tradition of Quatremère de Quincy, the dictator of French taste in the early part of the century. Hittorff had a passionate interest in art history and archaeology, and between 1822 and 1824 made an extensive survey of the classical remains of Sicily. It was intended to be a confirmation of all he believed about the centrality of the classical tradition in architecture, but the journey proved to be something rather different. Certainly the classical buildings of the island satisfied him as he expected, and in 1827 he included them in his first volume, *Ancient Architecture of Sicily*,[20] but he was also fascinated by the medieval, Arabo-Norman and Byzantine buildings of the island. He was attracted by their diversity, irregularity and their use of colour, so he published these in a second splendidly illustrated volume entitled *Modern Architecture of Sicily* (1835).[21] It included a three-page pull-out of a longitudinal section of the Cathedral at Monreale, and another showing the mosaics of the Cappella Palatina (fig. 47).

It was this new enthusiasm that Hittorff brought to Paris and to the building of St-Vincent-de-Paul. The original design for the church was not by Hittorff but his father-in-law, Jean-Baptiste Lepère, and Hittorff inherited the building partly built but emphatically classical in style. Lack of funds prevented much work on the existing structure, and when Hittorff finally took over from Lepère in 1833 he attempted to remodel it more along the lines of a Christian basilica. Like Lebas at Notre-Dame-de-Lorette, Hittorff employed artists to decorate *in situ*, but instead of the multitude of hands involved in that project, Hittorff chose just two men for the whole scheme – Picot and Hippolyte Flandrin. When in 1848 he commissioned Picot to design the apse, he urged him to consult his own book on Sicilian architecture, and probably also encouraged him to produce the vast figure of the Pantocrator that dominates the puny humans and angels kneeling on the steps

47 Jacob-Ignaz Hittorff, plate from *Modern Architecture of Sicily*, 1835, showing the apse mosaics of the Cappella Palatina, Palermo

of a monolithic altar (fig. 48). The Pantocrator, said Hittorff in his *Modern Architecture of Sicily*, 'leads the thoughts of the artist to the images of the colossal statues of the temples of Egypt and Greece',[22] but Picot, under Hittorff's direction, has borrowed the language of immobility, fixity, patriarchy and dominance for the central figure from Byzantium. It is a language which was determined by Hittorff's own authoritarian and conservative principles, views that go back to Ingres and were shared by Orsel and his companions at Notre-Dame-de-Lorette.[23] Flandrin's contrasting work is discussed below (p. 76).

At the same time there persisted in France, as elsewhere, a residue of hostility to Byzantine art inherited from the eighteenth-century Enlightenment. A good example is provided by Seroux d'Agincourt's *History of Art by its Monuments*,[24] which was published posthumously in 1823. It was a major illustrated source of material for art historians and artists, and offered one of the first attempts at a serious taxonomy (extremely inaccurate as it happens) of Byzantine and early medieval works of art in the context of medieval social and political movements. Seroux was resolutely dismissive of Byzantine art and architecture. 'Throughout the course of the Byzantine period,' he wrote, 'religious thought, taking advantage of the impotence of the art of the time, rendered it immobile in order to render it sacred; one knows that in effect this art of the Byzantines remained captive in its hieratic prototypes.' And in Seroux's condemnation of the 'ten centuries' of Byzantine rule, we hear the echoes of Gibbon and Voltaire when he speaks of the absence of 'a single ray of life, of liberty or of movement until the first rays of the sun of the Renaissance'.[25] As late as 1866, the critic Hippolyte Taine was still speaking of the 'ineptitude of the mosaicists' and of the way in which the figures in Byzantine art 'have no movement at all, they have no thought, they have no soul.'[26] But Seroux's distaste for Byzantine art is a Rationalist one, whereas Taine's is Romantic. Seroux saw the Byzantine period as an age when reason was suffocated by superstition; Taine saw it as a period when individual liberty and artistic creativity were suppressed by authoritarianism, and no doubt this view had been buttressed by the Ultramontane adoption of Byzantine art in the work of artists like Orsel and Picot.

Within Catholic aesthetic thought, however, there was an important distinction which has so far been overlooked. It is a distinction between Oriental Byzantine and Occidental Byzantine, between the art of Constantinople and the art of the Roman basilicas. The textbook of the Catholic renaissance in art was Alexis François Rio's *The Poetry of Christian Art* (1836),[27] and in this Rio expressed the orthodox hostile attitudes to Eastern Byzantine art. For Rio, as for many of his contemporaries, Byzantium had sunk into an 'abyss of moral and intellectual degradation from which no human power was able to withdraw it', and he claimed that Byzantium had exercised nothing but a 'pernicious' influence on the art of the West, including Ravenna. The art of Rome and the mosaic decorations of the Roman basilicas were, however, quite another matter. This 'Romano-Christian School'[28] came from a pure source; it derived from the early Christians and the images of the catacombs. So Rio had it both ways. He persisted in his conventional condemnation of Eastern Byzantium, but aligned himself with the growing Ultramontane admiration for Western basilican architecture and mosaic decoration, both of which went hand in hand with the belief in papal authority.

The changes taking place in aesthetic attitudes to Byzantine art are well illustrated in George Sand's *Letters of a Traveller* (1837).[29] Writing back from Torcello, Sand reports having seen the 'eleventh-century mosaics' which, she adds, 'like all those of that decadent period, [are] hideous in design' (see fig. 89). But the local priest stepped in and explained, in terms which were very up to date, that 'these eleventh-century mosaic virgins possessed an austerity and grandeur, better than the poetic grace of a more sophisticated art, the true faith.' By the time that the priest had finished his lecture, Sand was obliged to admit 'that in these great Byzantine figures with their almond eyes and Greek profiles there is something of the steadfastness and solemnity we associate with the teachings of the new faith.'[30] Nineteenth-century Romanticism was coming to the aid of Byzantine art, and there was a growing tendency both in France and elsewhere to interpret its Western manifestation in these terms. This is clear, for example, in the writing of the liberal Ultramontane Cyprien Robert, whose evocation of the beauty of the figures in the 'high tribunes of the imperial basilicas' of Rome is endowed with same strong feeling and emotion which Sand had attributed to her priest. 'It seems,' he wrote, 'as if these suffering souls are going to break their terrestrial envelopes by the very force of their sighs' as they 'incline toward the beholder as if from heaven' in order to 'embrace the earth'.[31] Similarly, in a series of lectures on the civilization of the fifth century given in the Sorbonne in the 1840s, the Catholic historian Frédéric Onzaman spoke breathlessly of the apses in the churches of this period with their 'great and resplendent image of Christ'.[32]

3 | Sainte-Marie-Majeure, Marseilles

In the world of modern architecture it was Léon Vaudoyer who took passionately to the idea of a Byzantine France. He came under the influence of Saint-Simonian thought in the early 1830s, and its belief in social scientific progress, and he established friendships with several of the editors of the Saint-Simonian journal called the *Encyclopédie nouvelle*. Pierre Leroux and Léonce Reynaud were among these men, as was Albert Lenoir, with whom he later collaborated on the *Magasin pittoresque*. He was also close to the historian Edgar Quinet and the journalist and politician Hippolyte Fortoul, both of whom were interested in things German, in reading the philosophy of Herder and in travelling to the Rhine.

It was at about this time in the early 1830s that the Byzantine style began to be distinguished from Romanesque. As we have seen above (p. 58), Albert Lenoir identified what he saw as two strains of post-antique architecture – *'style Latin'* and *'style Byzantin'*, as he called them. *'Style Latin'* was Western in its pedigree and derived directly from the basilicas of antique Rome; *'style Byzantin'* was the Eastern version, with an Oriental physiognomy that developed the pendentive and the dome. The two styles, in Lenoir's view, combined once again under Charlemagne, in the churches of Norman Sicily and in Venice.[33] Lenoir decided that sufficient architectural evidence was still lacking, so he set off for the Near East. In 1836 he toured the Middle East, returning in 1838 to give a series of lectures on Byzantine architecture at the Bibliothèque Nationale in Paris, and in 1840 publishing an important article in the *Revue générale de l'architecture et des travaux publics* entitled 'De l'architecture byzantine'.[34] Reynaud went to Lombardy, and Vaudoyer, accompanied by Fortoul, travelled to Prussia and Bavaria. Meanwhile Vitet, in his role as Inspector of Historical Monuments (see above, p. 56), was developing his enthusiasm for Byzantine work at home.

In the last chapter we saw Fortoul's enthusiasm for Ludwig I's work at the Allerheiligen-Hofkirche. It was his friendship with Vaudoyer that took him to Germany in the first place. He shared many of Vaudoyer's attitudes and opinions, though he lacked his training and experience. Eight years Vaudoyer's junior, Fortoul had come to Paris in 1829 to study law, but took instead to politics and to writing about art. Like his friend, he too knew Edouard Charton, the editor of the *Magasin pittoresque*, he wrote for left-wing journals, was a sympathizer with liberal Catholic aims and aspirations, and turned from the Romanticism of his youth to become a devotee of historiography. His tour of Germany in 1840 in the company of Vaudoyer was in order to test Sulpiz Boisserée's claim for the German source of Gothic, an assertion recently challenged by Augustin Thierry in his *Narratives of the Merovingian Era*. Germany was the envy of France, and particularly of the Saint-Simonians who saw in its dominantly Protestant culture the appearance of a progressive state. They felt that its philosophical scholarship, dominated by Fichte and Hegel, was second to none. Vaudoyer went to Munich, but missed Leo von Klenze who was away in Russia. Fortoul went to Berlin and was extremely impressed by the work of Schinkel, who was then suffering from a terminal illness. They both travelled to Cologne and, although the object of their pursuit was the Gothic, they were surprised to be confronted by 'Byzantine' work at every turn. They went to see the cathedral only to be overwhelmed by the 'twenty Byzantine churches' which surrounded it.[35]

Fortoul's *Concerning German Art* was the fruit of this trip. It appeared in two volumes in 1841 and 1842, and did much to establish the central importance of Byzantine architecture in the history of the West. Fortoul's view of art and architecture was societal and progressive. The artist, he maintained, was part of the continuing process of history, and artistic style was conditioned by evolving political and religious forces. In architecture two modes dominated: the rectilinear and the curvilinear. The first grew out of materialist religions, such as those of ancient Egypt, Greece and Rome. The second was a development of Christianity and its roots were found in Byzantium. Like Vitet and Lenoir, Fortoul opposed revival styles that were merely copies of ancient styles. This was why neoclassical and neo-Gothic building were both doomed to sterility. He argued that modern style might be developed by returning to the first inspirations for curvilinear architecture in Byzantine work and in the buildings of the early Renaissance. Fortoul's attitude to the origins of Gothic was that neither France nor Germany could be awarded precedence. Only when Roman and Byzantine had run its course was Gothic able to take root, which it did according to laws of universal progress rather than with reference to the national spirit. Fortoul's ideas had an enormous impact on Vaudoyer. Together with Albert Lenoir he worked them through in his articles for the *Magasin pittoresque*. In his concluding paragraphs of *Concerning German Art*, Fortoul had stressed the vital, revolutionary importance of Byzantine work in the progress of architecture. It was a moment, he wrote, when 'architecture freed itself from the orders … placed the arcade on the column … and began upon the road of its uncertain development.'[36]

For this group of architects and writers, Byzantine art was energetic, innovative and fresh. It was also exotic without being remote from the French tradition, and it fitted an interpretation of the relationship between art and society of which they approved. The outcome of their thinking can be seen in Marseilles. The cathedral church of Sainte-Marie-Majeure (fig. 49) and the pilgrimage chapel of Notre-Dame-de-la-Garde (fig. 50) dominate the city skyline. From the sea, the cathedral appears to be floating on a slim raft, its domes rising one behind the other and billowing like sails in the wind. The Byzantine style of both these buildings was the inspiration of Vaudoyer and his colleagues, but neither would have been possible without the efforts of a local priest, Eugène de Mazenod. The cathedral is in fact a symbol of many things. It is a monument to the ambitions (both spiritual and temporal) of Mazenod, and a symbol of the material prosperity of mid-century Marseilles. It represents the revival of Catholicism that took place under the Second Empire, since few buildings of the nineteenth century were more closely bound up with contemporary politics and the relationship between Church and State. Its origins lie in the Romantic mythology of the Mediterranean and the arrival of Christianity in France; and its physical structure is the architectural realization of the Saint-Simonianism sympathies of Fortoul and Vaudoyer. In terms of style, it symbolizes the triumph of a pan-European aesthetic over the narrower field of Northern European Gothic. A proud, striking and unusual building, Sainte-Marie-Majeure asserts itself at the heart of the port life of Marseilles. Its imposing presence on the seafront is reinforced by the architectural gesture of a companion, Notre-Dame-de-la-Garde, which was constructed nearby on the highest point of the city.

49 (overleaf) Léon Vaudoyer, Sainte-Marie-Majeure, Marseilles, 1852–93

The spiritual architect of Sainte-Marie-Majeure was Mazenod. Mazenod had been educated in the Paris seminary of St Sulpice in the spirit of Romantic Catholicism and the Catholic revival in France. On his arrival in Marseilles, with the help of the architect Pascal Coste, he began a church building campaign in the city that met with severe government opposition. In 1832 the two men travelled to Rome. Coste, who had an interest in the basilican style, went to see early Christian architecture. The result was his church of St-Joseph in Marseilles, which was based upon Sta Maria Maggiore, and the church of St Lazare, inspired by the restoration of San Paolo fuori le Mura. The reason for Mazenod's trip to Rome was less architectural than ecclesiastical. He had gone in an attempt to win the sympathy of the Vatican and came back with the promise that he would be given the sinecure bishopric of Icosie, a title that meant that he was able to communicate directly with Rome and not obliged to defer to the anticlerical establishment in Paris. He returned to Marseilles with a mission to Christianize the city which was then under the anti-Catholic central government of Louis-Philippe and his ministers – described by Mazenod as 'monsters vomited from hell'.[37] In 1837, when Louis-Philippe's government attempted a reconciliation with the Church, Mazenod was invested as Bishop of Marseilles and agreement was reached with Paris that a new cathedral might be built in the city. It was not, however, until 1839 that real progress was made, and this came about through the king's eldest son, Ferdinand, Duc d'Orléans. It seems that the Duc d'Orléans saw that political capital might be made out of an alliance between the clergy, the local administration and the House of Orléans.

50 Léon Vaudoyer, Notre-Dame-de-la-Garde, Marseilles, 1853–70. View showing the church's position above the city

Vaudoyer entered the picture in 1845, after the death of Ferdinand. He came down from Paris to advise on the site for the new cathedral and brought with him letters of introduction from Fortoul to Mazenod. Various locations were explored, but after much discussion the place settled on was one already occupied by the dilapidated Romanesque church of the Vieille Major. This was a legendary spot. Reputedly St Lazarus landed here, bringing with him the Three Maries; it was also believed to have been occupied by a Roman temple to Diana that had subsequently been Christianized. Just as the decision was about to be finalized, political turmoil erupted in the form of the 1848 Revolution. The outcome, however, was extremely favourable for Mazenod and his building project. Louis-Napoléon Bonaparte came to power with a government that was sympathetic to the Church. In an odd posture that mixed popular suffrage and authoritarianism, the government looked to the Church to help it battle against the forces of socialism and anarchy. In 1852 Louis-Napoléon (now Napoleon III) travelled through France attempting to win support for the new Empire. Marseilles had remained powerfully resistant to the Bonaparte charm, distrusting anyone who came to them in that hated name. Louis-Napoléon, anxious to curry favour with its citizens, determined at very short notice to use his visit to lay the cornerstone of the new cathedral. This he did after Mass on 26 September 1852, at the same time promising the sum of 2.6 million francs as a first instalment for the project. The whole venture was transformed by the inclination of its protagonists for myth-making. Napoleon, who wished to substantiate the authenticity of the Second Empire, saw himself as the heir of Vercingetorix and the Carolingian kings of France; the local politicians in Marseilles saw the cathedral as representing the developing role of the city as the capital of the South and as part of a utopian Saint-Simonian vision of social harmony and industrial development; and Vaudoyer, whose Saint-Simonianism was never far beneath the surface, also took a seriously historicist view of his role in designing the new cathedral for France's 'Gateway to the Orient'.

Saint-Simon had reserved a special, avant-garde mission for artists in interpreting modern society. In choosing the Byzantine style for the new cathedral, Vaudoyer was acting out that mission by creating a bridge between the ancient world and the modern, industrial world. The Byzantine mode was, in Barry Begdoll's words, 'the very seal on a marriage between the architect's belief in architecture as a product and even a form of historical knowledge, and the historical claims of Napoleon III's strategies.'[38]

As early as 1846, Vaudoyer had told Pascal Coste that the first cathedral to be built in France for a hundred years should be in a Byzantine-Romanesque style.[39] When Vaudoyer was commissioned to build the cathedral in Marseilles, Henri Espérandieu, his pupil and right-hand man, wrote to Charles Blanc that 'two things must have immediately occurred to him: the structure of the great thermal halls of the ancients and the decoration of St Mark's and Santa Sophia.'[40] Vaudoyer was also aware of the debate about the presence of Byzantine buildings on French soil. Charles Questel had successfully experimented with a neo-Romanesque style in the nearby church of St-Paul-de-Nîmes, and Vaudoyer wrote to him requesting copies of the drawings. He entered into a correspondence with local scholars about the relationship between Romanesque and Byzantine styles, and he corresponded with

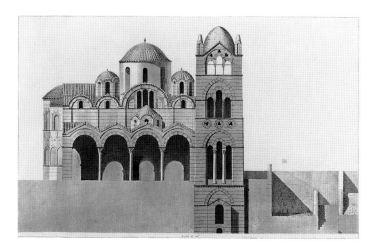

Armand Mallay, author of an *Essay on the Romanesque and Romano-Byzantine Churches of the Département of Puy-de-Dôme* (1838),[41] who sent him a substantial number of measured drawings of the churches from that region. Although Vaudoyer had never been to Greece, André Couchaud's *Selection of Byzantine Churches in Greece* (1841)[42] provided an array of drawings of domed churches designed as a source book of 'motifs' which might be 'applicable to modern architecture' (fig. 51).[43] He also sought the assistance of the French ambassador in Istanbul, who agreed to send measured drawings of Hagia Sophia and who reminded Vaudoyer that Fossati's *Aya Sofia* was about to be published.[44] Above all, he was convinced by the compelling argument of Félix de Verneilh's *Byzantine Architecture in France* (see above, p. 58).

Vaudoyer's original choice of a purely Byzantine style for the cathedral was gradually modified as he became more familiar with Marseilles, its needs and its myths. One of those myths was that the city was a kind of node or focal point between the Mediterranean and Northern Europe. The economist Michel Chevalier had promoted this idea in Saint-Simonian terms in his book *Mediterranean System* (1832),[45] and it was still current in 1868 when Pierre Puvis de Chavannes was commissioned by the city council to paint a mural to decorate the stairway of the newly opened Musée de Beaux-Arts. This was *Marseilles, Gateway to the Orient* (fig. 52), in which the viewer is located on a cargo ship approaching the city from the Mediterranean, the skyline punctuated by Vaudoyer's cathedral on the left and Notre-Dame-de-la-Garde on the right. The outcome of Vaudoyer's deliberations is that, although the controlling spirit of Sainte-Marie-Majeure is Byzantine, it incorporates many other architectural voices from France and overseas.

First, the Nouvelle Major was designed to pay homage to the ancient twelfth-century church whose territory it usurped. The shallow dome of the older structure was echoed and amplified in the new cathedral, and it was hoped that mosaics discovered in 1850 in a nearby fifth-century baptistery might find an equivalent in the decoration of the interior. Throughout the construction there were shifts and modifications. A decision to broaden the podium on which the whole building rested allowed Vaudoyer to open up the proportions of the bays, and in the mid-1850s the porch-façade was pulled out and developed into a freestanding triumphal arch of enormous size. On the main tympana are mosaic depictions of Jerusalem and Bethlehem, and underneath the arch mosaics closely based on the oratory of Galla Placidia in Ravenna.

51 André Couchaud, plate from *Selection of Byzantine Churches in Greece*, 1841–2, showing the church of Kapnicarea, Athens

Inside, Vaudoyer created a remarkable, dramatic space in pink and white stripes. The nave proceeds in three enormous bays down to the wide chancel, which is illuminated with light streaming from the tall narrow domes above: one above each transept and one above the chancel itself. The choir is plunged into a tenebrous half-light and features at its centre an elegant baldacchino in gold, pink and white. Wrapped around the outside of the choir is a narrow ambulatory which opens out into a procession of domical chapels. The whole area is full of mysterious places, with arches folding upon arches. The bays, corridors and domes have the feel of an endlessly complicated series of elegantly structured caves, where the light filters in from unexpected sources, all turning in upon themselves but eventually bringing the visitor back to the wide, open area of the chancel.

Vaudoyer went on to use this Romano-Byzantine framework as the basis for a highly allusive exercise in historicism, drawing upon what he called the great 'Mediterranean family of architecture'.[46] He experimented with Pisan banding, Lombardic patterning, and with turrets above the transepts based on the model of Périgueux. The soaring towers of Angoulême Cathedral and the clustered domes of St-Front can be readily discerned as the most recent influences on a design which became, in Bergdoll's words, 'the lost recension … of the great chain of buildings that led from the Baths of Diocletian … via Hagia Sophia and St Mark's in Venice to Périgueux and Angoulême.'[47] The violently eye-catching bands

52 Pierre Puvis de Chavannes, *Marseilles, Gateway to the Orient*, 1868. Mural, 4.25 × 5.65 m (14 × 18 ft 6 in). Musée des Beaux Arts, Marseilles

of red and white on the exterior probably derive in part from Coste's illustration of the El-Moyed Mosque in Cairo in his *Arab Architecture*,[48] and from the plates in André Couchaud's *Choice of Byzantine Greek Churches*. Throughout the building Vaudoyer set up links between East and West, between Byzantine in the East and Romanesque in the West, between Romanesque in Italy and its counterpart in France, between early Renaissance building in Florence and the Rhenish building of the Middle Ages, and between the Roman thermal bath and basilica and a vast modern liturgical space. It is, as Bergdoll says, 'a gloss on history itself'.

Vaudoyer's cathedral seems to float on the tide of commerce right in the busiest part of Marseilles. Complementing it, high and remote above the city, is the pilgrimage chapel of Notre-Dame-de-la-Garde. It stands proudly as the visual symbol of Marseilles itself, surveying both land and sea. Like the cathedral it is mainly the product of Vaudoyer's imagination, and it too derives substantially from Byzantium. There had been a chapel on this prominent chalk cliff since the thirteenth century. It was extended in 1477, then in the early sixteenth century François I decided that the position should be fortified and the chapel was incorporated into a garrison. In this way the land became the property of the state, and later, specifically, the Ministry of War, thus ensuring constant wrangles between Church and State about access and upkeep. During the French Revolution the chapel was largely abandoned, but it experienced a revival in the early part of the nineteenth century and went from strength to strength in the following years. In 1831 Mazenod's uncle, a former bishop of Marseilles, placed the responsibility for the chapel in the hands of a religious congregation recently founded by his nephew. The group was dedicated to the cult of Mary of which Mazenod was an enthusiastic supporter, and the 1840s saw a considerable increase in the number of pilgrims willing to climb the tortuous and steep path up to the top of the cliff. The new chapel rising above the city was to symbolize both this spirit of Catholic revival and the newly authorized doctrine of the Immaculate Conception.

Plans for a new chapel were first mooted in around 1848, but the Revolution temporarily halted their development. By 1851, however, negotiations with the army were completed successfully due to the sympathetic support of General Adolphe Niel, Inspector General of Fortifications for the South of France and a fervent Catholic. It was decided not to attempt to extend the ancient chapel any further, but to demolish it and put up a much larger and far more imposing building. As with the plans for the Nouvelle Major, there was scarcely a thought of attempting to preserve the older building, and in the case of Notre-Dame-de-la-Garde not a stone or statue of the original structure was introduced into the new. Instead, a competition was set up for a brand new chapel and by 1852 the building committee was divided between two plans, one neo-Gothic and the other Romano-Byzantine. Probably as the result of pressure from Mazenod the second was chosen. The successful plan had been produced by the 23-year-old Jacques-Henri Espérandieu, a pupil of Vaudoyer, but was almost certainly based upon drawings by Vaudoyer himself. Friction between the various parties broke out when it was discovered – to Mazenod's disgust – that Espérandieu was a Protestant, but the financial and moral support of Napoleon III pushed the venture onwards.

The Espérandieu–Vaudoyer plan deliberately echoed the design of the cathedral that was rising on the seafront below. The vibrant striped polychromy and the close relationship between dome and steeple of Notre-Dame are both reminiscent of the Nouvelle Major, but where the cathedral is at once expansive in its accumulation of chapels and the massing of its domes and towers, Notre-Dame is compact and fitted tightly into the walls of the strongly fortified site (fig. 53). Inside, side chapels are created by internalized buttressing which creates the sense of a number of private spaces without destroying the effect of a high vaulted space. A series of cupolas encloses a highly decorated interior reminiscent of the Byzantine churches in Couchaud's influential book. But the internal decoration of both Sainte-Marie-Majeure and Notre-Dame-de-la-Garde was part of a later phase of the Byzantine Revival (see below, p. 88). Vaudoyer died in 1872, and Espérandieu soon followed in 1874, after which Henri Révoil took on both projects. Révoil was architect-in-chief for the dioceses of Montpellier, Aix-en-Provence, Nîmes and Fréjus; he restored many of the most outstanding buildings of the region and was the author of the two-volume *Romanesque Architecture of the French Midi* (1867, 1868).[49]

53 Léon Vaudoyer, Notre-Dame-de-la-Garde,
Marseilles, 1853–70

4 | Hippolyte Flandrin and Dominique Papety

So far we have seen hieratic ecclesiastic decoration operating in the context of a rather socially reactionary Catholicism. This tendency was subverted, if not actually reversed, by one of the outstanding nineteenth-century ecclesiastical painters, Hippolyte Flandrin. In 1833, when he was a student in Rome, Flandrin had been deeply impressed by the mosaics of the basilicas, and of Sta Maria Maggiore in particular. He wrote in his diary about 'the figures in Greek mosaic which decorate the choir', which he thought possessed a 'great, terrible, character'.[50] Then in 1837 he was absorbed by the mosaics in San Marco, Venice, and by 'the different characteristics of Christian art and antique Greek art mixed with Arab and Saracen art' to produce a mixture which was 'unbelievably mysterious and strong'.[51]

That combination of strength and mystery is evident in the first commissions Flandrin received when he returned to Paris from Rome. In his rendering of the *Last Supper* in St-Séverin (1838), Christ is depicted in a full-frontal position and the disciples are grouped around the central figure like monumental sculptural effigies. The narrative is frozen and intensified; Christ is removed in both space and spiritual status from his followers who look upon him wonderingly and from afar. But, in contrast to the work of Orsel, that distance suggests transcendence rather than oppression. In the *Last Supper* Flandrin avoids the local and the particular in favour of something more contemplative and meditative. The murals for St-Germain-des-Prés followed soon after in 1842–4 (fig. 54). Here, again, the noisy event of Christ's entry into Jerusalem has become a passage of silent, almost paralysed stillness. The gestures of the men in the crowd on the right are frozen in mute fixity; the ordered group of onlookers' heads in the centre and the stately procession of disciples behind, all of whom are of equal height, contribute an even symmetry to the composition which is intensified by the horizontal lines of the architectural form behind. This eerie feeling of transcendence was something quite new in the 1840s and won for Flandrin an international reputation. Dante Gabriel Rossetti and William Holman Hunt made an artistic pilgrimage to Paris in 1849, declaring the Flandrin in St-Germain to be one of the most 'perfect' works they had ever seen.[52] The mute yet eloquent grouping of figures, who exist suspended in time and space, derives from a number of sources but principally from the mosaics of Sant'Apollinare Nuovo in Ravenna (see fig. 3). The figures occur not only in Flandrin's work (see fig. 57), but can also be seen in processional groups in the paintings of Rossetti, Millais and, above all, Burne-Jones (fig. 55), and they can be found again and again as a kind of Byzantine topos in mural, tile and mosaic, moving in stately dignity across the walls of churches and public buildings throughout Europe in the latter part of the nineteenth century.

One of Flandrin's most politically engaged designs was for the interior of St-Paul-de-Nîmes in southern France. This had been planned by a young Parisian, Charles Questel, in 1836 as a daring experiment in neo-Romanesque. Questel had been in Rome in 1831 and 1832 when Flandrin was a student there, and like Flandrin he had studied the mosaics. From the first he projected a hieratic design for the interior of St-Paul representing Christ enthroned and surrounded by standing figures. As the fabric of the church was nearing completion in 1846, Flandrin was

54 (above) Hippolyte Flandrin, *Christ's Entry into Jerusalem*, 1842–4. Mural. Saint-Germain-des-Prés, Paris
55 (below) Edward Burne-Jones, *The Wedding of Psyche*, 1895. Oil on canvas, 122 × 213.4 cm (48 × 84 in). Musées Royaux des Beaux-Arts de Belgique, Brussels

France Hippolyte Flandrin and Dominique Papety

56 Hippolyte Flandrin, apse mural,
1848–9. Saint-Paul-de-Nîmes

commissioned to execute interior paintings in encaustic, the very permanent wax-based medium that Orsel had used at Notre-Dame-de-Lorette in Paris. In Flandrin's apsidal composition, the figure of the enthroned Christ that Questel had suggested in his original design for the church ten years earlier remained, but the standing apostles were now replaced by the abject form of a slave and an emperor prostrate on the steps before the divine presence (fig. 56). Who chose this iconography is not known. Whether it was Questel, Flandrin himself or whether the idea came from the church authorities in Nîmes is uncertain. What is certain is that these three figures are a legacy of the turbulent political conditions that prevailed during the completion of the church.

In 1848 the July Monarchy collapsed. The Catholic community in Nîmes was broadly legitimist, respecting authority and particularly the authority of the Church. It feared the politically powerful Protestant minority in the town that was identified with republicanism and anarchy. For the Catholics, the rigidity and immobility of the group in the apse was redolent of authority and security – concepts which (as we have seen) had become associated with neo-Byzantine church decoration. But from what we know of Flandrin and his political sympathies it is unlikely that he shared these conservative views. In his youth he had experienced extreme poverty and had grown up with strong republican sympathies. Like many of his contemporaries he was torn between belief in the authority of the pope and the principle of personal liberty. In this way the political meaning of the apse at St-Paul is enigmatic and might be interpreted in a number of ways. Michael Driskel sums this up by saying: 'The figure of the slave could be read as either in the process of liberation or submission, so too could the prostrate figure of the king be interpreted as either in the act of renouncing his prerogatives or of offering them to a more powerful monarch, thereby preserving the principle of hierarchy.'[53]

What distinguishes Flandrin's version of the hieratic Christ from the similar figures in the tradition represented by Orsel is its benevolence. The authoritarian ferocity of Orsel's legitimist Christ, whose immobility corresponded with the unyielding authority of the law and who appears to sit in judgement, is replaced in Flandrin's version with a Christ who makes an asymmetrical gesture of welcoming acceptance. The lighter, gentler body movement in the Flandrin design speaks more of reconciliation than rejection, and more of authority than authoritarianism. Fortoul had written something very similar about Hess's treatment of Christ in the Allerheiligen-Hofkirche in Munich. The Old Testament figures, he said, derived from what he called the 'First Period' of Byzantine art – the stern hieratic mosaics of the fifth to eighth centuries. The New Testament figures, including that of Christ, had a gentleness about them which he thought derived from Hess's admiration for Giotto. Something similar seems to lie behind Flandrin's use of early Christian models in Nîmes, and it is confirmed to some extent by the contemporary painter and writer Jules Salles, who remarked that the king and the slave represented two extremes on the social scale and were 'the symbol of the equality of men before God'.[54] In spite of the fundamental differences between Flandrin and Orsel or Picot, Salles sees their work as a new development in Christian art. Consequently, his praise for Flandrin's work closely resembles that of Montalembert's for the decoration at Notre-Dame-de-Lorette (see above, pp.61–3). Flandrin, he said, avoided the models of Tintoretto and Michelangelo, and turned instead to the mosaics that decorated the first Romanesque churches. He avoided nudity or the Greek physiognomy which recalled 'a detested idolatry', and chose instead figures who were 'modestly dressed' and whose appearance was 'chaste and pure'. Flandrin's figures, he claimed, create a deeper and more powerful impression than posed figures, and appeal strongly to the 'heart and soul of the true Christian' through their sober demeanour, their naivety and their moral grandeur.[55]

The contrast between these two interpretations of hieratic Byzantine art is clearly seen in Hittorff's St-Vincent-de-Paul in Paris. The task for the internal decoration was shared between Flandrin and François Picot who, as we have seen (fig. 48), had produced an apsidal Christ in Judgement (completed in 1853) that conformed with Hittorff's political conservatism. Flandrin's contribution, however, was very different (fig. 57) and much more in the spirit of his work in Nîmes. The procession of figures around the side walls of the church is infused with an egalitarianism of scale and demeanour. It looks back to his work in St-Germain-des-Prés and owes much to the mosaics of Sant'Apollinare Nuovo.

Flandrin's most severe exercise in the Byzantine mode was in the church of St-Martin-d'Ainay, Lyons. Questel, who built no more new churches on the model of St-Paul-de-Nîmes, was employed by the Commission for Historical Monuments in survey and restoration work, and one of his tasks was the restoration of the Lyons church. In 1846 he proposed that the apse should be decorated in mosaic in the manner of the 'basilicas of Italy',[56] but during the period of restoration, 1846–55, the lack of both mosaicists and mosaic materials in France forced the use of painted decoration. Flandrin rose to the challenge by using a frontally posed Christ on the model of Cefalù in Sicily, and by placing the figure on a gold ground carefully painted to emulate mosaic tesserae (fig. 58). The double row of *trompe l'oeil* tiles painted around the standing figures is very similar to the practice in many Byzantine and early

57 Hippolyte Flandrin, processional figures, 1848–9. Mural. Saint Vincent-de-Paul, Paris

58 Hippolyte Flandrin, apse mural, 1855.
Saint-Martin-d'Ainay, Lyons

Christian mosaics.[57] Flandrin's work at Lyons was noticed by the French art Establishment, although it received very little public recognition. Another of his projects, this time at Strasbourg, placed the whole issue of neo-Byzantine decoration much more in the public eye. In the 1840s it was decided to bring the cathedral of Strasbourg back to its 'Romano-Byzantine' state, and the architect Gustave Klotz was appointed to the task. Between 1843 and 1844 he went to study, as he put it, 'that beautiful Byzantine architecture' of the Orient itself.[58] In this venture he had the support of the strongly Ultramontane bishop, Monseigneur Raess, who wished to return to the Roman liturgy and adopt the aesthetics of Byzantinism, and they both agreed that Flandrin would be ideal for the decoration of the interior. The hieratical mural designs for the *Coronation of the Virgin* in the apse (fig. 59) were halted by Flandrin's death in 1864, after which they were completed by the teacher of Frederick Leighton, Eduard von Steinle.

Flandrin's work was mainly monumental, whereas his friend Dominique Papety was responsible for taking Byzantinism to the Salon. Papety was one of that group of French painters who looked back to the traditions of the early Renaissance. He won the Prix de Rome in 1836 and spent five years at the Villa Medici under the directorship

59 Hippolyte Flandrin and Eduard von Steinle, *Coronation of the Virgin*, completed 1879. Strasbourg Cathedral

of Ingres. Towards the end of his short life (he died of cholera in 1849 at the age of thirty-four) he developed a strongly hieratical mode. The pictures he exhibited at the Salon of 1847 caught the attention of Théophile Gautier. One was entitled *Basilican Monks Decorating a Chapel of the Convent of Iviron on Mount Athos* (fig. 60).[59] It was an interesting realist study of a hieratic subject. The basilican monks of the title are depicted in readable Western perspectival space decorating an apse in an Eastern manner. In the semidome of the apse there is a full-frontal Theotokos – the iconic Byzantine image of the Mother of God – with the Christ Child standing before her. The stiffness of the figures, said Gautier, made one feel that they had stepped out of a distant era. In contrast with the murals at Notre-Dame-de-Lorette, whose clear didactic intent Gautier had disliked, he praised Papety's painting for its quiet tranquillity and its independence of story and drama. 'As people in France know,' said Gautier, referring presumably to the recent architectural debate, 'the Byzantine school has never died out.'[60]

Papety also submitted to the Salon twelve watercolour studies of saints copied from the walls of monasteries on Mount Athos, whose grace and Byzantine nobility Gautier found 'incredible'.[61] The myth of Mount Athos clearly fascinated Gautier as it fascinated many people around Europe, including Ludwig I of Bavaria. It had been much publicized by Paul Durand and Adolphe Didron's journeys in 1839 to the East, during which they documented the iconography of ancient art. They were already famous for their *Manual of Greek and Latin Christian Iconography Translated from the Byzantine Manuscript* (1845), which became a textbook for interpreting early Christian art. On Mount Athos they discovered a peculiar relic of Byzantium in the form of painter-monks who

(according to Gautier) seemed still to be practising an art 'unchanged from the days of Justinian and even Constantine'. The monks told Duran and Didron they rigorously followed a manual written by the eleventh-century Panselinos. Now that a proper name was attached to it, Byzantine art suddenly became more alive to an audience steeped in the Romantic tradition of the artist-hero. The two travellers dedicated their translation of the manual to Victor Hugo, whose *Notre Dame de Paris* had so excited Didron's imagination for the Gothic. He hoped that Europe would now turn towards Byzantine art, 'so profound and so strange',[62] in a similar way. Panselinos became the 'Raphael or rather the Giotto of the Byzantine school'[63] and Duran and Didron offered their manuscript to Ludwig I – 'that enlightened prince to whom one owes the renaissance of Catholic art in Germany' – in the hope that it would further the building of 'Byzantine and Gothic monuments in Munich and the rest of Bavaria'.

60 Dominique Papety, *Basilican Monks Decorating a Chapel of the Convent of Iviron on Mount Athos*, 1847. Watercolour, 32 x 25 cm (12½ x 9¼ in). Musée Magnin, Dijon

5 | Byzantine and Romanesque in French Architectural Writing

French attitudes to Byzantine building were profoundly affected by the way in which the French interpreted their own architectural history. Here it is almost impossible to disentangle the growth of interest in the Byzantine style from that of Romanesque, but from the 1830s onwards the shape of French architectural history changed radically as more and more previously neglected monuments were discovered to be of serious archaeological interest. The result was that contemporary architects felt free to experiment with styles that were beginning to make a real claim for architectural or ecclesiastic dignity. Charles Questel's St-Paul-de-Nîmes of 1836 is one of the earliest and, although to modern eyes it is clearly Romanesque in inspiration, it was thought to be Byzantine when it was first built. As we have seen, it was not until around 1840 that the French distinguished between the two styles, and even then that distinction was only for those with considerable knowledge and understanding of architectural history. Armand Mallay's publication on the churches of Puy-de-Dôme of 1838 was a significant contribution to the history of the development of a national style, and this was supported by growing evidence of the existence of a strong Byzantine tradition in the East put forward by writers such as André Couchard. One of the most ardent supporters of a Byzantine national tradition was Eugène Viollet-le-Duc. His name is usually associated with the Gothic Revival, but in his campaign against the formalism of the Beaux-Arts he invoked the Byzantine tradition as a link between classical Greek rationalism and the 'néo-grec'. Viollet-le-Duc had been excited by what he had found in Sicily on his grand tour of 1836, and when Verneilh's *Byzantine Architecture in France* was published he wrote to the author saying: 'I see Byzantine everywhere during the eleventh and twelfth centuries,' since 'our architecture is more or less saturated with it'.[64] Much later, in his *Lectures* of the early 1860s, he continued to promulgate the notion that Byzantine art was not the product of decadence but the repository of Greek thought and ideas.

Perhaps the most consistently influential worker in this field, however, was Charles Texier. Texier had been commissioned to survey the monuments of Greece and Asia Minor as early as 1834, and he continued to send back reports to the French government for the next two decades. His principal work was *Byzantine Architecture*.[65] It was published (with the assistance of Richard Popplewell Pullen) simultaneously in France and England in 1864. Rather surprisingly, this is not the Byzantium of Venice, Ravenna, Rome or Sicily. Instead the book deals exclusively with very early Byzantine work in the East – both architecture and decoration. There is a chapter on building before Constantine, and large sections on Thessalonika, Broussa, Edessa and Trebizond. Coloured plates accompanied the text, bringing such detail as a mosaic pavement from St Sophia, Trebizond, vividly to life (fig. 61). The explicit purpose of *Byzantine Architecture*, according to Pullen, was 'fill up a gap that exists in the history of early Christian art' and to challenge the view that Gothic was the only acceptable form of Christian architecture.[66] Another influential figure in this field was Fernand de Dartein, who in 1865 published two large volumes of 100 drawings entitled *A Study of Lombard Architecture and the Origins of Romano-Byzantine Architecture*.[67] It opened with plans of Hagia Sophia, Raventine buildings and San Paolo fuori le Mura, and contained sensitive and intriguing plates of Romanesque carving culminating in the doors at San Michele, Pavia. Like many of his contemporaries,

61 Charles Texier and Richard Popplewell Pullen, plate from *Byzantine Architecture*, 1864, showing a mosaic floor in St Sophia, Trebizond

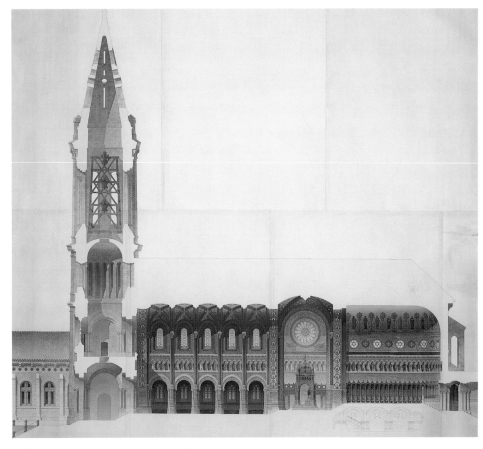

Dartein was fascinated by the origins of French architecture. In his discussion of 'the style we call Romanesque or sometimes Byzantine, or finally more justifiably Romano-Byzantine', Dartein asks his French readers the pertinent question whether it was perhaps 'born in France?'[68] The architect Georges Rohault de Fleury's *Medieval Pisan Monuments* (1866)[69] is similarly focused on the possible origins of French architecture in a Pisan tradition itself based on Constantinople. But the nationalistic tendencies of this genre emerged most clearly in Henri Révoil's *Romanesque Architecture of the French Midi* (1867 and 1868), a huge catalogue of then little-known buildings from the region, which, as he told his readers, 'had been too long overlooked'.[70]

These architectural histories played a direct part in the design and development of important new building in France. For example, on his return from the Middle East in 1863 Duthoit exhibited careful drawings of St Simeon Stylites near Aleppo, Syria, which in turn suggested to Émile Vaudremer a design for St-Pierre-de-Montrouge (1863-70), dominated by a tall Italian campanile rising above the west entrance (fig. 62).[71] Many of these new structures derived as much from Romanesque as from Byzantine models, but the combination was used widely for many types of building, including churches, museums and prisons. In Paris alone many churches owed allegiance to

62 (left) Émile Vaudremer, Saint-Pierre-de-Montrouge, Paris, 1863–70
63 (right) Julien Guadet, design for an Alpine hospice, 1864. Watercolour. École Nationale Supérieure des Beaux-Arts, Paris

France's presumed Romano-Byzantine past. Christophe Rémi's St-Joseph of 1863 (demolished in 1980) was one of the most purely Byzantine in design. Théodore Ballu's St-Ambroise of 1865 combined Romano-Byzantine with Gothic detail. Claude Naissant's Notre-Dame-de-la-Gare (1855–64) has a freely Romanesque exterior and a strong basilican interior, with forests of round arches and columns striding down the nave and around the apse behind the altar. Victor Baltard's larger and more prominent St-Augustin (1860–71; fig. 64) is essentially neo-Renaissance but utilizes many Byzantine details, especially in the huge dome which covers the chancel (see below, p. 95).

By the mid-1860s the spirit of Romanesque had spread to the Beaux-Arts. In 1865 the Prix de Rome was won by Julien Guadet with a Romanesque Alpine Hospice (fig. 63). The polychromatic detailing of the chapel is Byzantine, and Guadet was sufficiently proud of his design to give a signed photograph of it to his American friend Henry Hobhouse Richardson (see below, p. 90). Ten years later the churches of Thessalonika were explored once again, this time by the churchman Louis Duchesne, who worked on inscriptions and manuscripts, and the archaeologist Charles Bayet, who examined mosaics, sculpture and architecture. As with Didron many years before, the goal of their journey was Mount Athos, and in 1877 they published their *Memoir of a Mission to Mount Athos*.[72] When Bayet returned to France in 1876 he wrote a thesis on Christian art in the East before iconoclasm, was appointed to a Chair in Lyons and took up public offices in the French education system. His interest in Byzantine art persisted, and the real fruit of his pilgrimage to Mount Athos appeared in 1883 as *Byzantine Art*.[73] It was a popular account, published as part of a series dedicated

to the teaching of art and illustrated with rather crude engravings. But it was the first book in the nineteenth century to offer a comprehensive history of Byzantine art between single covers. Bayet's is a lively and spirited defence against the ancient objections to Byzantium, claiming for it a power to bring together and synthesize materials from antiquity, the Orient and Christianity. Above all, however, Bayet's work brought the subject of Byzantium to a much wider audience by providing a simple and lucid narrative.

64 Victor Baltard, design for Saint-Augustin, Paris, 1860–71. Pen, black ink and watercolour. Musée d'Orsay, Paris

6 | The Decoration of the Panthéon

The culmination of the Byzantine Revival in France took place in the aftermath of the Franco-Prussian War of 1870–1. The conflict was especially traumatic for the French. It resulted in the collapse of Napoleon's Second Empire and the siege of Paris; this in turn led eventually to the establishment of the Third Republic and the setting up of the Commune. France's crushing defeat at the hands of the Prussians, the loss of Alsace and Lorraine, the financial reparations, and the violence and the anticlericalism of the Commune all created a reaction in favour of piety, law, order and peace at any price. A brief period of government by Adolphe Thiers gave way to the reactionary republicanism of Marshal MacMahon. The resurgence of ecclesiastical power and influence led to Ultramontane hopes of a crusade for the restoration of the temporal power of the Church. On the one hand, the state encouraged pride in France, and French nationalism blossomed. On the other, the Church attempted to consolidate its own position by encouraging penitence and remorse for the sins of infidelity, materialism and violence. This new state of affairs under the Third Republic prompted two concurrent projects with strong Byzantine overtones. The first was the decoration of the Panthéon; the other was the building of Sacré-Coeur on the hill of Montmartre. One was an expression of French nationalism, the other an attempt at ecclesiastical consolidation.

There was nothing Byzantine about the church dedicated to Sainte-Geneviève, the patron saint of Paris. It was a neoclassical building designed by Jacques Soufflot in 1770 and was nearly finished by his death in 1780. It was not immediately consecrated and, at the suggestion of Quatremère de Quincy, in 1791 it was officially renamed the Panthéon – 'a monument for the great men, a national basilica'.[74] Several times in the course of the nineteenth century it underwent a change of purpose, and during the Revolution of 1848 it had returned to its secular role. Our interest here centres on its decoration. In the middle of the century the artist Paul Chevenard was commissioned by Charles Blanc, director of the École des Beaux-Arts, and by Alexandre Ledru-Rollin, minister of the interior, to produce a huge decorative scheme representative of 'the transformation of humanity and the moral evolution of mankind'.[75] This he did, and the original designs are preserved in his native town of Lyons. Chevenard was going to be assisted by Dominique Papety, who was sympathetic to the 'Early Italian', Nazarene manner of Chevenard, but nothing came of the project. Under Louis-Napoléon the building was once again reconsecrated and the Church would have no truck with Chevenard's iconographic syncretism in which Christianity was reduced to one episode in the 'moral evolution of mankind'. The Panthéon now fell into neglect. During the siege of Paris in 1870 the crypt was used to store gunpowder, and German bombardment severely damaged the dome and other parts of the building.

Following the Franco-Prussian War, in the early years of the Third Republic Philippe de Chennevières, the director of the Beaux-Arts, saw the possibility of promoting Catholic-monarchic propaganda and decided to turn the decoration of the Panthéon into a political project. He quickly put together a programme based on the life and works of Saint Geneviève and at the same time approached a number of well-known painters to produce designs. Gustave Moreau and Jean-Léon Gérôme turned the offer down, and Jean-François Millet died soon after beginning work on the project. Chennevières offered Chevenard the semidome of the apse as compensation for his efforts in the earlier part of the century, but Chevenard rejected the proposal. His place was taken by Ernest Hébert, who was an established painter in his mid-fifties. He was filled with a love of Italy which dated back to 1840 when, together with his friend Dominique Papety, he won the Prix de Rome under the apprenticeship of Ingres. Between 1867 and 1873, during the period of the Franco-Prussian War and the Commune, Hébert was Director of the French Academy in Rome. Upon finishing his term he was approached by Chennevières with the offer to design the apse of Sainte-Geneviève together with its surrounding spaces.

Up to this point all French neo-Byzantine decoration had been in paint or encaustic. Now Chennevières and Hébert agreed that mosaic would be the best choice, since its permanence and its traditional associations appealed to both men. Hébert's response to receiving the commission was to travel back to Italy to refresh his memory of the basilican mosaics. He was carried away by 'the superb Christ' in the mosaic in San Ambrogio, Milan, and he revisited San Marco, Torcello, and drew the Virgin in the duomo of Murano. He spent two weeks in Ravenna where he gathered so many images that he hoped there would be enough to furnish not only the Panthéon, but, as he put it, 'all the churches being built in Paris'.[76] In Rome he visited San Prassede, Sta Pudenziana, San Giovanni in Laterano, Sta Maria in Trastevere, San Lorenzo and, following in the steps of his august predecessor Ingres, he drew the figure of Christ in SS Cosma e Damiano (fig. 65). All the while he was working away at his design for the Panthéon. He was absent for so long that Chennevières was forced to send an emissary requesting his return to Paris. While Hébert travelled through Italy, Chennevières had been working on the problem of obtaining expertise and materials.[77]

As part of an exercise in national pride, Chennevières decided to request government money for the setting up of a mosaic studio at Sèvres. He reasoned that if they could do it in Italy, the French could do it in Paris. His argument was convincing, and he had his way. In February 1876 Édouard Gerspach, the minister for manufacturing industries, was sent off to Rome to the Vatican to see how mosaic was made and to get the blessing of Pius IX for a similar enterprise in France. Gerspach had an audience with the pope, who granted him the assistance of Italian mosaicists and was pleased that, in spite of the recent political turbulence, mosaics were planned both for the churches in Paris and for the Nouvelle Major in Marseilles (see above, p. 75).[78] Gerspach obtained the assistance of Angelo Poggesi, who had worked in the Vatican for twenty-two years, and a younger man, Devecchis, who had been involved in the redecoration of San Paolo fuori le Mura in Rome.

65 Apse mosaic, SS Cosma e Damiano, Rome, 526–30

On their arrival at Sèvres the Italian mosaicists set up studios for the manufacture of tesserae. They tried out their skills by turning a design by Charles Lameire into a frieze for the front of the new building and then set to preparing the material for the apse of the Panthéon. In 1879 Poggesi went to Paris to prepare the wall, the cartoon and the tesserae. Hébert drew the design directly onto the wall and by 1882 Poggesi had begun to place the pieces for the head of Christ 'following the techniques of Ravenna'.[79] In 1883 he had completed the head of the Virgin. More workmen were called in from Italy and France and by June 1884 the task was nearing completion (fig. 66). According to Chennevières it was finished with much official pomp and congratulation on France's contribution to the revival of 'this ancient and dignified art'. These plaudits were much to his satisfaction – he attached huge importance to this project which (he claimed with some exaggeration) was unequalled in terms of its strength, august dignity ('pompe auguste'), majesty and magnificence since the ancient world.[80]

Like many of his predecessors, Chennevières's insistence on the hieratic mode of Hébert's apse was linked to his belief in monarchism, tradition and the authoritarian values to which he wished to see French society return. The theme of Christ holding the book of destiny is closely connected to the legitimist rhetoric of the time, although it is ironic that when Chennevières was replaced by the radical republican Edmond Turquet in 1881, he too insisted that Hébert should avoid post-Renaissance pictorial values in the apse and should continue to think in terms of the 'means employed by the mosaicists of Ravenna'.[81] The pose of Christ clearly reflects the Christ of SS Cosma e Damiano which Hébert had studied in Rome, and it also picks up on Ingres's *Christ Giving the Keys to St Peter*

66 Ernest Hébert, *Christ, the Virgin, the Angel of Fame, Jeanne d'Arc and Saint Geneviève*, 1884.
Mosaic in the apse of the Panthéon, Paris

(see fig. 42), of which Hébert had made a watercolour copy when he was student. 'Christ', wrote Hébert in his own account of the work, 'shows the destiny of his people to the angel of France. To the right of Christ, the Virgin intercedes on behalf of the French people. Beside her is Joan of Arc and to Christ's left is the figure of St Geneviève, the patron Saint of Paris.'[82] In spite of its honourable precedents, however, there is something splendidly *fin-de-siècle* about this version of Byzantium. In the Panthéon Chevennières wanted the austere autocratic power of Picot's Pantocrator in St-Vincent-de-Paul, but what he got was an elegantly thin Christ gesturing gracefully to his people and half turning from the angel, rather like a monarch and his mistress, both of them dressed in chic sandals. Hébert might have tried to make his figures look formidable, but the big attractive eyes of the Virgin and the soulful appearance of the angel more closely resemble the voluptuous Italians of his portraits than figures from a Roman basilica.

In the Panthéon images of St Geneviève are everywhere, and her childhood is the subject of the finest decorations in the church.[83] Puvis de Chavannes's tripartite *Childhood of St Geneviève* (1877) and his *St Geneviève as a Child at Prayer* (1876) were certainly not self-consciously 'Byzantine', as was Hébert's mosaic, but there is little doubt that in the *Procession of Saints* for the frieze (1879) he saw himself following in a tradition established by Flandrin. As one contemporary critic, Réne Ménard, pointed out, the Panthéon frieze contained many reminiscences of Flandrin's work at St-Germain. Nothing, said Ménard, had 'risen to such a nobility of conception in the intervening years'.[84] He is surely correct and in Puvis's work we find the same archaic dignity, stasis and *gravitas* that Rossetti and Holman Hunt admired in Flandrin. Like the other participants, Puvis and Hébert realized that the decoration of the Panthéon was as much a political as a religious venture, and that it was to be, in Chevennières's words, part of a scheme that would reach 'the most severe and noble summits of religious and patriotic art'.[85] Earlier in the century the Church had adopted the hieratic aspects of Byzantium to enforce a conservative message about the relationship between society and its rulers; now the politicians had taken it over to nostalgically conjure up a period in French history undissipated by political fervour and anticlericalism. In the greatest neo-Byzantine monument in France, the Sacré-Coeur, government and Church united to produce a propaganda exercise of the greatest force. It is ironic that the vehicle for this propaganda was the most radical style of the period.

7 | The Building of the Sacré-Coeur

The calm, archaizing tendency of the Panthéon's decoration is deceptive, since it was the product of a period of political and religious turbulence. The contrast between the monument and the moment is even greater, however, in the case of the other major Byzantinizing project of the period – Paul Abadie's symbol of the spiritual power of the Church, the Sacré-Coeur on Montmartre (fig. 67). On a foggy morning in October 1872 the archbishop of Paris climbed the slopes of the hill of martyrs. As he reached the top, the fog cleared to reveal the well-known panorama of Paris, and he declared: 'It is here, it is here where the martyrs are, it is here that the Sacred Heart must reign so that it can

67 Paul Abadie, Basilica of the Sacré-Coeur,
Paris, 1875–1919

beckon all to it!'[86] The martyrs in question were not so much those of ancient history as the many Frenchmen who had died in the previous three years as a result of the war with Germany and the struggles of the Commune. The building of the basilica of Sacré-Coeur and the Byzantine silhouette which it shows on the Paris skyline are deeply rooted in the politics of the period, and to understand the shape that the basilica adopted it is necessary to turn, briefly, to those political conditions.

As he stood on Montmartre the archbishop hoped that he would be able to call Frenchmen back to the Church after a century of bloodshed, insubordination to the rule of God, rationalism, materialism and apostasy. The Sacred Heart was a symbol of the sufferings of Christ wounded by the sins of his people. Devotion to the physical heart of Jesus had existed for several centuries but first came to prominence with the visions of St Marguerite-Marie Alacoque in Paray-le-Monial in central France. The huge mural of Christ in the apse of the basilica bore beneath his breast the two words GALLIA POENITENS (France Penitent), since the cult of the Sacred Heart preached repentance above all things. In the eighteenth century it claimed among its devotees Louis XVI and Marie Antoinette, and in 1815, with the Restoration of the monarchy, Louis XVIII commissioned Pierre Fontaine to erect in Paris a Chapel of Expiation to his brother and his family in the name of the Sacred Heart. The cult appealed to the conservative monarchist element in French society and was the object of suspicion of liberal Catholics. The material prosperity, worldliness and decadence of Louis-Napoléon's Second Empire had created a backlash which enhanced devotion to the cult, and then in the 1860s France's relations with Italy gave it further impetus. During the Italian struggles for unification, Louis-Napoléon came down on the side of Italian unity and against the power of the pope. Pius IX retired to the Vatican, refusing to emerge until his temporal power was restored, causing a sympathetic reaction among France's religious. Meanwhile in 1864 the pope beatified Marguerite-Marie, setting in train great pilgrimages to Paray-le-Monial. Bismarck's victory over France in the summer of 1870 was interpreted by the pious as God's divine scourge against the country. In September Louis-Napoléon was defeated by the Prussians at Sedan and the Empire collapsed. In the same month Paris came under siege and was locked away from the rest of the world until the end of January of the following year. In December 1870 Alexandre-Félix Legentil, a rich Parisian textile merchant in exile in Poitiers, swore that if France were delivered from its woes and the pope from his self-imposed imprisonment he would organize the erection of a basilica in Paris dedicated to the Sacred Heart. What came to be known as the 'National Vow' received moral and material support from Georges Rohault de Fleury,[87] who also documented the building's progress, and these two figures remained at the forefront of the movement to the end.

In spite of papal endorsement for the project it was some time before Legentil and Fleury were able to rally enough material and ecclesiastical support to take the project forward, and in any case other events intervened to increase still further the repentant mood in France. Within Paris there had long been a class struggle between the bourgeoisie and the working classes of areas such as Belleville, swollen in size by immigration in times of prosperity. As the Empire began to collapse, economic growth slowed down, poverty increased and so did friction between these two groups. At the same time Louis-Napoléon was determined to improve the status of the capital through the extensive building projects organized by Baron Haussmann and, most splendidly of all, by supporting the building of Charles Garnier's Opéra. When war broke out with Germany all the cracks in French society began to appear. Hostility between the capital and the provinces was matched by hostility between rich and poor within Paris itself, and in January the Commune was declared. Meanwhile there was an armistice with Germany and Adolphe Thiers decided to use the conservatism of the country to smash the Commune. In March the French army descended on Paris to disarm the radicals. The 227 cannons on Montmartre were one of the army's principal goals, and in a stand-off between the military and the working class, General Le Comte ordered his troops to fire on the crowd. They refused and shot into the air. Le Comte and another general, Thomas, were taken prisoner and executed. For the conservatives these two instantly became 'martyrs … who died in order to defend and save Christian society', and the hill of Montmartre was the 'place chosen by Satan' for his attack upon the Church.[88]

With the connivance of Bismarck and an army strengthened in numbers, Thiers attacked Paris in April and within two months between twenty and thirty thousand communards had been killed by French troops. In a famous incident one of the radicals – Eugène Varlin, a member of the National Guard and a committed socialist – was tortured and killed on the same spot on Montmartre where Generals Le Comte and Thomas had been executed. The material and human destruction in Paris was terrible. The Commune's anticlerical rage was as great as it had been in the 1789 Revolution, and in its last week it shot seventy-four hostages, twenty-four of whom were priests. One of these victims was the archbishop of Paris.

The crushing of the Commune consolidated the bond between monarchists and conservative Catholics and guaranteed the building of the Sacré-Coeur. Monseigneur Guibert was persuaded (with some understandable reluctance) to take on the mantle of archbishop, and with it he embraced the Sacré-Coeur project. Guibert had been a close friend of the Mazenods in Marseilles up to Eugène de Mazenod's death in 1861, and until recently had held the archbishopric of Tours. In 1872 Guibert wrote to the instigators of the National Vow in terms which sum up the mood in which the new church was built: a mixture of humility and pride, of sanctity and sentiment, and of religious motives deeply interwoven with political ones. He said:

> You have considered from their true perspective the ills of our country … The conspiracy against God and Christ has prevailed in a multitude of hearts, and in punishment for an almost universal apostasy, society has been subjected to all the horrors of war with a victorious foreigner and an even more horrible war amongst the children of the same country. Having become, by our prevarication, rebels against heaven, we have fallen during our troubles into the abyss of anarchy. The land of France presents the terrifying image of a place where no order prevails, while the future offers still more terrors to come … this temple, erected as a public act of contrition and reparation … will stand amongst us as a protest against other monuments and works of art erected to the glorification of vice and impiety.[89]

One of those 'other monuments' erected to 'vice and impiety' was the Opéra, and for a while Legentil was keen to appropriate its newly laid foundations as the site for the Sacré-Coeur. As millions of francs poured in as the result of a propaganda campaign, however, Guibert selected a spot on Montmartre. Thiers had now been replaced in government by the arch-conservative Marshal MacMahon who two years before had played an important part in the repression of the Commune. With a great assertion of moral law and order the land on the top of the hill was seized by laws of expropriation. This in itself was deeply controversial and created a hostility that was to last for decades. Anselme Batbie, the Minister for Public Instruction, was obliged to ask the Assembly to vote for a law that allowed seizure of the land on the grounds that Sacré-Coeur was a work of 'public utility'. Figures like Georges Clemenceau, then mayor of Montmartre, bitterly opposed the move, as did other anti-Catholics in the Assembly. But at length, the law was passed (if only by a narrow majority) and a competition for the design of a new basilica was set in train.

A twelve-man jury was set up in February 1874, comprising representatives of the city of Paris, politicians and five architects. The judgement of the latter was clearly crucial for the outcome of the competition. There was Albert Lenoir, who pioneered the exploration of Eastern art in France in the 1830s; Théodore Ballu, architect of La Trinité (see above, p. 86), who had recently been a co-winner in the competition for the Hôtel de Ville (with Abadie on the jury); Joseph-Louis Duc, one of the Romantic architects who had been in Vaudoyer's circle in the 1830s; and there was Henri Labrouste, architect of the revolutionary Bibliothèque Sainte-Geneviève. The terms of the competition were closely related to the building site and the costs. It was suggested that there should be a porch on the façade, domes or towers, a crypt, and at least twenty chapels.[90] No style was specified. The response was considerable with seventy-eight projects submitted by eighty-seven participants. The majority of them were rather young and the winner, Paul Abadie, was exceptional in being sixty-two years old. As for the styles, the distribution was significant. There was almost no entry in the classical mode and only a small number of Gothic designs. Guibert himself passionately wanted a church in a thirteenth-century style and was greatly disappointed by the small number of medieval entries. The fact is that Gothic was played out in France, and for the last twenty or thirty years large ecclesiastical buildings had looked to Romano-Byzantine models. St-Augustin and La Trinité in Paris, and Sainte-Marie-Majeure and Notre-Dame-de-la-Garde in Marseilles had offered new possibilities for modern architecture, and entry after entry came in with domes, triumphal arches and polychrome stripes reminiscent of Vaudoyer's work in the south. In fact some were just too Oriental, too exotic for the jury and would (according to them) have been 'better placed in Jerusalem than in Paris'. It is not surprising in a competition where anonymity was hardly honoured that an established figure like Abadie was successful. Responses to his winning design, however, were divided between architects and writers and the Church. The architectural press accepted the verdict happily; not so the Catholic press. Like the archbishop the Catholics wanted something Gothic, something which they felt would meet national tastes and national religious attitudes. In short, they disliked 'Abadie's mosque'.[91] Nevertheless, building started in 1876, the basilica was consecrated in 1891, and work was to continue until 1919.

The Oriental quality of Abadie's design lies more in the imagination than in the structure itself, since it is in fact a remarkable synthesis of a number of styles that had become popular in the late nineteenth century. Both inside and out the church possesses a wonderfully soaring quality as it billows upwards like a white cloud on the hill of Montmartre. The domes are its most Eastern and outstanding feature, although in Abadie's original design they were shallower and more like those of Hagia Sophia. After Abadie's death they were extended vertically by H. Rauline, thus giving them a strongly mosque-like appearance. San Marco, of course, was an important domical model, but the much wider base of the Venetian church makes it appear to rise from the lagoon rather than, in the case of the Sacré-Coeur, shoot towards the skies. Again, the tight agglomeration of domes is reminiscent of Vaudoyer's Sainte-Marie-Majeure, but like San Marco that cathedral rises from a wide base and rests on a platform only a metre or two higher than the sea. Abadie's archaeological work on St-Front certainly played an important part in his design for the basilica, and like St-Front, the building is monochrome. In this it departs both from Byzantine tradition and from contemporary precedent. San Marco, encrusted with marbles that glow and burn in different lights and weathers, is famous for its polychromy. More recently, Vaudoyer's choice of northern Italian stripes picked out in black and red made his cathedral appear like some tropical insect. In contrast Abadie's Sacré-Coeur is built in blindingly bright, fine-grained, delicately cut limestone (calcaire) from Château-Landon. This whiteness, suggestive of purity and cleanliness, fits well with the ecclesiastical mode of abjection associated with the National Vow, but in its very intensity it expresses that pride and sense of political authority that was the Vow's flipside.

In Paris itself only Victor Baltard's St-Augustin (1860–71; see fig. 64), matched the Sacré-Coeur in its daring. Baltard's fusion of Renaissance, Romanesque and Byzantine on a framework of cast iron was less successful than Abadie's synthesis, but it provided both an inspiration and a warning. The development of Paris along the Boulevard Haussmann created a need for a new church, and St-Augustin was thus the product not of ecclesiastical fervour but governmental fiat. The triangular plot chosen for its construction was a very tricky one, but Baltard solved the problem by building a monumental and impressive west front, and stretching behind it a nave of eight bays that opens out into a vast chancel under a dome. As with Abadie's Sacré-Coeur, the dome of St-Augustin is flanked by four substantial towers, between which are two small semidomes and an apse. The dome owes more to Florence and Brunelleschi than to Byzantium, but all of the fenestration and all the doors are round-arched and many of them Oriental in inspiration. The portico has three small saucer domes, and the west door is decorated with a row of stiff, hieratic apostles grouped about a full-frontal Byzantine-like Christ.

Although Sacré-Coeur shares many of the features of St-Augustin, they are extended, simplified and integrated into a much more coherent and powerful unity. The shallow portico of the Sacré-Coeur has three saucer domes in its roof, not unlike the narthex of San Marco, but these are no preparation for the drama of the interior. The manipulation of space is breathtakingly imaginative. Instead of placing the dome over the chancel at the end of a long narrow nave as Baltard had done at St-Augustin, Abadie has brought it forward to create a vast open space over the nave itself. Here the experience of horizontal breadth and of soaring verticality produces something of the spatial jouissance of Hagia Sophia. The horizontal space is increased by the openness of the nave; only three enormous bays separate it from the two side aisles. As a result these become incorporated into the nave space, just as the enormous open chapels become

incorporated into the aisles. There is a crossing, but the transepts are vestigial and take the form of two chapels on either side of the nave. The tension between the round choir and the nave increases the feeling of spatial excitement. The choir is clearly a large area but appears flattened out by the stress on the nave, an effect which is strengthened by the apse mosaic (fig. 40). In this, the vast and vertiginous figure of Christ by Luc-Olivier Merson and Marcel Magne leans forward, arms outstretched like a diver leaving a high board and about to plunge into the nave.

Even more dramatic is the creation of spatial height in the Sacré-Coeur. This is not the narrow, soaring mysteriousness of Gothic but the forceful upward thrust of tall round arches. The verticality which the viewer sees on the outside is interiorized by the massive force of the pillars which rise cleanly from negligible bases and press their way upwards, uninterrupted by capitals of any significance or size. They give the appearance of stretching up to reach the light, since light is admitted only through the clerestory and the dome. This massive fountain of white stone froths into bubble after bubble of dome and semidome. The central dome continues this upward thrust even further, since its first row of round arches are blank and short, while the second row are stilted and are penetrated by windows through which the sunlight

68 (left) Léopold Hardy, Basilica of the Rosary, Lourdes, 1883–5
69 (right) Edmond Duthoit, Notre-Dame-de-Brébières, Albert, 1883–96

pours. That feeling of upward movement is enhanced by Abadie's choice of stilted arches throughout the building: over doors, in the clerestory windows, and particularly prominent over the row of pillars that run around the apse.

The spatial success of Abadie's interior is intensified by the austerity of the decorative detail. Not only are the mouldings kept to the bare minimum and the essentials – bases, capitals, coving, and arch hoods – all extremely unobtrusive, there are few pieces of sculpture and even fewer paintings. This absence of detail, far from creating a sense of impoverishment, allows the forms of the architecture to flow and to speak in their own language. The apse mosaic is an exception. It was not completed until 1923 and its colour makes a strong contrast with the whiteness of the interior. So much of it is versed in an unsubtle, sentimental language of ecclesiastical dogma, however, that it works against the genuinely impressive spatial organization of the architecture.

The animosity levelled against the Sacré-Coeur at its outset did not abate even when building had begun. The fierce anticlericalism in France at the end of the century was harnessed to undermine the legality of the original appropriation of the land for the church's foundations, and attempts were made to halt construction. This opposition failed, but to this day the Sacré-Coeur has tended to divide feelings in France between the pious, who hold it in high esteem, and those who dislike it as a symbol of religious imperialism. In terms of influence, however, its Byzantinism was very powerful, and for over half a century it inspired many imitations. Léopold Hardy took over its domical form for the Basilica of the Rosary at Lourdes (1883–5; fig. 68), as did Victor Laloux in St-Martin-de-Tours (1883–1924) and Edmond Duthoit in Notre-Dame-de-Brébières at Albert (1883–96; fig. 69). After World War I a second wave of similar basilican churches was built on the Romano-Byzantine model, including Albert van Huffel's Basilica of Koekelberg outside Brussels (fig. 71) and Louis-Marie Cordonnier's pilgrimage church at Lisieux. In Paris, Byzantium inspired Jacques Barge's Ste-Odile (1936–9) and, perhaps most spectacularly, that reinforced-concrete version of Hagia Sophia, Paul Tournon's St-Esprit (1928–35; fig. 70).

8 | Gautier, Moreau, Huysmans and Sardou

What we have traced thus far are the ecclesiastical uses of Byzantinism in France and the use of Byzantine motifs in wall decoration and in architecture. But Byzantium also appealed to many in late nineteenth-century France whose immediate interests were neither ecclesiastical nor theological. We saw (p. 83) how Théophile Gautier had been impressed by Papety's work in the Byzantine mode at the 1847 Salon. In the summer of 1850 he visited Venice and in his book *Italia* (1852) he wrote extensively about San Marco and its mosaics. In a sense this was an *annus mirabilis* for Byzantium, because Ruskin, as we shall see in the next chapter, was also in Venice at this time collecting material for the second volume of *The Stones of Venice* (1852). Both writers developed aesthetic responses conditioned partly by their respective sexual preoccupations, and their books drew particular attention to the sensuousness of Byzantine colour and the Oriental nature of Byzantine design in architecture and mosaic. In this way these two men between them laid down criteria for responses to Byzantine art which were to shape attitudes for the rest of the century.[92]

As the July Monarchy was collapsing in the Revolution of 1848, Charles Questel's St-Paul-de-Nîmes was receiving its mural decorations and Sainte-Marie-Majeure was being planned. The sudden change of political fortunes, however, had a detrimental effect on Gautier's financial position and he lost a number of his regular commissions as art, theatre and ballet critic in Paris. In the summer of 1850 he travelled to Venice with a view to making some money by writing a series of articles for the newspaper *La Presse* and to meet his latest mistress, Marie Mattei. The articles were published in 1852 as a book called *Italia*, a misleading title because the greater part of it is given up to an extended account of the art, architecture and life of Venice.

Gautier and Mattei met in Venice in August 1850, installed themselves in the Palazzo Vendramin-Calergi[93] and the ensuing period of hectic sexual pleasure was accompanied by a series of vivid and vibrant essays. The centrepiece of Gautier's Venice was San Marco. Henry James claimed that it was 'the best-described building in the world', urging the reader of *Italian Hours* (1909) to 'open the *Stones of Venice*, open Théophile Gautier's *Italia*' in confirmation of this fact.[94] The Byzantine architecture of San Marco was both strange and alluring for Gautier, and it impressed him with its primitive, almost antediluvian, appearance. 'One might say,' he wrote, 'that it was the temple of a Christianity which pre-dated Christ, a church built before religion.'[95] It was, however, the 'barbaric', 'wild', 'primitive', 'powerful' mosaics which most arrested his attention. He noticed the Deluge in the narthex ('powerful' but 'gloomy'), and like Ruskin in the first volume of *Modern Painters* compared it favourably with the version of the same scene by Poussin in the Louvre. Also like Ruskin, Gautier saw San Marco as a magnificent text, part visual, part verbal, describing it as 'a great historiated flower-covered, illuminated golden Bible, a medieval missal on a huge scale'.[96] 'The first impression,' he continues, 'is of a golden cave encrusted with precious stones, splendid and sombre, simultaneously sparkling and mysterious.' 'Are we in a building or in an immense casket for jewels?' Gautier asks.[97] He goes on to speak of the way in which surfaces filled with the 'irrepressible imaginations' of the mosaicist glitter like the scales of a fish and make no attempt to reproduce nature. The human figures are 'imperial', 'imperious' and 'magisterial'. The large eyes of a Madonna 'penetrate you without seeing you', and she has the aspect of an idol or an icon.[98] Like Ruskin, Gautier is attracted to the dreamlike sumptuousness of the mosaic work, but where Ruskin finds exuberant purity, Gautier sees excess verging on decadence. This is felt most prominently in Gautier's enumeration of the stone, marble and gold of the surfaces, a 'vast pile of riches and works of art … a pile which assaults and overwhelms the senses'.[99] It is significant, too, that he is intrigued by the lasciviousness of the figure of Salome (fig. 72): in his account, her suggestive lubricity looks forward to Gustave Moreau's pictorial treatment of the subject in 1876 and Huysmans's descriptions in *Against Nature* of 1884. 'Dressed', Gautier writes, 'in long dalmations fringed with fine fur, she brings to mind those dissolute empresses of Constantinople, those great courtesans of Byzantium, Theodora, for example, lustful, lascivious and cruel.'[100]

In 1878, as the decorations of the Panthéon were under way and the cornerstone of the Sacré-Coeur was being laid, two pictures were shown at the Exposition Universelle that employed Byzantine imagery in a startling and curious way: Moreau's oil painting *Salome Dancing before Herod*[101] (1876; fig. 73) and his pendant watercolour *The Apparition* (1876; fig. 74). The tension in these works between the rigidity of the figure of Salome, held as it were on the point of her toes, and the vibrant sparkling movement of light across the decorations, the jewels and the exotic architectural setting stirred the imagination of visitors. The most famous account of these paintings appears in Huysmans's *Against Nature* (1884),[102] and it is he who identified the setting of the oil as Byzantine. 'This painting', he wrote, 'showed a throne like the high altar of a cathedral standing beneath a vaulted ceiling … in a palace which resembled a basilica built in both the Muslim and the Byzantine styles.'[103] In fact there is very little in the architecture which might identify it precisely as Byzantine, and in the syncretic arrangement of the decorative objects surrounding the figures Julius Kaplan notices objects from Egypt, Persia, India and Rome.[104] We know that Moreau avidly copied decorations from Owen Jones's *The Grammar of Ornament*, which has a strong Byzantine section (see fig. 98), and when Moreau visited the fifth exhibition of the Union Centrale des Beaux-Arts Appliqués in 1876 he carefully studied photographs of mosaics in Ravenna, Rome and Palermo. During his two trips to Italy in 1858 and 1859, however, he seems to have shown no interest in Byzantine mosaic. Where, then, does Huysmans find Byzantium in these pictures? The answer must surely lie in Moreau's formal placing of Herod in the centre, flanked by Salome and the executioner. In some of the preliminary drawings Herod is enthroned in an apse; this creates a strong resemblance to the hieratic placing of God the Father between the Virgin and Christ not only in the Byzantine originals, but also in the numerous nineteenth-century versions that had proliferated in France during the previous twenty years. It is probably to these that Moreau had looked.

Clues to the connection between the work of Orsel or Picot in the earlier part of the century and these pictures by Moreau lie partly in Moreau's religious beliefs, partly in his attitude to contemporary culture, and partly in his sexual predilections. Moreau was religious, but in a strongly mystical way. His affinities were not with the rational elements of Thomist philosophy that the Church was trying to reintroduce, nor with Pius IX's call for support for the Third Republic. In common with many of the leaders of the Catholic literary movement, such as Barbey d'Aurevilly

and Sâr Joséphin Péladan, he looked back beyond the Ultramontanism of Montalembert to the proto-Romantic Chateaubriand with his 'supreme disenchantment, his hopeless reverie of a high order [and] his pilgrim's faith'.[105] For Moreau the core of art was supernatural, providential and divine, and he considered primitive art 'closer to the state of our modern soul' than that of the 'so-called Renaissance'.[106] He opposed all artistic positivism and was repelled alike by Realism and Impressionism. Like many of his fellow countrymen he was deeply disturbed by the Franco-Prussian War and the events surrounding the Commune. He tended to the kind of

France Gautier, Moreau, Huysmans and Sardou

73 (left) Gustave Moreau, *Salome Dancing before Herod*, 1876. Oil on canvas, 144 × 104 cm (56¼ × 50 in). Armand Hammer Foundation, Los Angeles

74 (right) Gustave Moreau, *The Apparition*, 1876. Watercolour, 106 × 72 cm (41¼ × 28½ in). Musée du Louvre, Paris

authoritarianism we have identified in other artists, with its desire for a 'well-ordered, well-balanced, well-directed country full of respect and obedience'. It seems that he felt alienated by the turbulence of revolution, by 'the general decay', and by what he called the 'greedy and sensual wants' of modern society.[107]

Moreau's anxieties about the necessity for severe personal and social control and his abhorrence of sensuality may, as some commentators have suggested, be related to a latent homosexuality. Art, he claimed, represented the effort to free oneself from sensuality: 'It is the poor, pretentious and tense simpletons … who confound earthy passion, eroticism, etc. with artistic creative passion. They have never suspected what superhuman efforts, what superior will are required of a creator of art to elevate himself to this superior region …'[108] What emerges from both his painting and his writing is a strong unease about women, developing at times into a hysterical response to women and their supposed power. Many of his female figures appear emotionless, depersonalized and rigid, and many of them, including Salome, Delilah and Cleopatra, were historical *femmes fatales*. Moreau was fascinated and repelled. His picture of Messalina painted in 1874 (just before *Salome*) represented, he said, 'the insatiable desire of woman in general',[109] and his remarks about Salome are similarly misogynistic. He claimed that his painting was a warning to those who submit to the pleasures of the sensual life. 'This woman represents eternal woman, a frivolous, often fatal character, passing through life holding a flower, searching for her vague ideal.'[110] In Huysmans' account of the far more scantily dressed figure of Salome in *The Apparition*, the combination of misogynistic loathing and erotic fascination is similar but more boldly stated. 'Here she was no longer just the dancing-girl who extorts a cry of lust and lechery from an old man by the lascivious movements of her loins … she had become, as it were, the symbolic incarnation of undying Lust, the Goddess of immortal Hysteria.'[111] What Moreau seems to have done with the iconic tradition as it came down to him in the work of his contemporaries is to have taken the forbidding figures of scriptural authority, released them from their specifically Christian or religious roles and made them actors in a violent and terrifying sexual drama. In *Salome Dancing before Herod*, the awesome enthroned Pantocrator or Christ in Majesty has been transformed into Herod, diminished, corrupt and voyeuristic. The sightlines of the picture suggest an identification between the viewer and the lustful king – like him, we are fascinated by the dancing figure of Salome. Byzantine convention would dictate that we see the Virgin at the foot of the throne of God, but what we have instead is the sexually insatiable 'eternal woman'. Like the Virgin she intercedes, but for the head of a man; she prays for his symbolic castration and ultimately his death. The panchronistic, eclectic elements of the setting – architecture, jewellery, furniture – serve to generalize the symbolic significance of the *femme fatale* across time, whereas the stiff, hieratic, frontal and profile Byzantinism of the figures lifts them out of time. In this way Moreau is using Byzantium, with its archaic and eternal associations, to suggest that femininity is intrinsically damaging and that the struggle between the sexes is absolute and final.

The year 1884 saw not only the publication of *Against Nature*, but also Sarah Bernhardt playing the leading role in Victorien Sardou's *Théodora*, and there is a recognizable conflation here of the figures of Salome and Theodora.

75 Chromolithographic poster advertising
Victorien Sardou's *Théodora*, 1885

Gibbon's denunciation of the Byzantine queen makes her sound remarkably like the late nineteenth-century version of Salome. He described her as 'the prostitute who, in the presence of innumerable spectators, had polluted the theatre of Constantinople, was adored as a queen in the same city, by grave magistrates, orthodox bishops, victorious general and captive monarchs.'[112] Sardou created the part especially for Bernhardt, whom he had recently met, and the collaboration was hugely successful. The play, with music by Massenet, ran consecutively for 257 performances and was revived with Bernhardt in the same role seventeen years later. Sardou was careful about his archaeology and got a Signor Gattieri 'from Venice' to send drawings which schematized the costumes of the mosaic figures in San Vitale, Ravenna. No expense was spared, and Bernhardt 'wore a reproduction of Theodora's mantle decked with heraldic peacocks and priceless gems'.[113] The poster advertising the play's first performance in the Porte St-Martin, with its rows of Byzantine columns and capitals, stresses the sumptuousness of the costumes and interiors (fig. 75). Sardou's attention to historical detail was, perforce, less meticulous. Ever since Karl Wilhelm Dindorf had published the so-called 'Secret History' of Procopius in his *Corpus Scriptorum Historiae Byzantinae* in 1833, the stories of Theodora's alleged sexual appetite and spectacular erotic display had been available. By Sardou's time they were common knowledge in France, and in his book *The Empress of Byzantium* (1870)[114] Benjamin Gastineau treated his readers to a version of the famous episode of the geese and Theodora's reputed sadness at possessing only three orifices for her pleasure. The coverage of the play was enormous in France, England and America. Illustrations of the costumes and sets appeared in the French press, and in England the *Sunday Mercury* devoted many pages to a detailed account of the complex and rambling plot. Of course, even had he wished it Sardou could not have allowed Sarah Bernhardt to abandon herself in the manner outlined by Procopius, and in the play Theodora comes to the notice of Justinian through her fine acting ability rather than her lubriciousness. Nevertheless Sardou depicts her as a cruel and heartless *fin-de-siècle femme fatale*. Sarah Bernhardt's acting without doubt helped to shape the popular idea of Byzantium in late nineteenth-century France. Even the eminent Byzantinist Charles Diehl, when he came to write his *Theodora, Empress of Byzantium*[115] in 1904, was careful to take into account not only the image of the queen as she was represented in Ravenna, but also as she had been represented 'on the boards of Porte St-Martin'.[116]

9 | Maurice Denis and the Iconic Mode in Painting

Both Sardou and Moreau developed a fantasy world of Byzantium which drew upon myths of excess and evil. Moreau in particular stressed what was thought to be the Byzantine preoccupation with objects and materials. A little later in the century the Nabis also found inspiration in Byzantine art, but it was inspiration of a very different kind. Émile Bernard, Albert Aurier and Maurice Denis saw themselves as the children of Flandrin, Puvis de Chavannes and Cézanne, and they reinvented the iconic mode in a new form. They all wrote approvingly of the spiritual, symbolic language of the 'Primitives', whose non-material values they urged against contemporary naturalism, and whose expression of permanence they contrasted with the fluidity of Impressionism. Bernard in 1890 described Cézanne's work as 'essentially hieratic';[117] for Aurier Primitive art was 'simultaneously subjective, synthesizing, symbolist and ideal';[118] and for Denis Byzantine art was the 'most perfect

type of Christian art'.[119] In the modern period, said Denis (thinking of Puvis de Chavannes and Odilon Redon), the revival of religious art corresponded to a return to Byzantium and Byzantine symbolism. 'A Byzantine Christ', he said in 1890, 'is a symbol; the Jesus of our modern painters is merely literary. In the first it is form which is expressive; in the second, expression is attempted through the imitation of nature.'[120]

In his 'Notes on Religious Painting' (1896),[121] Denis spoke of how Byzantine art had transcended the *trompe l'oeil* effects of late classical art and 'invented a complete visual language' to express the dogmas of Christianity. In the mosaics of Rome, Milan and Ravenna he claimed that Byzantine artists had created modes of expressing sacred history which they communicated to Cimabue, Giotto, Raphael and Ingres. As a practising artist, however, Denis's focus was on the present, and the whole tendency of his criticism was to inscribe the ancient within the modern. For him Byzantine symbolist ideas were imprinted in all good modern art.[122] 'In the work of Cézanne, Gauguin, Bernard,' he wrote, 'there was a close correspondence between form and emotion. Phenomena signify states of the soul and that is Symbolism … which takes me back to the Byzantines.'[123] Driskel sums this up by saying that Denis, in his demand for a return to Byzantine hieraticism, wanted 'a renunciation of narrative modes of representation' and 'a revival of an iconic one, dictating an attitude of non-discursive contemplation and direct

76 Maurice Denis, *La Mystère catholique*, 1891.
Oil on canvas, 27 x 41 cm (10½ x 16¼ in).
Kröller-Müller Museum, Otterlo

emotional response to the forms constituting the image'.[124] Denis's own iconic paintings were developed in the context of his response to the work of Bernard and Gauguin at the Café Volpini in 1889. At this time he began to work on his famously iconic *Mystère catholique* (fig. 76), of which he produced three versions. He had already been impressed by the writings of Sâr Péladan, who spoke warmly of the Primitives, and in the next few years, together with the other members of the Nabis, he began to work out an avant-garde theory which favoured non-mimetic art and whose historical basis lay as much in Byzantium as in the Western classical tradition.

It is remarkable that by the end of the nineteenth century the Byzantine style had been adopted in French painting for both a pious asceticism and an extreme form of decadence. It might be said that they both had their roots in a reaction against the dominant mode of materialist realism and both pursued a symbolist pathway to distinct destinations. The use of the Byzantine mode in church decoration also had its roots in an earlier pietistic reaction. In its desire to stimulate a spiritual revival, the Ultramontane wing of the Church saw in the hieraticism of Byzantine art an appropriate vehicle for what it felt to be the expression of its own dignity and authority. It therefore encouraged many artists to abandon the elegant studio manner of an earlier period and to fill large ecclesiastical spaces with murals reflecting the stern certainties of neo-Catholicism. These spaces were found, however, not in new Gothic buildings, where columns and sculpture occupied the walls, but in Byzantine and Romanesque structures which provided large areas of uncluttered stone. Not that the Romano-Byzantine buildings of nineteenth-century France were built specifically to accommodate the new kind of decoration. Architects like Vaudoyer and Abadie were driven more by a purely secular desire to experiment with forms which were neither Gothic nor classical but were, nevertheless, linked to French architectural traditions. Although the French neo-Byzantine tradition rolled on across Europe taking twentieth-century forms as it went, its greatest achievement was the Sacré-Coeur, which stands now, as it did at the end of the nineteenth century, as a symbol of the Church's attempt to reappropriate the past in the interests of its survival.

3 | Britain In Germany and France interest in Byzantium centred on Byzantine architecture and emerged out of an earlier curiosity about the Romanesque. This pattern was repeated in Britain, but happened more slowly. The reason for this may have been that Byzantium was more remote for the British than for the rest of Europe. Germany saw connections between the churches of the Rhine and the buildings of ancient Byzantium, and in the figure of Charlemagne in particular their history was linked to that of the East.

The French, too, perceived both direct and indirect links between their own architecture and that of the Byzantine Empire. In the middle of the nineteenth century the ancient domed churches of southwestern France came into prominence in such a way that the Oriental origins of early French architecture became something of an orthodoxy. This was not the case in Britain, however. It is true that the terms 'Norman' and 'Romanesque' were used indifferently and that the two were often identified as 'Byzantine', but the extremely widespread use of the term 'Byzantine' to describe any pre-Gothic building was the result of blurring and confusion, rather than of strong historical connections.[1] Religious issues also played a part in the shaping of attitudes. The Gothic Revival in Britain was a doctrinaire affair: Catholics claimed one thing and Anglicans another, but both perceived Gothic as the Christian style *par excellence*. In terms of this odd way of thinking Romanesque was seen as 'foreign', and Byzantine even more remote. It was Oriental and alien, and its long-standing associations with Christianity were almost totally ignored.

Historians of Gothic architecture, however, could hardly overlook its precursors, and in the late 1830s British architectural writers began to take a serious interest in early medieval and basilican styles. At the same time a small number of architects, independently of one another, built churches in variations of Romanesque, each of which was called 'Byzantine' at the time: Sara Losh at St Mary's, Wreay, Cumbria (1842); James Wild at Christ Church, Streatham (1845); and Sidney Herbert at St Mary and St Nicholas, Wilton (1845) (figs. 78–80). The first (and perhaps the most remarkable) was ignored;[2] the other two were much publicized, and their use of round-arched forms, large undecorated wall surfaces and other un-Gothic features set in train a vigorous debate about the place of non-Gothic styles in modern church design (see below, p. 112). This in turn contributed to the growing interest in the art and architecture of the so-called 'Dark Ages'. In the 1840s both Byzantine art and Byzantine architecture began to take a prominent place in people's understanding of the post-classical European past, and in the 1850s Ruskin's account of San Marco and other Veneto-Byzantine buildings focused British minds on Byzantium. This was a Western form of Byzantium, and its architectural result was a crop of secular and ecclesiastical Veneto-Byzantine buildings built in the 1850s and 1860s. Ruskin's account of San Marco also stimulated interest in mosaics. Exhibitions in the 1850s and early 1860s contained both replicas of ancient mosaics and examples of modern work. It had been difficult to make mosaics without suitable materials, but when in around 1860 Antonio Salviati set up his business in Venice for the manufacture of tesserae, the picture changed. In Britain Henry Layard engaged royal patronage for mosaic, and the decision (after endless discussion) to decorate the interior of Wren's St Paul's Cathedral with mosaic placed Byzantium and Byzantine art firmly in the public eye. It was, however, archaeology and the Arts and Crafts movement that gave the strongest impulse to the Byzantine Revival. William Morris was its leading figure in Britain, and during the 1880s he turned to Byzantine design and Byzantine architecture as an alternative to the ubiquitous Gothic. The younger William Lethaby took up Morris's ideas. His account of Hagia Sophia linked Byzantine architecture with late nineteenth-century symbolism and exercised, in turn, a strong influence over John Francis Bentley's Westminster Cathedral and other neo-Byzantine buildings of the period.

77 (previous spread) St Paul's Cathedral, London, view of the saucer domes with mosaics by William Blake Richmond, 1894

78 (top left) James Wild, Christ Church,
   Streatham, London, 1845
79 (top right) Sara Losh, St Mary's, Wreay,
   Cumbria, 1842
80 (above) Sidney Herbert, St Mary and
   St Nicholas, Wilton, Wiltshire, 1845

1 | Early Nineteenth-Century Responses to Byzantine Architecture

In the early years of the nineteenth century British understanding of Eastern Byzantium was picturesque rather than archaeological or historical. Gibbon's less than complimentary account of Byzantium continued to dominate attitudes right through the century, and *The History of the Decline and Fall of the Roman Empire* was issued again and again.[3] Hagia Sophia failed to conform to eighteenth-century aesthetic criteria and Gibbon's criticism was extensive, ambivalent and well known. 'The architecture of St Sophia,' he wrote, '... has been imitated by the Turkish sultans, and that venerable pile continues to excite the fond admiration of the Greeks, and the more rational curiosity of the European travellers. The eye of the spectator is disappointed by an irregular prospect of half-domes and shelving roofs: the western front, the principal approach, is destitute of simplicity and magnificence; and the scale of dimensions has been much surpassed by several of the Latin cathedrals. But the architect who first erected an aerial cupola, is entitled to the praise of bold design and skilful execution.'[4]

In the early part of the century accounts of Hagia Sophia came from the rather confused, if influential, experiences of British travellers. In 1810 Byron was moved by its romantic history but was unimpressed by the building. In the 1830s the romantic tone was taken up by Julia Pardo. In 1835, at the age of twenty-four, she accompanied her father to Constantinople and recorded her experiences in *The City of the Sultans* (1837). Twice she gained admission to Hagia Sophia and her account of adopting a disguise and risking death to get a glimpse of the interior is exciting and well told. She found the mosque 'a creation of enchantment ... of such unearthly magnificence',[5] but when she returned as part of a visiting foreign delegation, her attitude changed. The 'marble, porphyry, jasper, and verd-antique' continued to amaze her, but now she was confused by the 'medley of different orders and materials'.[6] As in Gibbon's case, Hagia Sophia did not conform to her idea of 'the beautiful and the symmetrical', and when she published the *Beauties of the Bosphorus* in 1838 Hagia Sophia was not one of them. It is a mark of the shift in taste for Byzantium during the nineteenth century that when this same book was reissued in 1874 Hagia Sophia was included. Now it was described as 'strikingly majestic' and 'despite all its incongruities ... decidedly an architectural wonder, and well worthy of the admiration which has been lavished upon it for centuries'.[7] William Bartlett provided the illustrations for this volume (fig. 81), as well as some soft-focused views of Constantinople for Guizot's 1850 edition of Gibbon. The well-known Orientalist painter J.F. Lewis went to Constantinople in 1840 and also made some beautifully sensitive drawings of the interior of Hagia Sophia, but never made use of them in his larger oeuvre (fig. 82). In 1846 Thackeray was impressed by the 'light swelling domes and beautiful proportions' of the building;[8] and back in London in the same year Robert Burford exhibited a huge panorama of Constantinople in Leicester Square.[9]

81 William Bartlett, plate from *The Beauties of the Bosphorus*, 1874, showing the interior of Hagia Sophia

82 J.F. Lewis, *Interior of Hagia Sophia*, 1840–1.
Pencil, chalk and watercolour, 36.2 x 47.6 cm
(14¼ x 18¼ in). Victoria and Albert Museum, London

Outside of travel literature there was not much discussion of Byzantine architecture. Architectural criticism in Britain was dominated by Gothic, though in their search for the origins of the pointed arch a number of architectural writers and historians touched on Romanesque and Byzantine precursors.[10] One writer in particular who had considerable enthusiasm for pre-Gothic building was Thomas Hope. Hope had come from Amsterdam in 1796 and was a rich and cultivated admirer of the arts. He died in 1831 but his most influential book, *An Historical Essay on Architecture*, was published posthumously in 1835. It was the fruit of a lifetime of travelling, drawing and observing buildings. It was breezy, ebullient, compendious and unorthodox. In contrast to many of his contemporaries, Hope writes warmly about Byzantine architecture, which he characterizes as: 'Arches thus rising over arches, and cupolas over cupolas.' 'We may say', he adds, 'that all which in the temples of Athens had been straight, and angular, and square, in the churches of Constantinople became curved and rounded – concave within, and convex without.'[11] Hope gives an outline of the development of Byzantine architecture starting with Hagia Sophia and continuing with a spirited description of the cathedral of Torcello. Like many of his contemporaries he saw early German churches as a combination of the Roman basilica and Byzantine arch, and he pointed to the connections between medieval German and Byzantine work. Speaking of the eleventh-century church of St Aposteln in Cologne, for example, he says: 'on entering its ancient gates, I almost thought myself at Constantinople' (fig. 83).[12]

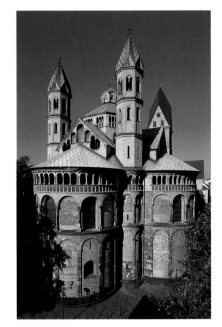

In England two other books helped fire this enthusiasm for the pre-Gothic round-arched style: J.L. Petit's *Remarks on Church Architecture* (1841) and Henry Gally Knight's *The Ecclesiastical Architecture of Italy from the Time of Constantine to the Fifteenth Century* (1842). The former was a two-volume anthology of drawings by Petit made on a continental trip in 1839, and accompanied by a commentary in which he suggested the adoption of a round-arched architecture in Britain. Knight's was a magnificent historical panorama of the history of pre- and early medieval architecture illustrated with sumptuous drawings of Italian, German and French buildings by Domenico Quaglio.[13]

Petit's suggestion that the British might adopt round-arched building met with stiff opposition from the High Church. The Cambridge Camden Society recognized him as 'a non-high-church-man'[14] and conducted a campaign against him in its journal, the *Ecclesiologist*. Worried by the appearance of new basilican churches, especially Herbert's at Wilton and Wild's at Streatham (see figs. 78, 80), it lamented the 'introduction of foreign styles of Church Architecture, essentially discordant with our national feelings and associations'.[15] After a long and acrimonious debate on the subject, the *Ecclesiologist* put its foot down and enunciated three fundamental principles. '1. That Gothic Architecture is, in the highest sense, the only Christian Architecture. 2. That, during the period in which it flourished, our Country churches are, *in their way*, as perfect models as our Cathedrals. And 3. The proposed introduction by Mr Petit and his followers of a new style, whether Romanesque, Byzantine, or Eclectic, is to be earnestly deprecated, as opening a door to the most dangerous innovations, and totally subversive of Christian Architecture as such.'[16]

83 St Aposteln, Cologne, begun *c.*1032

2 | Byzantium and the History of Art

Just as the English High Church was intolerant of the use of Romanesque or Byzantine styles in modern architecture, it was equally unsympathetic to Byzantine art. In France (see above, p.65) Rio's *The Poetry of Christian Art* had denounced Byzantine art as emanating from an 'abyss of moral and intellectual degradation'.[17] Nicholas Wiseman, a leading British Catholic who had earlier been much moved by the art of Ravenna, was converted by Rio's argument into condemning Byzantine mosaic. How sad, he said, that the 'artistic type' of the Virgin should have been 'locked up in the hard and dark delineations of the Byzantine school, waiting as it were for a germ of life to bring them into the warm and bright existence of the Christian school'.[18] The most widely read guide to art history took an even stronger line. Franz Kugler's *Handbook of the History of Painting* was first published in 1837 and translated into English in 1841. Like Rio, Kugler distinguished between the mosaic art of the Roman basilica that was pervaded by 'solemn tranquillity' and produced 'a feeling of awe',[19] and the mosaics of the Eastern empire characterized by 'spectral rigidity' and 'dull, servile constraint'.[20] Kugler's British editor, Sir Charles Lock Eastlake, a pillar of the art Establishment,[21] endorsed Kugler's views and excused, on the basis of 'completeness', the fact that Byzantine art should have been included at all.[22] In the second edition of the book (1851), Kugler augmented the sections on early art with more vilification of Byzantium. Ravenna, San Paolo fuori le Mura, SS Cosma e Damiano and Sta Maria Maggiore all helped to bring art into a state of 'corruption' and 'kept her stationary there for many a long century'. Byzantine art was guilty of the 'superficial and defective representation of the human form', presenting 'half-animated corpses'. In Kugler's opinion the mosaics of San Marco in Venice have nothing to recommend them. Here, he says, is 'an utter extinction of all freedom of form', where figures are merely 'lifeless shadows' and the product of 'the decrepit theology of the period'.[23]

The aesthetics of Romantic individualism had nothing to say about Byzantine art, and it took Romantic Christianity and an aesthetic that linked piety, poetry and art to 'rediscover' it. The change took place in the 1840s, and it was sudden and bold. In the face of all this denunciation, Lord Lindsay asserted in his remarkable *Sketches of the History of Christian Art* (1847) that 'St Mark's is the glory of Byzantine architecture.' The whole building, he continued, is 'completely incrusted with mosaics; the lower walls are lined with precious marbles; the pavement is of rich opus Graecanicum, undulating and uneven like a settling sea – the whole blending into a rich mysterious gloom.'[24] Alexander Lindsay, the 25th Earl of Balcares, swept away all talk of stiffness and rigidity; he abandoned the tests of realism or Renaissance perspective, and wrote of both Byzantine mosaic and architecture with an uninhibited pleasure and delight. This was indeed a new note.

Lindsay knew that he was being unorthodox. 'The respect with which I have spoken of the arts of Byzantium', he told his reader, 'must have appeared rather strange to you.' He was familiar with Gibbon, of course, and had bought Kugler's *Handbook* when it appeared in 1841. Summarizing them he said: 'We are apt to think of the Byzantines as a race of dastards, effete and worn out in body and mind, bondsmen to tradition, form and circumstances, little if at all superior to the slaves of an Oriental despotism – and that too from the very first hour of

Constantine's migration to the Bosphorus.'[25] But the strength of Lindsay's account of Byzantium is his acceptance of its Orientalism and his refusal to judge it by Western standards. That openness to Eastern influence was the result of a journey to the East he made in 1836, and which laid the foundation for a catholic response to art and architecture.

Lord Lindsay was rich and privileged. In 1829 at the age of seventeen he paid his first visit to Italy, and even then his fascination with the 'curiosities' of early art was clear. In Brescia he bought 'a very curious old Greek picture, painted with a background of gold', and was hugely impressed by his first sight of San Marco.[26] In 1833, aged twenty-one, he came into the substantial estate left to him by a distant relative, Lady Mary Crawford, which included books and works of art. This stimulated his bibliomania, and as the direct result of an early purchase – Léon Laborde's *Journey through Arabia Petraea* (1830)[27] – the young Lindsay decided to visit this mysterious world for himself. In 1836 he set off with his cousin William Ramsay on an aristocratic tour of the Near East. Though money and connections opened doors and brought the two men into contact with the most sophisticated levels of society, the absence of any organized tourism resulted in travelling conditions that were often harsh and demanding. One of the most difficult journeys was to Mount Sinai where, in the monastery of St Catherine, Lindsay had his first experience of Eastern Byzantine work. In the chapel he found 'mosaic work, contemporary with Justinian, the Transfiguration of

84 Apse mosaic, *c.*565. Monastery of St Catherine, Mount Sinai

the Saviour' (fig. 84).[28] In order to see the more remote sights they were obliged to walk great distances in desert conditions, and the heat and the lack of clean water and of good food took their toll. Outside Damascus William Ramsay contracted cholera and was dead within a few days. Lindsay brought his body back by sea.

In 1839 Lindsay visited Munich where he developed an enthusiasm for the modern Nazarene work that (as we saw in Chapter 1) was being encouraged by Ludwig I, and discovered a taste for Hess and Overbeck in particular. In common with many German and French critics of the period, Lindsay linked painting with what they called 'poetry', that is, the expression of strong feeling. Furthermore, this group read both painting and poetry in terms of religious piety. During this period a new kind of pious ecstasy was identified in the art of the Middle Ages, and was being translated into modern terms by Overbeck and the other Nazarenes. Lindsay shared this tendency and planned a project on the 'poetry and prose of painting', since 'poetry', he claimed, 'began with religion.' For him, the great 'poets' of painting were 'Giotto, Fra Angelico … Overbeck, Hess, etc.'[29] He claimed the Nazarenes as modern artists *par excellence* because they had taken up the 'chain' of early Italian art and continued it in the present. This was the thrust of *Sketches of the History of Christian Art*, and it resulted in one of the earliest accounts of Byzantium in which Byzantine art and architecture were treated enthusiastically and seriously in an intimate and readable way. The book was widely appreciated; it was, said Ruskin, 'unquestionably the most valuable which has yet appeared in England' on the subject, but Ruskin regretted that Lindsay had become bogged down in a theory which was both 'unworkable and untenable'.[30] Ultimately it was Ruskin himself who was to become the most powerful figure in rehabilitating Byzantium in Britain, but he was by no means the first. He was preceded by a number of now rather neglected figures whose work he knew well, and to trace their interest in Byzantine art and architecture we have to turn to the colleges of Oxford and Cambridge and to the highly influential Camden Society.

3 | Oxford, Cambridge and a New Architectural History

The application of Hegel's ideas to world history was widespread in the 1840s. The German historian Barthold Niebuhr developed the general Hegelian dialectic of progress through action, reaction and synthesis to explain the division between the Aryan ethnic group that inhabited the north and central Mediterranean and the Oriental group that inhabited the eastern Mediterranean. Niebuhr's ideas were enthusiastically imported into Oxford and taken up by Edward Freeman, who believed that Aryans were unified by language, habits and institutions and were in creative oppositional struggle with the nations of the Orient. As Mark Crinson puts it: 'In this scheme of things Byzantium was to occupy a curious position. It was Christian in religion, its peoples polyglot, its culture rich in Graeco-Roman forms and skills, yet by the very fact of its relative geographical position it had to be Oriental and non-Aryan and, consequently, without historical change.'[31] Freeman published his *History of Architecture* in 1849, and in this he expressed strong views about Byzantium, but even before that he was a major protagonist in the debate about the suitability of 'foreign' or racially alien styles for British buildings.

Freeman came up to Oxford in 1841, and at the age of only nineteen threw himself into the theological and architectural controversy that was being waged between the Cambridge Camden Society and the Oxford Society for Promoting the Study of Gothic Architecture. The two societies had been founded at about the same time in 1839, and their creation was an indication of how seriously ideas about church building and restoration were taken. Under the early direction of Benjamin Webb and John Mason Neale the Cambridge society wielded great power; its only serious challenge came from the more liberal sister society in Oxford.[32] Both were passionately committed to Gothic, but the Oxford society distrusted the Cambridge obsession with a single Gothic style and was open to ideas of architectural pluralism. In the 1840s the Camden Society, with its interest in early Church history, had become more and more associated with Roman Catholicism. This was a source of considerable embarrassment to the membership and in 1844 a rift developed between the absolutist Neale and the more moderate factions in the society. In order to save itself from destruction the society attempted to change its identity by transferring its headquarters to London and adopting a new name – the Ecclesiological Society. Neale temporarily retired and Webb remained as secretary. The chairmanship was taken up by Alexander J. Beresford Hope, who was to become a symbol of the reorganized society. Hope was the wealthy son of Thomas Hope and had inherited his father's passion for architecture. His views were more broadminded than those of his predecessors, and in 1846 he confessed in the pages of the *Ecclesiologist* an appreciation of Romanesque. Although he thought that it was not suitable for direct emulation, he felt that it possessed fascinating features worthy of serious study.[33]

Some of these elements can be discerned in All Saints', Margaret Street, London, which was masterminded by Beresford Hope and William Butterfield. Although not itself a Byzantine building it incorporated one powerfully Oriental characteristic – colour. The polychromatic effects of the interior (fig. 85) owed much to the awakening of interest in San Marco and Ravennite architecture, and it opened the way for a much more liberal and extensive 'Byzantine' use of colour in the architecture of the second half of the nineteenth century.

85 William Butterfield, interior of All Saints', Margaret Street, London, 1849–59

In 1846 Freeman and Beresford Hope struck up a friendship. The result was that Freeman (from Oxford) joined the Ecclesiological Society and Beresford Hope (chairman of the Cambridge group) joined the Oxford Society. In his first Oxford address, Beresford Hope urged open-minded pluralism on his audience and suggested they follow the 'great example' of Giotto in glorifying the 'forms of Byzantine art'.[34]

Freeman, too, gave Byzantium a new role in his *History of Architecture* (1849). Hitherto Byzantium had been something of a curiosity; in Freeman's scheme it took a prominent place in the historical development of world architecture. In spite of its importance, however, in Freeman's eyes it was fundamentally the product of alien culture: 'it is not ancient, modern, or mediaeval … it is Oriental … alien in language, government, and general feeling.'[35] He treats it as dangerously alluring, attractive yet foreign. He expresses great enthusiasm for the Byzantine dome, 'the very life and soul of Byzantine architecture', and he rhapsodizes, in terms drawn from the Romantic writing of Friedrich Schlegel, on 'the mighty cathedral dedicated by Justinian to the Divine Wisdom' which had 'more influence on architecture than any other single building'.[36] For Byzantine details he was very dependent on A. Couchard's *Selection of Byzantine Churches in Greece* (1841–2),[37] which he hoped would be followed by yet more scholarly productions.[38] Freeman also waxed lyrical about the 'magnificent cathedral of St Mark's', about Sta Fosca on Torcello, and San Vitale in Ravenna – 'the most completely oriental building in western Europe'[39] – but his pleasure is entirely theoretical, since he did not actually visit these places until 1856.

4 | British Travellers in Byzantine Italy

The institution of the Grand Tour, which had been such an important part of British aristocratic life in the seventeenth and eighteenth centuries, had finally faded when hostilities with France at the turn of the nineteenth century prevented foreign travel. In the 1830s new kinds of traveller emerged and old itineraries were changed. With the increase in aesthetic pietism, sites such as the medieval Campo Santo in Pisa and the Byzantine churches of Ravenna were included in the growing number of guidebooks and travellers' manuals. Ravenna in particular rose in prominence. Previously it had not been much visited because it had no important classical monuments like Rome and was not picturesque like Venice. But as the Christian traveller was beginning to discover, it was filled with some of the earliest architectural relics. One of those travellers was Nicholas Wiseman, a leading figure in the Catholic Church. As early as 1839 he visited the 'sadly neglected' town of Ravenna, and what he found there was something which even Rome could not offer. Unlike Rome, association with paganism (he claimed) had not polluted Ravenna. Lamenting the 'decay of [Ravenna's Byzantine] imperial magnificence', Wiseman waxed lyrical over the mosaics in San Vitale and the tomb of Gallia Placidia, and he urged the readers of the Catholic *Dublin Review* to include the town in their Italian pilgrimage.[40] Such was the force of Wiseman's prose that Octavian Blewitt reprinted large sections of the article in his early *Handbook for Travellers in Central Italy* (1843).

Unlike Ravenna, Venice had never been entirely neglected on the conventional European art tour, but its sensuous pleasures came much lower on the list than the bracing medievalism of Florence or the rigorous classicism of Rome. Francis Palgrave, a Jew who had converted to Christianity, compiled one of the first guidebooks intended for mass tourism. Ten years before Ruskin, Palgrave enthused about the Byzantine work in San Marco in his *Handbook for Northern Italy* (1842). 'As soon as you cross the threshold' of San Marco, he wrote, 'you feel admitted into the Byzantine empire.' For travellers brought up on Gibbon this would have been an unwelcome experience, but not for Palgrave. 'From the resplendent cupolas and apsides above,' he continued, 'to the rich and variegated pavement below, the whole is pervaded by the same character of mystic solemnity: dark and shadowy, but not gloomy, and full of complexity without confusion.' 'The gold-grounded mosaics,' he went on, 'spread over the roof and wall, give to the building the appearance of being lined with precious metal,' and he drew his readers' attention to the Pala d'Oro as 'one of the most remarkable specimens now in existence of Byzantine art'.[41]

While Palgrave's enthusiasm for San Marco derived from its antiquity, others were fascinated by its exotic Orientalism. For Charles Dickens, who was there late in 1844, Venice was 'An Italian Dream' and his visit to San Marco the highlight of a somnambulistic experience. 'I thought I entered the Cathedral, and went in and out among its many arches: traversing its whole extent. A grand and dreamy structure, of immense proportions; golden with old mosaics; redolent of perfumes; dim with the smoke of incense; costly in treasure of precious stones and metals, glittering through iron bars; holy with the bodies of deceased saints; rainbow-hued with windows of stained glass … unreal, fantastic, solemn, inconceivable throughout.'[42] Dickens's version of San Marco derives originally from the enchanted view of Venice offered by Byron in *Childe Harold*, but it is clear that it is Palgrave's *Handbook* rather than Kugler's upon which he is relying.

The ecclesiastical associations of San Marco moved neither Palgrave nor Dickens, but there was one English writer in this period who combined the kind of enthusiasm for early Christian art with a sympathetic attention to architectural detail that we associate with Ruskin. Ironically, it was one of the high priests of the Cambridge Camden Society, Benjamin Webb. The intimidatingly dull title of his book, *Sketches of Continental Ecclesiology* (1848), disguises a fascinating guide to the most important religious centres of Europe. In Munich he was impressed by the neo-Byzantine efforts set in motion by Ludwig I. The Allerheiligen-Hofkirche is 'a kind of adaptation of the Byzantine idea' whose 'inside is certainly very beautiful'. The Ludwigskirche, in 'a sort of pseudo-Byzantine style', is 'sumptuous'.[43] It was the real Byzantine at Venice, however, that fully occupied Webb's attention. In San Marco, a church 'unique in the world in almost every point of view', Webb is mesmerized by the 'porphyry, jasper, serpentine and alabaster, verde, and rose antique' and hundreds of other marbles; they create 'a truly eastern magnificence' and he is awestruck by their 'deep symbolism and ornament'.[44]

5 | Ruskin and Byzantine Venice

But where, one wonders, is Ruskin in all this? We know that Ruskin had experienced the fascinating influence of San Marco long before Webb set foot there. His interest in the church began back in 1835 when, as a boy of sixteen, his parents took him to Venice. In the early 1840s Ruskin's attitude to Venice and San Marco was picturesque rather than historical, though in 1841 he made a large number of drawings of the church. He was particularly intrigued by the mosaics in the outer porch, which he described in the first volume of *Modern Painters* (1842). Though they are 'archaic' and 'rude', he also found them 'suggestive', 'inventive' and 'sublime'.[45]

Ruskin returned to Venice in 1845. He was now drawing the city energetically in the face of a systematic and destructive programme of 'restoration'. It is during this visit that he seems to have made his first visit to Torcello. 'A decent distance,' he wrote to his father, 'but a most interesting church, about the best preserved of its age – 8 or 900 – that I have seen', but the largely deserted island location which contributes so much to the austere image of Torcello in the second volume of *The Stones of Venice* is dismissed as 'a horrible marsh'.[46] During this visit Ruskin's main interest was in painting, but a number of architectural drawings treat Byzantine subjects, including the arches of the Ca' Loredan (fig. 86). At this point Ruskin was still assimilating his impressions and had not yet worked out the historical relationship between Byzantine and Gothic architecture. It would be rash to insist on the point at which he came to a full realization of the significance of Byzantine work, but one might conjecture a Sunday evening in Beauvais in November 1845. He was on his way home from his hectic Italian trip, and was beginning to order in his mind all that he had seen there. He wrote to his father of thoughts that came to him as he sat for 'an hour or two' in the choir of the cathedral. 'I wanted to compare the effect of the pure Gothic with the Byzantine and Lombard schools,' he said, adding that 'the northern Gothic shows decidedly barbaric after them.'[47] He was in Italy again the following year and produced a number of Venetian studies which reflected his growing interest in the Byzantine, notably the Palazzo Dario (fig. 87) and a watercolour of San Marco after rain (fig. 88).

Ruskin's first published views on Byzantine building came in *The Seven Lamps of Architecture* (1849). This is a thematic approach to architecture in which Ruskin uses style to illustrate or to exemplify human values. One of those values is connected with the vitality of art and architecture, and in a chapter entitled 'The Lamp of Life' he treats buildings 'in proportion to the amount of energy [of mind] that has been visibly employed upon them'.[48] One of those buildings that bears the strong impress of mind is San Marco, whose west front, 'though in many respects imperfect, is in its proportions, and as a piece of rich and fantastic colour, as lovely a dream as ever filled human imagination'.[49]

It is, however, the chapter 'The Lamp of Power' in which Ruskin says most about Byzantium, and which forms a basis for his historical account of architecture in *The Stones of Venice* (1851–3). The two great intellectual lamps of architecture, says Ruskin, are those of Beauty and Power. These, he says, are linked to our response to the eighteenth-century theory about the Beautiful and the Sublime in nature. In architectural terms, however, Beauty is

Casa Loredan,

86 John Ruskin, *Study of the Marble Inlaying on the front of the Casa Loredan, Venice*, 1845. Pencil, watercolour and bodycolour, 32 × 26.7 cm (12½ × 10½ in). Ashmolean Museum, Oxford

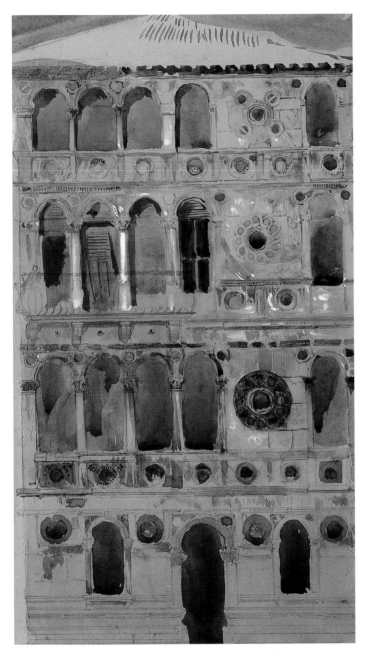

87 (left) John Ruskin, *Palazzo Dario, c.*1846.
Pencil and watercolour, 23 × 12.7 cm (9 × 5 in).
Ruskin Foundation, University of Lancaster
88 (right) John Ruskin, *Part of St Mark's, Venice, Sketch after Rain, 1846.* Pencil, watercolour, ink and bodycolour,
42.1 × 28.6 cm (16½ × 11¼ in).
Ashmolean Museum, Oxford

suggestive of preciousness and delicacy, while Power is suggestive of mystery, majesty and 'undiminished awe'. Power is a generative principle; it is connected to the elemental forces in nature and to masculinity in mankind. To illustrate the difference between the Beautiful and Powerful Ruskin contrasts Greek and Byzantine architectural sculpture. 'While the arrangements of *line* are far more artful in the Greek capital,' he says, 'the Byzantine light and shade are … incontestably more grand and masculine.'[50] This 'masculinity' in Byzantine work he likens to 'natural arrangement of grand form', such as 'the thunder cloud', the 'majestic heave of the mountain side' and 'the head of every mighty tree'. For Ruskin, Byzantine work is strongly gendered. The Byzantines were in his estimation originators in the manner of God the Father, and had 'truer sympathy with what God made majestic' than the feminized 'self-contemplating and self-contented Greek'.

Ruskin added a new ingredient to the current treatment of Byzantine art and architecture: sensuous pleasure, and an ability to articulate that pleasure in mesmerizing prose. His pleasure may be contained within a firm moral structure, but it is pleasure nonetheless. By the time that the second volume of *The Stones of Venice* appeared in 1853, there was as yet no real consensus about the status of Byzantium either historically or aesthetically, nor about its place in the history of art and architecture. At about this time George Finlay was attempting to rewrite its political history (see below, pp. 130–1), and it featured prominently in handbooks of art and tourist guidebooks, but its architecture was still confused with Romanesque and its art misunderstood. Thomas Hope had generated an antiquarian enthusiasm for Byzantine building, and Lord Lindsay had brought eccentric warmth and delight to its art, but Ruskin short-circuited all this by a love affair with one building and its decoration: San Marco. His language is effusive, tactile, corporeal, even erotic: 'Round the walls of the porches' of San Marco, 'there are set pillars of variegated stones, jasper and porphyry, and deep-green serpentine spotted with flakes of snow, and marbles, that half refuse and half yield to the sunshine, Cleopatra-like, "their bluest veins to kiss" – the shadow, as it steals back from them, revealing line after line of azure undulation, as the receding tide leaves the waved sand.'[51] But Ruskin's romanticism is not uncritical. His account of San Marco shifts between meticulous observation, moral rhetoric and intense personal responsiveness. The first readers of *The Stones of Venice* were simultaneously astounded by his language and puzzled by his ideas. Throughout these volumes Ruskin consciously manipulates his audience; his range of linguistic 'voices' is far greater than that of any writer we have so far mentioned, and he employs those voices to entice, to fascinate and to convert his readers.

The journey to San Marco is prefaced by the far more sober lessons of the first volume of *The Stones of Venice* (1851), which, as the subtitle explains, form the 'foundations' of the later volumes. In the Byzantine sections of the second volume Ruskin maintains a curious balance between scientific empiricism and romantic moral narrative, while the vehicle is a pseudo-travelogue. Like the many true volumes of travel literature available to Ruskin – Curzon's or Webb's, for example – Ruskin's object is as much to instruct as to entertain, and he employs the form of the travelogue to lull his reader into a kind of complicity with an author who sets himself up as guide not merely to the physical monuments of Venice but to their understanding and interpretation. In other words, it is a form that appears denotative but is in fact connotative.

89 Apse mosaic, late 12th century.
Duomo, Torcello

The journey begins in the reflective, sombre, even melancholy Byzantine and Romano-Christian world of Torcello. The romantic narrative of the early settlers of Torcello is a nostalgic tale involving the privation, the hardship and the nobility of a people exiled from their homes on the terra firma, and these human characteristics are inscribed in the details of the duomo, 'built by men in flight and distress'.[53] Everywhere Ruskin meets with 'simplicity and dignity' under the 'frank diffusion of light': the pulpit is 'severe', as are the famous raised seats and episcopal throne in the apse; there are mosaics of 'the most solemn character' but reduced to two subjects only – The Last Judgement and Ruskin's favourite weeping Madonna (fig. 89).[54] There may be 'bluntness and rudeness of feeling' in the early settlers of Torcello but it is offset by the 'redundance of power'.[55] What Ruskin elicits from these details is a sense of primal authenticity, integrity and, above all,

unaffected masculinity. There is something Adamic about these earliest inhabitants of Torcello. In the book of Genesis Adam dreams one female, Eve, into being; in Ruskin's myth of the creation of Venice men create two females – 'Torcello and Venice, mother and daughter'.[56]

The intermediate resting place on the reader's journey to Venice is Murano and the church of San Donato. Austerity has now passed into muted Byzantine richness and Ruskin relishes the subtle but largely geometric polychromy of the church (fig. 91). The beauty of San Donato is contrasted (as so often in Ruskin) with the grotesque appearance of modern Venetians with their 'animal misery', 'glittering eyes and muttering lips'.[57] They are the product of the fallen Venice, while the Madonna of San Donato is the creation of Byzantine innocence (fig. 90). She is a solitary figure wearing 'a robe of blue, deeply fringed with gold'. But this is not the robe of the Queen of Heaven; it is 'simply the dress of the women of the time'.[58] Similarly, the floor of the church, 'one of the most precious monuments in Italy', provides evidence of the earliest uses of Venetian colour. For Ruskin, colour is associated with holiness and purity, and here in its Byzantine form is 'the beginning of that mighty spirit of Venetian colour, which was to be consummated in Titian'.[59]

The unaffected masculinity of Torcello and the subtle use of colour in Murano provide the framework for the climax of the first part of The Stones of Venice, and as Ruskin approaches the central Venetian complex his narrative tone becomes more intimate, and the pressure on the metaphorical elbow of the reader more insistent. The English Victorian traveller is conducted to what is unfamiliar, rare and strange by way of what is known and familiar. 'And now I wish that the reader, before I bring him into St Mark's Place,' says Ruskin, 'would imagine himself for a little time in a quiet English cathedral town, and walk with me to the west front of its cathedral.' The cathedral close, with its 'secluded, continuous, drowsy felicities' and its 'diminutive' houses, is small in scale, ordered and Anglican;

90 (opposite) Apse mosaic, c.1140. San Donato, Murano
91 (above) San Donato, Murano, completed c.1140

it is a product of a culture that is English and unthreatening. The *sestieri* that press around San Marco are very different. Here, 'we find ourselves in a paved alley,' Ruskin tells the reader, and it is an alley which is encumbered, blocked and obstructed by people and by things. Everything here is disorderly, fragmented, shattered, noisy, incomprehensible and Catholic. 'Overhead, an inextricable confusion of rugged shutters, and iron balconies, and chimney flues, pushed out on brackets to save room, and arched windows with projecting sills of Istrian stone, and …'[60] The accretive, asthmatic 'ands' intensify the sense of claustrophobia generated by the press. But, says Ruskin, bursting through the restraints, 'we will push fast through them into the shadow of the pillars at the end of the "Bocca di Piazza".' Suddenly everything changes: 'for between those pillars there opens a great light, and, in the midst of it, as we advance slowly, the vast tower of St Mark seems to lift itself visibly forth from the level field of chequered stones.' Ruskin's excitement is aroused by the sight of this feminized Byzantine monument, the 'Cleopatra' of San Marco (fig. 92). Even the cramped and clogged buildings of the area are 'struck back into sudden obedience and lovely order'. 'And well may they fall back,' he exclaims, since 'there rises a vision out of the earth, and all the great square seems to have opened from it in a kind of awe that we may see it far away;– a multitude of pillars and white domes clustered into a long low pyramid of coloured light.' The erotic charge is intensified by a religious awe derived partly from the Book of Revelation and partly from Milton's *Paradise Lost*, while the jouissance which Ruskin experiences before the façade of San Marco reaches a climax in the 'crests of the arches' which 'as if in ecstasy … break into a marble foam, and toss themselves far into the blue sky in flashes and wreaths of sculptured spray'.[61]

As in his account of San Donato, Ruskin intensifies the documentary immediacy of his narration by contrasting the beauty of the building with the loitering repulsiveness of modern Venetian men, 'like lizards', and noisy Venetian children with 'eyes full of desperation and stony depravity', drawing the reader into the silence of the Baptistery. The tone now drops to a whisper. 'We are', he tells us, 'in a low vaulted room; vaulted not with arches, but with small cupolas starred with gold, and chequered with gloomy figures' (fig. 93). Slowly the figure of Doge Andrea Dandolo is revealed in the half-light, a recumbent figure on his own tomb, and Ruskin issues further instructions to his companion. 'Look round at the room in which he lies.'[62] The account of the encrusted, shattered, gloomy interior is masterly, but the best is reserved for the mosaics and floor of the interior of the basilica (fig. 94). Here, the mosaics on the wall have an effect upon Ruskin reminiscent of Dickens's 'Italian Dream': 'Under foot and overhead, a continual succession of crowded imagery, one picture passing into another, as in a dream; forms beautiful and terrible mixed together dragons and serpents, and ravening beasts of prey, and graceful birds that in the midst of them drink from running fountains and feed from vases of crystal.'[63] In contrast to many contemporary accounts of Byzantine mosaic which stressed the static, rigid, hieratic quality of the images, everything in Ruskin's is moving, flowing and active. From the details of the encrusted outer surface of the building to the variegated marble and glass of the interior Ruskin perceives energy and motion everywhere. Yet the first impression is not enough, and Ruskin immediately retraces his steps around the building in a more ordered procession in order to consider some of the recent debates about the virtues and vices of the Byzantine style and to set out some of the principles of Byzantine art. He addresses two main issues. First, whether Byzantine architecture is truly Christian, and second, whether mosaic is really art. *Contra* Pugin and the Cambridge Camden Society, Ruskin makes a strong case for the Byzantine as authentically Christian, and dismisses claims for the superiority of Gothic on these grounds as 'a piece of absurdity'.[64] As for the argument that Byzantine is essentially 'foreign', Ruskin provocatively delights in the alien appearance of the domes of San Marco because, he says, they increase the 'fantastic and unreal character' of the church. Their 'chief charm', he adds, is 'that of strangeness'.[65] As for mosaic, his principal argument against those (like Eastlake and Kugler) who 'suppose the mosaics of St Mark's, and others of the period, to be utterly barbarous' is to point out how 'solemn', 'majestic' and 'sublime' they are. What they communicate to Ruskin is religious awe. 'And the man must be little

93 Baptistery, San Marco, Venice, *c*.1354

capable of receiving a religious impression of any kind,' he writes, 'who to this day, does not acknowledge some feeling of awe, as he looks up to the pale countenances and ghostly forms … or remains altogether untouched by the majesty of the colossal images of apostles, and of Him who sent apostles, that look down from the darkening gold of the domes of Venice and Pisa.'[66]

In his account of Byzantine architecture, Ruskin says that the characteristics which most appeal are the subtle, irregular use of proportion, the marble encrustation and the colour. Ruskin loved colour in both painting and architecture, but he was always anxious about its traditional association with sensuality and licence. This was especially true of Venetian colour, and he expended much effort throughout his life justifying its use in the work of Venetian artists.[67] Colour was too easily associated with luxuriance and with effeminacy, and the volumes of *The Stones of Venice* are punctuated with Ruskin's attempts to dissociate the vestal, female Byzantine Venice and her coloured architectural clothing from the vulgarity and sinfulness of the fallen post-Renaissance Venice.

On the issue of the racial contributions to Byzantine art, Ruskin was at first enthusiastic about its Orientalism. Having recently seen examples of Eastern industrial design at the Great Exhibition of 1851, he pointed out that San Marco 'possesses the charm of colour in common with the greater part of the architecture, as well as of the manufactures, of the East'. Generally speaking, he added, 'Venetians deserve especial note as the only European people who appear to have sympathized to the full with the great instinct of the Eastern races.' Later he is more anxious about the implications of Byzantine Orientalism and feels that he should have dwelt more 'upon the distinction between the Byzantine and Arab temper', stressing the difference between Byzantine work and 'the mindless luxury of the East'.[68] Edward Said points out that running through European Orientalism is the notion that Western 'rationality is undermined by Eastern excess.'[69] For Ruskin the female Venice is particularly susceptible to the corrupting temptations of irrational Eastern excess, so he counteracts the possible accusation of effeminacy against the early Venetians by invoking their essential masculinity. Though 'the Venetians', he wrote, 'were compelled to bring artists from Constantinople to design the mosaics of the vaults of St Mark's, and to group the colour of its porches … they rapidly took up and developed, under more masculine conditions, the system of which the Greeks had shown them the example.'[70]

Thus in the gender economy of *The Stones of Venice* the masculine, rude, but honest, unaffected and expressive Byzantine builders provided, in their moral integrity and simple Christian faith, a solid base for the female Venice. Their buildings inherited something of the splendour of the East but their colour was not the expression of dissipation. Instead, colour indicated 'a peculiar seriousness'.[71] The 'daughter' of the masculine Byzantine is Venice, and Venice is always female for Ruskin. Clothed by Byzantium, her life cycle takes her from virgin to whore, from innocence to corruption, and from joy to desolation. In the chapter 'Byzantine Palaces' Ruskin traces the fate of Venice from Byzantine origins to Renaissance depravity. 'The bright hues of the early architecture of Venice', he writes, 'were no sign of gaiety of heart, and … the investiture with the mantle of many colours by which she is known above all other cities of Italy and of Europe, was not granted to her in the fever of her festivity, but ... her glorious robe of gold and purple was given her when she first rose a vestal from the sea, not when she became drunk with the wine of her fornication.'[72] Ruskin, who was so seduced by Byzantine colour, was concerned to protect it from the charge of sensuality by stressing its 'chastity', purity and rectitude. Even the tactile surfaces of Venetian building have an erotic appeal for him, but it is one which is kept strictly within bounds.[73]

6 | Responses to Ruskin   Ruskin never answers his own questions about the suitability of Byzantine architectural style for modern Britain, nor does he convince his reader that Byzantine mosaic is able to communicate the range of human experience contained in later styles. Nevertheless, *The Stones of Venice* fired readers' imaginations and focused nascent interests in Byzantium. Its publication had a powerful impact but its reception was not unanimous. Many noted his unusual interest in Byzantine work and even hostile critics were amazed by his command of language.[74] The most antagonistic group of readers, however, were the professional architects. This was not architectural writing as they knew it, and Ruskin's pleasure in the Byzantine architecture of San Marco was perverse. Responding to Ruskin's comment that the church was 'as lovely a dream as ever filled human imagination',[75] the architect George Wightwick said that 'to us it is a very un-lovely nightmare ... we think it extremely ugly.' William Tite, who regretted Ruskin's involvement with San Marco, told the Institute of British Architects in 1855 that 'of all the ugly types of Gothic architecture to be found on the continent, that of Venice was ... the most ugly';[76] and a reviewer in *The Builder* was amazed at Ruskin's admiration for so 'grotesque a pile' as San Marco.[77] Yet the tide was turning, and by 1855 G.E. Street, who was to exert such a powerful practical influence over the Arts and Crafts movement, was writing in praise of Venice and San Marco. In his *Brick and Marble Architecture in the Middle Ages* he claimed that he had never seen an interior like that of San Marco to inspire religious awe. After his visit to the basilica, Street insisted that architects should not 'as now, venture to design cold shells'. Instead, the lesson of San Marco pointed 'most forcibly to the absolute necessity for the introduction of more colour in the interior of our buildings, either in their construction, or afterwards by the hand of the painter'.[78]

The Byzantine material in the second volume of *The Stones of Venice* sharpened public awareness of a style and a period that had already been developed in other publications. A few years before Ruskin's work on Venice appeared, George Finlay had challenged Gibbon and the French rationalists by trying to set the record straight in a new history of the Byzantine empire, and by expressing views, as he put it, 'in direct opposition to these great authorities'.[79] Finlay had a colourful life. After a course of study at the University of Göttingen, he became intrigued by the history of Greece. In 1823 he met Byron in Cephalonia, became his friend and, fired with ardent philhellenism, threw himself into the Greek War of Independence. After the war he settled in Greece and, filled with idealistic ambitions about its social future, invested his own money which he promptly lost. He began to study the history of his adopted country, and in 1844 the first volumes began to appear. In *Greece under the Romans* Finlay reversed the old notion of Byzantine decline in favour of the continuity of Greek society and politics up to the eighth or ninth century. The story continued in the sequel, *The History of the Byzantine Empire from 716 to 1453*, which came out in 1853. This is even more powerfully recuperative than the first volumes, describing Greek Byzantine influence as a positive force in resuscitating the Empire up to 1057. Alas, however, Finlay's history did not match his life in either warmth or colour. William Morris was later to find it 'somewhat dreary' (see below, p. 164), and the pedestrian prose was not calculated to stimulate the imagination.

One of the liveliest debates about the afterlife of Byzantine architecture took place at the Institute of British Architects in January 1853. T.L. Donaldson, who was Professor of Architecture at University College, London, read a paper on the Byzantine influence on French architecture which he introduced by means of a general account of the development of the Byzantine style and its influence in the West.[80] For the French material he was openly dependent on Albert Lenoir and Félix de Verneilh, whose opinions he entirely endorsed, and he went on to suggest that the English, too, might look more closely for Byzantine influence in Britain. 'Iffley Church', he said, 'was very like some of the simple Byzantine churches', and others were to be found in Herefordshire. George Gilbert Scott agreed with Donaldson, suggesting the church at Kilpeck as a Byzantine candidate, and wondered whether the Byzantine dome might not 'be introduced into modern Gothic design'. George Godwin enthusiastically took up the theme, saying that he had long ago been struck by the Byzantine origins of many of the churches of southwestern France, and he had no doubt that 'their principal forms and peculiarities derived from Byzantium'. 'It was clear', he went on, 'that in England, as in France, Byzantium had exercised a great influence.' Finally, a Dr Henszlmann directed his audience's attention to the Byzantine origins of the churches of the Rhine and elsewhere, suggesting that 'the churches of St Martin, and of the Apostles, at Cologne' were instances of the same phenomenon. Within a year the British had the opportunity of testing some of these fledgling enthusiasms. The Byzantine Court at the Crystal Palace brought casts of a wide range of early medieval building to London where their Byzantine qualities could be examined at leisure.

7 | The Byzantine Court at the Crystal Palace

So far the British had only read about Byzantium, but in the 1854 Crystal Palace Exhibition in Sydenham, Byzantium came to Britain (fig. 95). Matthew Digby Wyatt was the force behind this project and he made a fine watercolour of the outer façade of the Court (fig. 96). In the late 1840s he had worked with Owen Jones on *Geometric Mosaics of the Middle Ages* (1848), and in 1851 he was elected to the post of secretary to the executive committee of the Great Exhibition. When its site moved from Hyde Park to Sydenham, Wyatt, together with Jones, was instrumental in designing a number of the new Crystal Palace courts. Apart from the Byzantine Court, they provided drawings for the Pompeian, English Gothic, Elizabethan and Italian Renaissance

spaces, and these were already under way when Wyatt asked J.B. Waring to write guide books to all of them. Waring, a friend of Owen Jones, was primarily an architectural draughtsman. In 1850 he had published *Architectural Art in Italy and Spain,* the result of a journey through those countries. The splendid plates in this volume illustrate a number of items from which casts were taken for the Crystal Palace exhibition, such as the capitals in the cloisters of San Giovanni Laterano, Rome (fig. 97). Also included were chromolithographs of mosaic work in Palermo, Venice, Salerno and Rome. But in order to write his introduction to the Byzantine Court, Waring was obliged to undergo a crash course in architectural history. Wyatt pointed him in the direction of works in English, French, German and Italian with which he was unfamiliar.[81] Though Wyatt's role was only supervisory, he insisted that his own name should appear on the catalogues. So pleased was he with the result that he suggested to Waring that they should collaborate on a series of books, with one entitled *A History of Byzantine Architecture*. Wyatt invested money and Waring

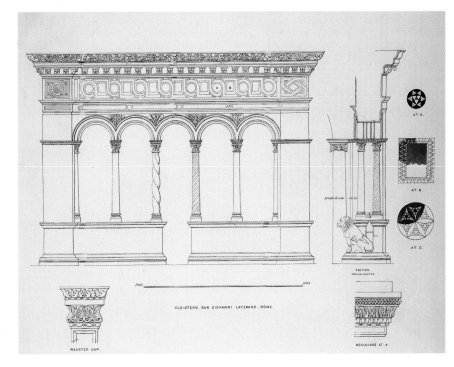

invested time, but the project came to nothing. Meanwhile, the art historian James Fergusson published his two-volume *Illustrated Handbook of Architecture* in 1855 with extensive sections on Byzantium.

The procession of courts in the Crystal Palace exhibition must have been a remarkable sight, but since there had been no real attempt to distinguish Byzantine from Romanesque the choice of casts provided a particularly eccentric view of the Byzantine style. At first sight one might have been forgiven for believing that Byzantinism was a German phenomenon. The Crimean War may have prevented casts from being made in Constantinople, with the result that the architecture and sculpture of Germany supplied many of the displays. The internal façade came from Gelnhausen near Frankfurt, and the whole of the outer arcade was replicated from St Maria im Kapitol, Cologne – 'one of the most interesting churches in Europe' in which were combined 'the Roman basilica and the Byzantine church'.[82] Italy was well represented: the central arcade was taken from San Giovanni in Laterano (the plaster carefully encrusted with mosaic work), and the court included sculpture from San Ambrogio, Milan, and objects from 'that great encyclopaedia of art', as the guide-book called it – San Marco.[83] Mosaic was confined to replicas of the portraits of Justinian and Theodora in San Vitale, Ravenna (placed somewhat incongruously in the cloisters from St Maria im Kapitol) and some work from Sta Maria in Trastevere, Rome. French 'Byzantine' was not prominent, while Britain was represented by, among other things, the Norman church of Kilpeck near Hereford and two sculptures from Chichester Cathedral. These depicted the arrival of Christ at the house of Lazarus and the raising of Lazarus, and were, it was claimed, strongly 'influenced by the spirit of Byzantine art'.[84]

95 (opposite above) *The Byzantine Court in the Crystal Palace, Sydenham.* Engraving in *The Builder,* 12, 23 September 1854

96 (opposite below) Matthew Digby Wyatt, *The Byzantine Court, Crystal Palace, Sydenham,* 1854. Gouache, 55.8 x 119 cm (22 x 47 in). Victoria and Albert Museum, London

97 (above) J.B. Waring, plate from *Architectural Art in Italy and Spain,* 1850, showing San Giovanni Laterano, Rome

98 Owen Jones, plate of Byzantine designs from
The Grammar of Ornament, 1856

At the very moment that Ruskin was urging the centrality and importance of Byzantine art, so too were the members of the Jones–Wyatt circle, yet they arrived at this position from very different points of view. Though Wyatt and Waring introduce their catalogue with a gesture towards the 'deep emotion' generated by mosaics in Ravenna and Sicily, with 'their majesty and richness', their primary focus is not on the sublime but on the design. There are echoes of Saint-Simonianism and its stress on progress and science in their suggestion that variations in Byzantine work can be understood only in terms of the 'commerce, the social life, and the differences of religious creed' of local artists, and that these are open to rational explanation.[85] Their treatment of the examples is entirely secular, and the authority of science is invoked as the primary basis for their methodology: 'But as all science informs us of the mutual dependence of everything on earth,' they write, 'so in this case, a well-directed spirit of inquiry has revealed to us a kindred law of relation.'[86] This law of relation takes the form of a tracing of stylistic similarities and affinities across Europe, pointing to the extraordinarily widely spread influence of Byzantium in both space and time. But this catholic interpretation of Byzantine style had cold water poured upon it by James Fergusson, who scoffed at the use of the term 'Byzantine' for 'every building possessing a dome, every style in which that form was at all usual, and every form of architecture in which polychromy was adopted to any extent'.[87] Fergusson felt that Byzantine architecture had 'no claim to rank among the great styles of the earth',[88] but was nevertheless highly enthusiastic about the idea of Hagia Sophia as a model for large Protestant congregations in Britain.

The so-called 'South Kensington Group' led by Owen Jones continued to look to the East as a source of new possibilities in design that had not been dulled by over-familiarity, and Byzantine was prominent amongst them. J.B. Waring wrote the section 'Byzantine Ornament' to accompany three magnificent Byzantine plates in Jones's *The Grammar of Ornament* (1856; fig. 98), and in 1858 he edited a lavish volume illustrating the famous 'Art Treasures' exhibition in Manchester, with extensive discussion of Byzantine ornament, enamels, textiles and ivories. Other names, too, continued to advocate the suitability of the Byzantine style for modern architecture. J.L. Petit, who had earlier suggested the adoption of Romanesque in Britain (see above, p.112), gave a lecture in March 1858 at the Institute of British Architects. Inspired by André Couchard's *Selection of Byzantine Churches in Greece* (1841), Petit had made a trip to Greece and Turkey in 1857–8, which in turn fired his enthusiasm for the modern application of Byzantine architecture. In his 1858 lecture he attacked followers of the Gothic for working 'in the style of an age very different from our own', whereas classical buildings, including Byzantine, are 'grounded on forms and principles of beauty which neither age nor fashion can affect'.[89] Even the liberal Beresford Hope protested at this, and Wyatt intervened with a characteristically historicist compromise. Turning away the propensities of what he called 'Greek and Goth' he took an eclectic view, urging the use of any style that was appropriate to the 'natural wants' of the age. But enthusiasm for Byzantium was on the increase and in the same volume of *Building News* that reported Petit's lecture, William Burges, who was to play an important part in the mosaic decoration of St Paul's Cathedral, published an enthusiastic account of his 'Architectural Experiences at Constantinople'.[90]

8 | George Gilbert Scott and Secular Byzantine

The most prominent secular example of the Byzantine style in this period appeared in one of the rounds of the 'Battle of the Styles'. This was the well-known struggle between George Gilbert Scott and the Prime Minister, Lord Palmerston, over the design for new government offices in Whitehall. Few architectural events had received more publicity since the competition for the Houses of Parliament in the 1830s. The Foreign Office competition was set up in 1856 and, although Scott's Gothic Revival design did not win, the Prime Minister, Lord Derby, set aside the successful entries and appointed the project to Scott anyway. A change of government brought Palmerston back into office in 1859, and he was convinced that Gothic was uncomfortable, gloomy and fundamentally Romanist. He criticized Scott's design for being neither northern nor English Gothic, but a mixture of French and Italian. It received the support of both Edward Freeman and Ruskin, but Palmerston rejected it. An energetic public debate broke out in 1860 between those who supported Scott's Gothic design and those who wished for a building in the classical style. The opposition to Scott was led by a fellow architect, William Tite, who as MP for Bath took the debate to Parliament. The upshot of Tite's furious and unfair challenge was that Scott went into self-imposed exile in Scarborough to prepare a new design that he hoped would satisfy the reactionary views of Palmerston. 'It struck me', Scott wrote, 'that not wholly alien to this [i.e. Italian Gothic] was the Byzantine of the early Venetian palaces, and that the earliest renaissance of Venice contained cognate elements. I therefore conceived the idea of generating what would be strictly an Italian style out of these two sets of examples; Byzantine, in fact, toned into a more modern and usable form, by reference to those examples of the Renaissance which had been influenced by the presence of Byzantine works.'[91]

Scott, a powerhouse of architectural energy, had tried his hand at most styles. Before 1838 he had designed at least twenty buildings in the classical mode, and after that his name had become closely associated with Gothic building. Before 1859 he had been to Italy only once, when he made a continental tour with his friend Benjamin Ferrey in 1852. The highlight of this trip for Scott was Venice, where 'all was enchantment'. Here he met Ruskin, who was writing *The Stones of Venice*, and Scott's observations at the time show clear evidence of Ruskin's enthusiasms. As he recalled in his memoirs, 'My impressions of St Mark's were stronger than I can describe. I consider it, and still continue to do so, the most impressive interior I have ever seen.' He went on to recount how 'the Byzantine palaces also attracted my attention a good deal,' especially one of Ruskin's favourites, the Fondaco dei Turchi.[92] His discussions with Ruskin soon bore fruit. By 1853 he was known to be sympathetic to the possibility of introducing Byzantine elements into modern building (see above, p. 131) and in 1854, the year of the Byzantine Court in nearby Sydenham, he designed a Byzantine extension for the very church in which the Ruskin family worshipped in Camberwell. The alternating dark and light patterning of the chancel of Camden Chapel (fig. 99) looked foreign and incongruous with the rest of the building, but almost certainly derived from one of Ruskin's favourite early churches, San Miniato al Monte near Florence.[93]

All this came back to him in Scarborough, as did his reading of Thomas Hope and his first-hand experience of modern *Rundbogenstil* building in Hamburg.[94] The new Byzantine design for the Foreign Office (fig. 100) was approved by Lord

99 George Gilbert Scott, Camden Chapel, Camberwell, 1854. Engraving in *The Builder*, 12, 8 July 1854

Elcho, a member of the Select Committee on Foreign Office Reconstruction, and by William Francis Cowper, Palmerston's stepson, but once again it was rejected by Palmerston as 'a regular mongrel affair'.[95] Finally Scott was forced into producing a third, classical design, the one from which the present buildings were constructed. In spite of this frustration Scott seems to have retained a real enthusiasm for Byzantine work. In 1862 he was stimulated by a letter to *The Builder* by a certain 'A.W.' on the subject of 'Byzantine Decorative Colouring'. A.W. said that Byzantine (by which he meant 'all Christian work before Gothic') is 'manly and massive'. He continued: 'If Byzantine had only had the pointed arch it would have been perfect. There is life in it, and plenty of grotesque – the best sign of healthy minds. Gothic grotesque is sensual compared with the open-hearted vigour of Byzantine.' This association of Byzantine with robust masculinity reminds us of Ruskin's account of the early builders of Torcello, and A.W. concludes in the same vein, praising Byzantine work as 'noble, thick, massive [and] manly in form'.[96] Signing himself 'A Goth', Scott wrote appreciatively about A.W.'s remarks, adding that 'Byzantine is the connecting link between Classic and Gothic: its interiors, excepting Gothic, are the most beautiful in existence; and offer *without any exception*, the finest field for decorative painting.'[97] In the following year Scott submitted an elaboration of the Camden Church design for a new chapel at Worcester College, Oxford (fig. 101), which was far more heavily decorated than his earlier piece. The round apse would have contained niches resembling semidomes, and the central space was to have been covered with a decorated dome supported by Byzantine pendentives.[98] Scott's final brush with Byzantium came in the competition for the Royal Albert Hall which was announced in 1862. For this he submitted a Byzantine design based on Hagia Sophia which employed sculpture, painting and mosaic. Once again his idea was rejected and a building designed by Major General Henry Scott occupies the spot. Looking back seventeen years later, Scott felt that his 'design was worthy of more consideration than it has received'.[99]

100 (above left) George Gilbert Scott, rejected Byzantine design for the Foreign Office, Whitehall, London, 1860. Pen and ink. Royal Institute of British Architects, London

101 (above) George Gilbert Scott, rejected Byzantine design for Worcester College Chapel, Oxford, 1863. Engraving in the *Civil Engineer's and Architect's Journal*, 26, December 1863

Ruskin's Venetian version of Byzantine architecture had greater success elsewhere, and Thomas Deane and Benjamin Woodward's Trinity College Museum, Dublin, was one of the first in this style (1852–7). When the poet William Allingham saw it in a half-completed state in 1855 he told Dante Gabriel Rossetti that it was 'early Venetian', while Deane himself called the building 'fifteenth-century Byzantine Period'.[100] The Byzantinism of the exterior is expressed in the fenestration which echoes that of the Palazzo Dario. Inside, the dome of the stair-hall is tessellated in a design reminiscent of the pavements of San Donato and San Marco (fig. 102). What marks this building out is its confident employment of Byzantine round-arched openings and coloured surfaces.

In the 1840s the High-Church *Ecclesiologist* had taken up the cause of colour in architecture. 'We would have every inch glowing,' it said, whereas 'Puritans … would have every inch colourless.'[101] By the mid-1850s the issue of colour in architecture and design had become prominent. As Paul Thomson points out, the High Victorian revival of colour was the reverse of puritanical austerity.[102] Sensuousness, sensuality and idolatry were closely allied in the evangelical mind, and William Butterfield's work, first at All Saints', Margaret Street, London, then later at Keble College, Oxford, was colourful and had 'papist' overtones. Ruskin was on the defensive and denied that colour was a 'mere source of sensual pleasure'. 'None of us', he stressed, 'appreciate the nobleness and sacredness of colour', since 'colour is the purifying or sanctifying element of material beauty'.[103] Both Ruskin and Street argued in favour of architectural polychromy, and by 1863 it had become sufficiently important to qualify as the subject for an essay prize offered by the Institute of British Architects. On 18 May T.L. Donaldson presented the silver medal for an essay entitled 'On the Application of Coloured Bricks and Terra Cotta to Modern Architecture' to an aspiring architect, poet and novelist: Thomas Hardy.

Byzantine colour blossomed during this period. Deane and Woodward's splendid Crown Life Assurance Office of 1856–8 looked strange and intriguing to the contemporary observer (fig. 103). With 'Byzantine and Saracenic features

102 (left) T.N. Deane and B. Woodward, Trinity College Museum, Dublin, 1852–7, domed entrance hall and staircase

103 (centre) T.N. Deane and B. Woodward, Crown Life Assurance Office, London, 1856–8. Engraving in *Building News*, 16 July 1858

104 (right) George Aitchison, Mark Lane Offices, London, 1864. Watercolour, 73 × 53.5 cm (28¾ × 21 in). Royal Institute of British Architects, London

105 Archibald Ponton and William Venn
Gough, The Granary, Welsh Back, Bristol, 1869

so prominent', said *The Builder*, 'the whole effect is very different from that of Gothic, to the English eye.'[104] Both exterior and interior were characterized by the use of a wide range of materials in variegated patterns and textures. The sculpture was designed by Hungerford Pollen and executed by the famous O'Shea brothers, who filled the little spaces with birds, rabbits and dogs. The new Veneto-Byzantine work delighted the Pre-Raphaelites Rossetti, Madox Brown and Thomas Woolner,[105] but in 1866 it was demolished to make way for the London Chatham and Dover Railway. The building had been so successful, however, that a very similar design was used in Deane's Crown Life Assurance Building in Fleet Street (1864–6).

Commercial building in the late 1850s and early 1860s adopted the Venetian-Byzantine arcade as a way of creating long rows of well-lit office space, while at the same time using the façade as a way of creating dazzlingly original effects of polychromy.[106] Prominent among these structures were George Aitchison's Mark Lane Offices of 1864 (fig. 104). Here the three rows of repeated arches are distinguished only by the detail of their ornamentation and, as Louis Sullivan was soon to discover, they could be repeated as often as necessary until the whole building became monumentally high-rise. The most splendid examples, however, came in the 'Bristol Byzantine' sequence of the late 1860s, culminating in Archibald Ponton and William Venn Gough's exquisite Granary, Welsh Back (1869; fig. 105). In its balance between downward and upward thrust and in its finely detailed use of coloured bricks, this is a building worthy of the Grand Canal itself.

Scott had bad luck with his Byzantine designs, and it is an irony that his chief professional opponent in the Foreign Office fiasco, William Tite, had at this time just completed a small Byzantine-style church: St James's at Gerrards Cross[107] (1859; fig. 106). Tite's choice of style, however, may not have been his own. The church was paid for by the sisters of a friend of Tite's, Major General Reid, who had had a long-standing interest in early Italian architecture, and the sisters may have requested a domical building. Tite himself justifed the Byzantine mode for St James's by reference to James Fergusson and Henry Layard.[108] In a contemporary article in *The Quarterly Review* Layard, reviewing Fergusson's *Illustrated Handbook of Architecture*, traced the dignified history of the dome back to the early Christians, Romans and Etruscans, and heartily endorsed Fergusson's views on the possibility of Hagia Sophia as a model for future large Protestant churches.[109] It was not long, however, before a much more influential figure endorsed the choice of Byzantine for British building: Queen Victoria.

106 William Tite, St James's, Gerrards Cross, Buckinghamshire, 1859

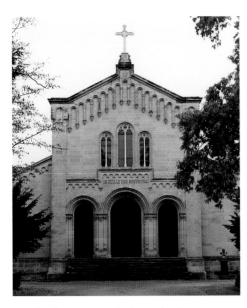

Not far from Gerrards Cross, in the sequestered parkland of the Royal Gardens at Frogmore, stands the Royal Mausoleum. This was a singular project for the Queen because in Britain monarchs were not buried in their gardens, nor were they buried in Byzantine mausoleums. The two issues were related. Mausoleum burial may not have been usual in Britain, but it was in Saxe-Coburg, and as early as 1843 Victoria and Albert had seriously considered building a monument for themselves at Windsor. In 1844 Albert's father, Duke Ernest I of Saxe-Coburg, died, and Albert together with his elder brother decided to erect a mausoleum for him and their mother in Coburg.[110] In 1851 Albert was still urging the architect, Gustav Eberhard, to submit plans and expenses,[111] and the building finally went up between 1854 and 1858 (fig. 107). In September 1860 Victoria and Albert paid a state visit to Coburg, which included 'the beautiful Mausoleum, which has been erected by the whole family, after Albert's and Ernest's designs, carried out by the architect Eberhard. It is in the Italian style; beautiful inside, with a marble floor and marble altar in the Chapel.'[112] By December of the following year Albert was dead and Victoria's immediate impulse was to build him something similar. The design that Albert and Ernest had adopted for Coburg was unashamedly Romanesque. It was a basilican building with a low pitched roof, no dome or octagon, and with a gable on the west front whose rising blank arches and disposition of doorways and fenestration strongly resemble the drawing of San Michele, Pavia, in Thomas Hope's volume. Victoria consulted Ludwig Grüner, who had been one of Albert's principal artistic advisers, and he came up with a design which, in spite of its huge cost, pleased the Queen. The result was much more Ravennite than Eberhard's building (fig. 108). Externally the tall octagon, reminiscent of the mausoleum of Galla Placidia, is its dominant feature. This covers a Greek cross with low convex ambulatories. If not pure Byzantine, it is certainly not very English. Instead of the delicacy of North Italian Romanesque or the warm brick of Ravenna, the combination of granite and Portland stone gives it a feeling of sombre massiveness and weight. It is, as Pevsner suggests, a very Germanic version of a southern style. The foundation stone was laid on 15 March 1862 and it marked not only the beginning of this building, but also a new phase in the acceptance of Byzantine building in Britain.

107 (left) Gustav Eberhard, Herzog Mausoleum, Coburg, 1854–8
108 (right) A. Jenkins Humbert and Ludwig Grüner, Royal Mausoleum, Frogmore, 1862

9 | Salviati and the Mosaic Revival

The decoration for the Royal Mausoleum at Frogmore was rapidly put in place, though there is a contrast between the interior and the portico outside. Inside, Grüner used a Renaissance Revival style favoured by Albert himself; under the portico was something rather different. Here there is a lovely blue ceiling dotted with golden stars that echo the decoration in the mausoleum of Galla Placidia. Beneath them on the walls are six angels in white with golden wings, each holding a palm frond in one hand and a floral crown in the other (fig. 110). Once again the model is undoubtedly Ravenna, but this time it is the procession of apostles in the Arian Baptistery who are depicted holding their triumphal crowns (fig. 109). In both mosaic groups the figures are separated by etiolated palm trees with fronds springing from their tops and vegetation from their bases. The decoration of the Frogmore portico was one of the first British projects by Antonio Salviati and was also one of the first attempts in Britain to revive the ancient art of Byzantine mosaic.

Though mosaic decoration was never extensively employed in Britain in the nineteenth century, it did play a conspicuous role in a number of extremely important and influential projects. The most prominent of these were the decoration of the interior of St Paul's Cathedral by William Blake Richmond, Salviati's mosaics for the Albert Memorial, the decoration of Keble College, Oxford, and other work by William Butterfield. It continued into the twentieth century with the decoration of Westminster Cathedral. Some of these projects are more strictly Byzantine in their inspiration than others, but they all have their roots in a renewed interest in mosaic that dates from the mid-century.

The initial desire for a more permanent decorative system than painting came from the Oriental interests of Matthew Digby Wyatt, Owen Jones and J.B. Waring, combined with technological advances in the manufacture of 'encaustic' tiles in around 1839. Wyatt was commissioned by the manufacturer Blashfield to collect designs while he was touring Europe, which he later published as *Specimens of the Geometrical Mosaic of the Middle Ages* (1848). Meanwhile another manufacturer, Minton, employed Owen Jones in a similar role.[113] At this stage interest in tiles was confined to abstract polychromy. Quite a number of designs were Byzantine in inspiration (fig. 111), but few were figurative. The 1851 Great Exhibition and the development of Government Schools of Art gave a stimulus to the design and manufacture of patterned tiles, which in its turn prompted works such as Owen Jones's The *Grammar of Ornament* (1856; see fig. 98), and was further encouraged by Street's passion for polychromy as expressed in *Brick and Marble Architecture of the Middle Ages* (1855). As yet pictorial mosaic using vitreous tesserae was out of the question since there was simply no way of manufacturing the glass medium.

At this point Antonio Salviati enters the picture. He was a prosperous Venetian lawyer who, spurred on by a passionate love for Venetian culture, decided to abandon his profession and devote himself to the restoration and repair of the mosaics of San Marco. In the late 1850s he met a glass master from Murano named Lorenzo Radi.[114]

109 Dome mosaic, *c*.500–52. Arian Baptistery, Ravenna

110 Antonio Salviati, mosaics in the portico of the
Royal Mausoleum, Frogmore, 1862

With Radi's technical expertise and Salviati's business acumen, Salviati's Venetian Enamel-Mosaic Works was an instant success and Salviati, quoting liberally from Ruskin's *Stones of Venice*, Street's *Brick and Marble Architecture* and Gautier's *Italia*, travelled through France and England to generate business. International exhibitions provided a useful platform. At the Italian Exhibition in Florence in 1861 Salviati and Radi exhibited copies of two Byzantine mosaics, one from Hagia Sophia and the other from San Marco,[115] and at the International Exhibition in South Kensington the following year they showed a much-publicized glass table. But they were not alone. At South Kensington the Imperial Manufactory from St Petersburg entered a monumental 20-foot-high iconic representation of St Peter (fig. 112), but with its price tag of £4,000 this type of product was dismissed as having little potential for widespread use in Britain.[116] A marble mosaic by Baron Henri Triqueti also featured in the same exhibition. For a while Triqueti was an artist favoured for the completion of the decorations of St Paul's Cathedral and, though his attempt to marmorialize Renaissance painting in mosaic had nothing Byzantine about it, the technique did gain acceptance with some architects, including William Butterfield. But at South Kensington it was Salviati who gained most public interest, with *The Times* claiming that his work was 'the most successful imitation of the ancient Byzantine mosaics which modern art has produced'.[117]

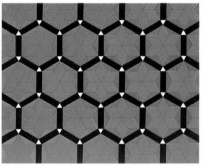

In the early 1860s there was considerable interest in the history of mosaic. We have seen how Lord Lindsay and then Ruskin were the first to attach aesthetic worth to mosaic in the 1840s, but the idea that Byzantine art was cold, lifeless and empty was slow to disappear. By 1859, however, the tide had begun to turn. In *Painting Popularly Explained*, for example, Thomas Gullick and John Timbs devoted a substantial chapter written in dispassionate prose to 'the Byzantine style' of mosaic. The eminent architectural historian from Oxford, J.H. Parker, published a substantial three-part illustrated account of the history of mosaic in *The Gentleman's Magazine* in 1861;[118] and Wyatt wrote an extensive history of the subject in *The Builder* in 1862 with a view to effecting, as he put it, 'its practical revival'.[119]

Interest in the use of mosaic for public projects was increased by the technical failure of the frescoes in the House of Lords and the cancellation of further contracts in 1863. Many suggested that 'the beauty of mosaic art' should replace the crumbling paintings at Westminster.[120] After all, if 'the wall mosaics of Venice, Ravenna, and other Italian cities … impart to their buildings a glory and richness peculiar to them alone', then why not on the walls of the British Parliament?[121] 'Anyone', wrote the critic J.H. Parker, 'who has seen the mosaic pictures at Rome, and especially at Ravenna, must feel a wish to have them introduced into his own country.'[122] This sentiment was put to a Parliamentary Committee set up to investigate the 'abundant promise' of mosaic, a group that included the MP for Southwark, Henry Layard. Layard was almost certainly the *éminence grise* behind Salviati's success in Britain. He had been brought up in Tuscany where he had developed an extensive knowledge of art, and had made his reputation as the 'discoverer' of Nineveh. He first saw Constantinople in 1842 as attaché to the British embassy, and went there often during the Crimean War. In the early 1850s he made an extensive study of fresco with a view to its possible use in public buildings, and he was instrumental in creating the Arundel Society for the promulgation of finely recorded details of Italian art. Venice in particular was dear to him, and it was there that he probably first met Salviati during a two-week stay in 1860. [123] Layard was certainly behind the decision in 1865 to employ this unknown Italian to decorate the porch ceiling in the

111 Matthew Digby Wyatt, plate from *Specimens of the Geometrical Mosaic of the Middle Ages*, 1848, showing mosaics in San Lorenzo fuori le Mura (above) and San Giovanni Laterano, Rome (below)

mausoleum at Frogmore, though it is unlikely that Layard suggested Salviati directly. The Queen, who was very antipathetic to Layard's radicalism, strongly resisted his appointment by Palmerston to Foreign Undersecretary. There must have been an intermediary, and that was undoubtedly George Gilbert Scott.[124] The Queen had already employed Scott to convert the Wolsey Chapel in Windsor into an Albert Memorial Chapel, and Salviati was busily at work for him, supplying florid and highly coloured Gothic mosaics for the ceiling. Scott, who, as we have seen, was especially sympathetic to Byzantine design in this period, argued that since 'Venice is the very land and home of mosaic', it would be foolish to compete with those 'who have been brought up among the ancient productions of this noble art'.[125]

By 1868 Salviati realized that Britain would be a useful base for his operations. Since Layard had come to believe that 'that mosaic is the only external and internal decoration on a great scale which will suit our climate',[126] the Englishman invested money, and the Venice and Murano Glass Company opened in London. Commissions came in fast, including mosaics for the Albert Memorial, Kensington Gardens, and the Bishop's Palace in Southwark. Its legacy remains in Regent Street, though few notice the mosaic decorations above the windows of nos. 235–241. On one side the Royal Coat of Arms (fig. 113) is flanked by the arms of the City of London and the City of Westminster, and on the other the Lion of Saint Mark is accompanied by the emblems of Murano and Burano.

112 (left) Mosaic of St Peter by the Imperial Manufactory of St Petersburg. Engraving in J.B. Waring, *Masterpieces of Industrial Art and Sculpture at the International Exhibition, 1862*, 1863

113 (right) Antonio Salviati, mosaic on the façade of 235–241 Regent Street, London, *c.*1870

10 | The Decoration of St Paul's Cathedral

One of the largest mosaic projects of the nineteenth century was the decoration of St Paul's Cathedral. The preface to this larger event was the appointment of Francis Cramner Penrose in 1852 as architect to the Dean and Chapter. As early as 1859 he knew that Salviati was making mosaic tesserae in Venice,[127] and at about this time he went on a journey to Palermo, Rome and Venice to investigate the costs of doing some work on the spandrels in the cathedral. In 1863 Salviati was commissioned to put in place mosaic figures of Isaiah and Jeremiah designed by Alfred Stevens. These were followed by St Matthew (1866; fig. 114) and later St John, both by G.F. Watts. Penrose was a classicist and muscular Christian and he preferred so-called 'Renaissance' mosaic to the Byzantine version. This took the form of vitrified pictures rather than hieratic designs, and on several subsequent occasions he submitted grandiose plans for covering the whole cathedral in this style. He had both his supporters and opponents, but for many, Salviati included, the ancient Byzantine model could not be improved upon and Renaissance mosaic was simply an inappropriate and debased version of the art.

The architect William Burges shared Salviati's view. 'What building would *not* look well, covered with mosaics on a gold ground,' he asked, even before Penrose started work. This, said Burges, is 'the only way to treat our own St Paul's'. He suggested Torcello and San Marco as models since 'Renaissance' mosaic would only produce 'the boudoir effect of St Peter's'.[128] Burges is a key figure in the St Paul's project. He may have been associated with Matthew Digby Wyatt in assessing the entries for the design of the Great Exhibition in 1851. In 1853 a long European tour took him to Rome, which he disliked, and to Palermo and Monreale where the mosaics bowled him over. In 1855 he entered into partnership with Henry Clutton and developed a reputation as a Goth. They won a competition for Lille Cathedral, which was never executed, and in 1856 Burges provided the winning design for a Crimean memorial church in Constantinople, which likewise remained unbuilt. His work in Constantinople,

146 | 147   **Britain** The Decoration of St Paul's Cathedral

114 G. F. Watts and Antonio Salviati, *Saint Matthew*, 1866. Mosaic. St Paul's Cathedral, London

however, brought him into close contact with Byzantine and Islamic art, and when he visited the city in 1857 to collect information for the Crimean project he was fascinated with the decoration of Hagia Sophia. All this played its part when he was later invited to submit a proposal for the completion of St Paul's.

The St Paul's project was a long-standing problem for the British Establishment and a hornet's nest of conflicting theological, political and aesthetic considerations. Few other architectural projects attracted more public attention and the successive waves of interest it provoked correspond with the terms of office of three Deans of the cathedral.[129] The first period, from 1858 to 1869, was dominated by the Low Churchman Dean Milman, and it was during this time that Penrose organized the decoration of the spandrels. During the second period, between 1870 and 1889, Dean Church was the significant figure, and his attitudes were more High Church than those of Milman. The election of Dean Gregory in 1890 marked the third period, and it was only under his autocratic rule that the issues about the decoration were finally resolved.

In 1870 an appeal, full of nationalist fervour, was launched to bring in the money necessary to complete the decoration of the cathedral. A committee was set up to oversee the project. This was effectively controlled by a group of High Church men under the leadership of Alexander Beresford Hope: Benjamin Webb, one of the founders of the Camden Society; the new Dean, Dean Church; Canon Gregory; and the Puseyite Canon Liddon. Their choice of architect was Burges, who had already demonstrated his High Church affiliations. They were deeply opposed, however, by three other powerful figures, namely the classicist William Tite, the rationalist James Fergusson and the Liberal Protestant MP George Bentick. The committee's brief was to 'carry out the intentions' of Christopher Wren, who had left the interior decoration unfinished but had also suggested the possibility of mosaic. The problem was that no one knew what Wren's intentions were, since he had not been specific in his instructions and had probably never actually seen mosaic. Into this gulf marched the members of committee and the architect, each man with his own agenda.

In July 1870 Burges drew up a plan. It was hugely elaborate, involving a Christ in Majesty in the apse at the east end (fig. 115) and the Angelic Hierarchy in the spandrels of the choir and transepts. At the west end he envisaged the Creation and the Fall, and in the nave, transepts and aisles, scenes from the New Testament. The great dome would teem with figures from the Heavenly Jerusalem and the Apocalypse.[130] Though the hundreds of figures would have been scrutinized for their acceptability to Protestant doctrine, the whole scheme looked like a magnificent Anglo-Catholic scheme to outdo Catholics in expense and extravagance. For this reason it aroused the suspicions of the Broad Church members who made up the bulk of the St Paul's congregation, but the committee pressed on. In 1873 Burges set out for Italy in search of details for the design. On his return he constructed two models. The first was

115 William Burges, design for the decoration of St Paul's Cathedral, *c*.1870. Watercolour. St Paul's Cathedral Library, London

exhibited in December 1873, the second in March 1874, and the cathedral's Fine Arts Committee rejected both. A public storm broke out.[131] Anglo-Catholics welcomed the decorative splendour of the enterprise but the Broad Church faction was anxious about the suggestion of Byzantine idolatry. The Christ in Majesty was singled out as 'a ludicrous … fetish of the barbarous ages of Christianity'. St Paul's, argued *The Builder*, was the epitome of Englishness and Protestantism, and therefore an unsuitable vehicle for this kind of iconography.[132] T.L. Donaldson, now seventy-nine, a senior member of the Royal Institute of British Architects,[133] classicist and evangelical, abandoned his liberal ideas of the 1850s and betrayed a terror of Byzantium in language which mixed religious denunciation with sexual innuendo. He would hear nothing of Burges's 'semi-barbarous … medieval monstrosities', nor of turning 'the noblest Protestant Cathedral' into a 'mass-house' decorated by Burges in 'the sensuous allurements of the harlot … tawdry, meretricious and luscious'.[134] It would be wrong to describe Burges's plan as pure Byzantine, however. It was a kind of eclectic amalgam involving early Renaissance and classical with Byzantine adjuncts. But the problem was that no style could be easily developed in the mid-nineteenth century that would fit in a baroque setting. As a result, no decision was reached, and in 1874 work was suspended and Burges dismissed from his post.

Beresford Hope was not to be defeated, however, and in 1877 he thought of resuscitating Burges's plans. The whole debate was reopened and in 1878 a new sub-committee commissioned Frederick Leighton and Edward Poynter to draw up another plan. With Penrose in control of the whole operation, the glass-makers Powell and Son and Salviati were once more asked to provide estimates for tesserae. Again no consensus was reached and again the mosaic idea was shelved. Finally, in 1890, the 'bulldog cleric of adamantine disposition' – Canon Gregory – became Dean.[135] Many of the participants in the original discussions of 1870 were now dead or too frail to be bothered. In 1891 Burne-Jones was asked to take on the commission by the architect G.F. Bodley, who was doing extensive work in the cathedral, but his response was a vehement 'No. I couldn't face it.' 'Yet,' he went on, 'I love mosaics better than anything else in the world. It's nonsense to put mosaic there – nonsense I think to try to do anything with it but let it chill the soul of man and gently prepare him for the next glacial cataclysm.'[136] Instead Sir William Blake Richmond, with his 'colossal self-confidence, verging on insanity',[137] was brought in, and he and Gregory bulldozed the mosaics into place.

Richmond was an arch-classicist who was best known as a portrait artist. He moved in aristocratic circles, knew Gladstone and was a member of the Athenaeum Club. It was here that he met G.F. Bodley, who had been commissioned by Dean Church to build a new high altar and reredos at St Paul's. Richmond had at one stage been singled out by Burges to help with the St Paul's project and was well known for his interest in monumental decoration. He made it clear to Bodley that he felt able to complete the interior, and Bodley took him seriously. The newly appointed Gregory concurred, and Richmond's plans for the apse were accepted. Like Burges before him, he went on an Italian tour, visiting Monreale, the Cappella Palatina in Palermo, Sta Maria Maggiore in Rome, the Baptistery of Florence Cathedral, and finally Ravenna.[138] When he retired to London he set up a Byzantine 'workshop' training mosaic workers in his back garden. His foreman, Gaetano Meo, was Italian; the rest were

English. Powell and Son were commissioned to provide tesserae, for which Harry Powell studied Byzantine examples in the South Kensington Museum. They collectively decided on half-inch-deep pieces set into a special Florentine cement and mounted on pieces of slate.

Work began on the completion of the eight spandrels of the dome, and by 1894 the mosaics were appearing across the saucer domes beginning with the creation of the fishes (fig. 77). Powell and Son were now producing vast numbers of tesserae and the men trained by Richmond were putting them in place. Unlike Salviati, Richmond did not prefabricate the mosaic. Instead the tesserae were slowly assembled and located *in situ*, producing a less polished, rougher, but more dramatic effect. The archaism and the cost (£78,000) of the decoration provoked a backlash. Just as Richmond was about to start work in the choir, *The Times*, in the name of Englishness and Protestantism, attacked him. Petitions were signed. There were protests in the House of Lords, and in a famous outburst the Earl of Wemyss denounced what he called these 'barbarous, anachronous … Byzantine mosaics'[139] without seeing them. Holman Hunt wrote supportively to Richmond from Ravenna. Yes, he said, the mosaics were Byzantine in technique, but they made no attempt to enforce Church dogma; the modern designs, he insisted, were 'essentially of nineteenth-century invention', the 'creation of a living Church'.[140] Richmond agreed. He worked in the spirit of Burges, and in the spirit of Byzantium, and he preferred the ancient hieratic style to the more recent Renaissance mosaic. After the ninth century, he said, 'mosaic went off, and eventually the pictorial system began to come in.'[141] In a passionate and vigorous letter to *The Times* he defended polychromy against Puritanism: 'colour is surely appropriate' in 'a metropolitan Cathedral'. A church like St Paul's 'should not strike cold to the soul', rather it should 'arouse emotions which tend to possess the imagination with joy'.[142] Unlike original Byzantine mosaic, Richmond's version of biblical legend is far more humanized and corporeal. *The Persian Sibyl*, an early panel at clerestory level of which Richmond was especially proud, mixes a childlike naivety with a playful use of busy decoration (fig. 116). As with many of the monumental figures the body is treated balletically, and the figure revealed rather than hidden by the mosaic clothing. When no clothing is called for, as in the Adam and Eve sequence, Richmond does not hesitate to exploit sensuousness in a way that would rarely be found in Early Christian work. In *Eve Amongst the Beasts* a particularly feline tiger cuddles up to the side of the naked woman while she looks apprehensively at another one which is settling itself between her legs (fig. 117). Again, in the

116 (above) William Blake Richmond, *The Persian Sibyl*, 1899. Mosaic. St Paul's Cathedral, London
117 (left) William Blake Richmond, *Eve Amongst the Beasts*, c.1899. Mosaic. St Paul's Cathedral, London

Christ in Majesty (fig. 118), which fills one of the quarter domes (and which is derived from Sicily via Burges), Christ is seated on a rainbow with a sun and moon beneath his cloudy throne. Unlike the austere Byzantine originals, however, he holds up his hands in an expression of naïve surprise and with a look of startled amazement on his face.

The decoration of St Paul's marks a considerable change in what British Protestants were prepared to tolerate in church interiors. The cathedral had long been a 'sacred cow' of austere ecclesiastical decoration where the introduction of colour was viewed as an attack on Protestant principles. The resolution of the issue must be attributed to Dean Gregory and William Blake Richmond, but the real inspiration came from William Burges. Though he had been a victim of the scheme, it was his love of Byzantine and other Oriental designs that had spurred the project on. Outside the precincts of the cathedral it had been the Camden Society and Butterfield's All Saints', Margaret Street, which, in a sense, had infiltrated Protestant chromophobia, and it is to Butterfield's contribution to the Byzantine Revival that we now turn.

11 | Butterfield, Burne-Jones and Byzantium

One of the prime movers behind the St Paul's mosaics had been Alexander Beresford Hope. During the St Paul's debate he had also lent considerable support to another project of mosaic revival, this time in Oxford. In 1876 Keble College Chapel had been consecrated with considerable pomp and ceremony.[143] In an article entitled 'Classical and Byzantine' Beresford Hope pointed out how 'two modern works of great importance have attracted due attention within the last few years: the greater remains a fragment, the lesser has been completed.' The 'greater' was, of course, the decoration of St Paul's which had 'become a weariness to the world'; the 'lesser' was the decoration of William Butterfield's Keble College Chapel, which Beresford Hope saw as an outstandingly successful Byzantine Revival design.[144] Beresford Hope thought that Butterfield's mosaics had the potential to 'disarm suspicion of "idolatry" in the English Church for all forms of decoration', and he was at pains to locate them historically while pointing out the degree to which they conformed with Protestant doctrine. These mosaics, he said, 'make one understand what real and good Christian art is and always has been; rich, genuine, imposing, and historic, intelligible to the learned and unlearned.'[145]

Butterfield studied the mosaics of San Marco and sent his designer, Alexander Gibbs, off to Venice in preparation for the work at Keble.[146] Gibbs brought back a chemist and some Italian craftsmen to operate a furnace for the manufacture of the tesserae, while the 'numerous designs and cartoons', we are told, were 'executed under Butterfield's own hand'.[147]

Beresford Hope was very keen on the Byzantine pedigree of these mosaics, insisting that they were 'those of the second or Byzantine period of Christian art to the 13th century', and claimed that they derived principally from the

118 (opposite) William Blake Richmond, *Christ in Majesty, c.*1899. Mosaic. St Paul's Cathedral, London

mosaics at Torcello and the 'early work in St Mark's'.[148] The doom on the west end (fig. 120) certainly has affinities with the Last Judgement at Torcello (fig. 119), but the total effect has little of the warmth, glow, sparkle and brilliance of any Byzantine mosaic in Italy, and the use of rather pallid pastels gives the interior a soapy, washed-out look.

More successful because they are more strictly Byzantine are Butterfield's mosaic figures of the twelve apostles, together with the heads of eight patriarchs from the Old Testament, in the church of St Andrew's at West Tarring near Worthing (1882–6; fig. 121). The idea for the decoration here came from the rector, Henry Bailey, who until 1878 had been warden of St Augustine's Missionary College in Canterbury. Butterfield's design, said Bailey, came from 'his vivid remembrance of the marvellous ancient mosaics at Ravenna'.[149] The money for the venture was donated by families who were closely connected with the parish. One of them paid for as many as seven of the twelve apostles who line the nave, and another put up money for a further three. In his defence of the mosaic Bailey is very careful to cover himself against the accusations of idolatry and popery which so quickly sprang to the British Protestant mind when faced with this type of decoration. But by the time he was writing in 1886, a far greater mosaic scheme was under way in which neither of these issues seemed to matter. In a subject which is full of ironies and curiosities, one of the greatest is the fact that the largest mosaic project of the late nineteenth century should be designed by a Protestant Englishman for Americans in a Protestant church in Rome! The Englishman was Burne-

119 (left) Last Judgement, *c.*1100. Mosaic.
Duomo, Torcello
120 (right) William Butterfield, *Last Judgement*,
1876. Mosaic. Keble College, Oxford

Jones, and the church is G.E. Street's St Paul's American Church in the Via Nazionale. St Paul's was founded in the wake of the liberation of Rome from papal rule in 1870, when the ban on non-Catholic churches within the city walls was lifted. As Richard Dorment points out, this was the most extensive ecclesiastical project undertaken in late nineteenth-century Rome.[150]

In the early 1870s Dr Robert J. Nevin gathered $34,000 from American Episcopalians and commissioned Street to design a new church. Street had had much experience of building Protestant churches abroad and his work could be found in Paris, Geneva and Constantinople, but the Americans were nearly pipped to the post by the British who asked him to design All Souls in the Via del Babuino. The cornerstone of St Paul's was laid in 1872 and from it arose a neo-Romanesque church with banded interior brick decoration like many of those he had illustrated in his *Brick and Marble Architecture in the Middle Ages* (1855). He intended to use interior mosaic decoration, but only for the apse. 'All parts of our churches must not be equally gorgeous in their colouring,' he wrote, 'and … a distinction must be established between the part around the altar and the rest.'[151] But Nevin had other ideas. By 1877 he was talking of a much bigger project. Large sums of extra money were needed, and in 1881 the first donation came from Junius Morgan, the rich father of the even richer John Pierpont Morgan. Nevin and Street now needed a designer. Street had known Burne-Jones since the 1860s when he and William Morris had worked briefly in Street's office at Oxford. In July 1881 Burne-Jones agreed to draw up some ideas for mosaics in St Paul's, but when street died in December 1881 he nearly gave up the project.

It is not surprising that Burne-Jones, with his interest in stained glass, should also have been interested in the potential of mosaic. He had long been associated with firms who were central to the mosaic revival. In 1857 he designed a stiffly formalized window for Powell and Son for St Andrew's College, Bradfield, in Berkshire; and a window depicting Christ in Glory which he designed in 1873 for Morris and Co. in Oldrid Scott's St Mary the Virgin, Speldhurst, Kent, anticipates the apsidal mosaic of St Paul's by some ten years (fig. 122). Burne-Jones's interest in mosaic went back to his introduction to the art of Venice under the auspices of Ruskin in 1862. He had been on a brief visit in 1859, and expressed a boyish enthusiasm for the place, but now, employed by Ruskin to look and make copies of works of art, his attitude was much more intense. After seeing San Marco and Torcello he wrote to Ruskin saying that his 'heart was full of mosaics', and this love was strengthened by his visit to the 'heavenly churches' of Ravenna in 1873.[152] St Paul's in Rome thus offered the prospect of fulfilling his long-standing ambition to work in 'vast spaces' and to have 'big things to do'. Unlike Burges, who was fascinated by the purely decorative potential of

mosaic, or Butterfield, who was strongly motivated by religious impulses, Burne-Jones saw in this work the possibility of creating democratic art along the lines suggested by William Morris. He wanted 'common people to see them and say and say Oh! – only Oh!'[153]

It took him many years to complete the work for the first section, the 'Heavenly Jerusalem' destined for the apse. The preparatory design was done between 1881 and 1882, the cartoon between 1882 and 1884, and the mosaic was not unveiled until 1885. Compared with the Speldhurst Christ in Glory, this figure is much younger and more formally Byzantine in his fully frontal pose. He is beardless and androgyne, much more lightly clad and with more exposed flesh. His orb has become a crystal ball in which we can see the earth, the water and the sky entwined together, and he is seated on a narrow Byzantine throne. Burne-Jones set out on this task with a romantic attitude towards reviving the values of Byzantium in art. He was doing it, he said, for 'love of Venice and Ravenna and the seven impenetrable centuries between them'.[154] Reality was much harder. 'It would be impossible', noted his wife, 'to describe the anxiety and labour connected with mosaic.'[155] Robert Nevin was in Rome and, although he knew the ancient mosaics and understood the tradition in which Burne-Jones was working, had his own priorities.[156] Giovanni Castellani, whom Burne-Jones had once met in Venice, was director-general of the Salviati works with responsibility for assembling the mosaics from the cartoons, while Burne-Jones's surrogate abroad, his faithful studio assistant Thomas Rooke, was responsible for interpreting his master's voice in Italy. At the start of the process that voice was full of imprecations and expletives. Burne-Jones would spend his Sunday mornings with Morris at The Grange in London creating a system of keys by which the colours on the cartoon could be matched to the colours on the tesserae supplied by Castellani. During this period Morris was taking a considerable interest in Byzantine art, now deepened by his personal involvement in the craftwork associated with mosaic production.

After early failures the apse mosaic was unveiled on Christmas Day 1885, after which the money ran out and the operation stopped. Three years later a local parishioner offered to pay for one of the arch mosaics and selected the *Annunciation*. The cartoon was ready by 1890. Money then became available for *The Tree of Life* (or *The Tree of Forgiveness*, as is sometimes called; fig. 124), but everything was further delayed until the two could be put in place together. They were eventually unveiled in 1894.

122 Edward Burne-Jones, *Christ in Glory*, 1873. Stained-glass window. St Mary the Virgin, Speldhurst, Kent

Burne-Jones shared with other mosaicists of this period a delight in the thought that their work would defy time. They were also attracted to the idea that mosaic was removed from consumerism and those realms of art tainted by commercialism. In the course of discussing his work, Burne-Jones described his own beliefs in relation to the mosaics' Christian content: 'There are only two sides of Christianity for which I am fitted by the Spirit that designs in me – the carol part and the mystical part. I could not do without medieval Christianity. The central idea of it and all it has gathered to itself made the Europe that I exist in.' His list of Christianity's contributions to European culture includes 'enthusiasm and devotion', 'learning and art' and 'humanity and romance'. This is a far cry from the impassioned commitment of the Ecclesiologists, or the evangelical intensity of Ruskin. For Burne-Jones, Byzantium and 'medieval Christianity' represented romance – withdrawal and separation from the distracting, invasive aspects of modern life. Yet at St Paul's, in the cartoon for *The Earthly Paradise*, he included members of his family, friends, residents of Rome, and even prominent American political figures. The precedent was, of course, the mosaics of San Vitale in which Theodora is surrounded by her court and members of her family, and is facing Justinian, who is similarly grouped with important figures of the Byzantine military and bureaucracy. Here the Archbishop of Canterbury makes an appearance as Pope Gregory I (fig. 123); Thomas Rooke appears as Longinus; and among the Doctors of the Church Robert Nevin appears in the guise of St Anastasius. Nevin became the driving force behind the completion of these mosaics after Burne-Jones's death in 1898, and he persuaded Thomas Rooke to finish The *Earthly Paradise* on the authority of Burne-Jones's designs. Nevin's end was in keeping with his obsessions. He died in Mexico where he had gone to prospect for gold for the ground of this same mosaic. Burne-Jones himself never saw the inside of St Paul's American Church. It is remarkable that, though the design of these mosaics absorbed so

124 Edward Burne-Jones, *The Tree of Life*,
1894. Mosaic. St Paul's American Church, Rome

much of his time during the last seventeen years of his life and though they fulfilled one of his highest ambitions, he preferred to let their realization remain a fantasy and to leave the practicalities to Rooke and Nevin in Italy.

Burne-Jones's mosaics at St Paul's American Church had strong links with the British Arts and Crafts movement. William Morris, as we have seen, was instrumental in helping Jones design the first panels and in developing a system of communication between artist and craftsman. Morris was also interested in the wider role of Byzantium in Western art history, and became a crucial figure in reviving interest in Byzantine design in the latter part of the nineteenth century (see below, p.166). Morris's interest coincided with a period during the 1870s when the conceptual framework for understanding Byzantine mosaic art (and, most especially, Byzantine architecture) was being revised. Up to the 1860s the terms Byzantine, basilican and Romanesque had often been used synonymously. During the 1860s, probably as the result of publications such as Texier and Pullen's *Byzantine Architecture* (1864), Byzantine was more carefully distinguished from Romanesque, and both began to be separated from basilican. While Byzantine looked more specifically to Eastern sources in Constantinople, Romanesque was linked with Northern Italy, France and Germany, and basilican was more closely identified with Rome. This was a slow process, and was prefaced by the ambitions of two or three slightly eccentric figures who, for quite separate reasons, wished to build in a Byzantine style.

12 | Some Early Neo-Byzantine Churches

St Barnabas in Jericho, Oxford, was built from money donated mainly by Thomas Combe, the Anglo-Catholic superintendent of the Oxford University Press.[157] Keen to bring enlightenment to the slum area of nearby Jericho, in 1868 Combe had Arthur Blomfield design 'the first perfect Basilica in this country', modelled (as he told Holman Hunt) on 'the cathedral of Torcello, near Venice'.[158] Like a Ravennite building it was intended to be simple on the outside but sumptuous within. The exterior of Portland cement with brick banding[159] is truly primitive and solid – some might say 'crude' (fig. 127). But it embodies something of the 'severity', 'simplicity' and 'dignity' that Ruskin had attributed to the duomo at Torcello in the second volume of *Modern Painters* (see above, p. 125). Inside, the richly decorated space was designed, according to Blomfield, as 'a vehicle for coloured decoration',[160] and it was this interior that caused problems. Many of the early visitors saw it as 'papist', and the apse paintings in particular seemed very un-English, very un-Protestant and distinctly 'Roman'. The large figure of Christ in blessing (fig. 126) is reminiscent of those in Sicilian churches, especially the twelfth-century Pantokrator in the Martorana in Palermo (fig. 125), but the immediate inspiration may have come from a source much closer to home – the Oxford Architectural Society.

Combe had been elected to the Society's committee in 1868, and among the members there were two, J.H. Parker and E.G. Bruton, who were professionally interested in early medieval architecture. Parker, as we have

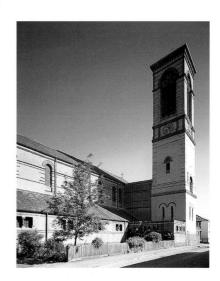

already seen (above, p.144), had written about the history of mosaic, and Bruton was restoring the ancient apsidal church of SS Peter and Paul, Checkendon, Berkshire. In 1868 Bruton published an enthusiastic paper on the subject with a large illustration of the mural he had found under the plaster of the apse. This showed six apostles lined up on each side, with SS Peter and Paul in the middle.[161] Above is the outline of a seated figure in majesty with a nimbus and one hand held up in blessing (fig. 128).

It is this arrangement that Combe and Blomfield adopted for St Barnabas. In Combe's church Saints Paul and Barnabas join the apostles, and the fourteen figures are paired off within niches that combine to form a round-arched colonnade with Byzantine capitals. Above them the full-length figure of a seated, bearded Christ looms out of the semi-darkness. He is painted in black and gold on a blue ground. The gesture of his right hand is identical to that of the Checkendon Christ, and the other hand holds an orb on his knee. Behind him the blue firmament is filled with gold stars.

Before this impressive apse is a triumphal arch in black and red on a gold ground, surrounded by rectangles containing the animals of the Evangelists. The nave has six bays separated by short heavy columns on square brick bases. These contribute to the stocky appearance of the columns, adding in turn to the building's feeling of weight and solidity. Inserted into the carving at the west end are portraits of Combe, Blomfield, Bishop Wilberforce and the first incumbent, M.H. Noel. The 'solidly constructed Latin cross', as Thomas Hardy called it in *Jude the Obscure* (1895), is still 'set with large jewels' and hanging over the chancel as it was when he wrote the novel. It was under this cross in the church of 'St Silas' that Sue Bridehead prostrated herself with grief after

125 (top left) Pantokrator, *c.* 1143. Apse mosaic.
La Martorana, Palermo
126 (top right) Arthur Blomfield, apse mosaic of the
Pantokrator. St Barnabas, Oxford
127 (above) Arthur Blomfield, St Barnabas,
Oxford, 1868–72

the death of her children.[162] Her passive submission to ecclesiastical authority in a neo-Byzantine church picks up on the 'popery' of which many Anglicans suspected St Barnabas. The diarist Francis Kilvert, who visited in 1876, was not the only visitor to find 'pure Mariolatry' at the church[163] and a series of contemporary cartoons about St Barnabas made fun of its supposed connections with Rome. In one of them, entitled *The Bridge of Sighs* (fig. 129), St Barnabas is separated from St Peter's, Rome, by only the Oxford canal, and linked to the centre of Catholicism by a spider's web woven by the arachnoid figure of Cardinal Newman. Already struggling in the web is the young 3rd Marquess of Bute, who had recently converted to Catholicism (see below, p.163), while M.H. Noel is flying towards the trap.[164] The suspicion that the Byzantine style was associated with Catholicism was one of the issues that fuelled the debate at St Paul's Cathedral, and was confirmed for many people when Bentley chose it for Westminster Cathedral (see below, p.173).

In 1874, two years after the completion of St Barnabas, Gilbert Scott's son, John Oldrid Scott, was asked to design a Byzantine church about which there was no controversy. The reason for this is that St Sophia in Bayswater (fig. 130) was built for the Greek rather than the Anglican community. It has an orthodox Byzantine plan: a Greek cross under a central dome. The High Victorian exterior, solid and compact, would convince no one familiar with the buildings of Constantinople, and the interior, dominated by a forty-foot dome, is an odd mixture of Byzantine decoration and Renaissance illustration. The lower parts of the walls are covered with richly coloured marble, and the elaborate stalls and the post-Raphaelesque iconostasis made of coloured woods and inlaid mother of pearl were designed by Scott and made by Farmer and Brindley. The space works well, however, partly because large arches support a high dome in a confined area, lending the interior a compactness and unity, and partly because there was no need here to compromise or minister to the needs of

128 (left) Christ in Majesty with Apostles, 13th century. Apse mural. SS Peter and Paul, Checkendon, Oxfordshire

129 (right) 'The Bridge of Sighs'. Cartoon by an unknown hand, reproduced in Arthur Tilney Bassett, *S. Barnabas' Oxford* (London, 1919)

Anglican or Catholic rituals. The dome and vaults are brilliant with mosaic, and these too bring the interior together (fig. 131). They were designed by A.G. Walker, and unlike Salviati's work, the tesserae were inserted *in situ* so that the unevenness of the surface serves to catch the light and contributes a liveliness and brilliance to the images. The critic of the *The Builder* liked it. He pronounced that it was 'one of the most important pieces of interior church decoration in London … carried out in accordance with what the late Mr. Burges, with much less reason, proposed to introduce into the interior of St Paul's'.[165]

The shift between the basilican and the Byzantine is beautifully illustrated by St Catherine (1874) – 'the little Byzantine church', as *Building News* called it – at Hoarwithy, near Ross, Herefordshire.[166] The small church was attached to the parish of Hentland, and was the brainchild of the wealthy rector, William Poole, who had been vicar of the parish since 1854. For his new building he turned to his friend John Pollard Seddon, one of the local diocesan architects of Llandaff, who was then in partnership with Richard Phené Spiers. Continental and Eastern building fascinated Poole, and his motives, unlike Combe's, were more aesthetic than evangelical. In 1843 Poole's long summer vacation from Oriel College, Oxford, took him to Constantinople, Greece, Venice, Milan, Genoa and Rome. In one undated notebook he made studies of 'Old Basilicas converted into Churches', including Sant'Agnese and San Prassede, and in San Clemente he also examined the mosaics and made drawings of Byzantine colonnades.[167]

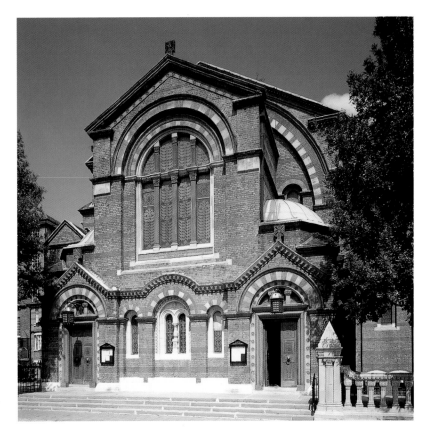

At Hoarwithy the architects made good use of the hill-top location overlooking the Wye valley by creating a building whose outside has a strong Tuscan-Romanesque quality (figs. 132, 133). The Romanesque planning is done sensitively and well, but the triumph of the church is inside at the magnificent east end. In contrast to St Barnabas, which is theatrical-Byzantine, the work here is extremely fine and carries a strong sense of authenticity. It is given a prelude by a small but pure white ambo, possibly modelled on a pulpit in Fiesole.[168] Behind it stand four massive columns of grey Devonshire marble supporting an inner cupola. This, as Pevsner noted, is 'purely Byzantine'.[169] These marble columns support large Byzantine capitals, and above them is a cupola from which radiate tunnel vaults to the north and south. To the east is an apse with a figure of the Pantocrator on a gold ground. There are more Byzantine capitals throughout the church, and the mosaic pavements that extend to the cloister outside were still being laid in 1885.

131 A. G. Walker, dome mosaic, 1874.
Aghia Sophia, Moscow Road, London

At about this time the Byzantine Revival was beginning to appear in Scotland, imported under the auspices of the hugely rich John Patrick Crichton-Stuart, 3rd Marquess of Bute. Bute built his own Byzantine churches and had a considerable influence on the design of Westminster Cathedral. He first experienced Byzantine architecture in Constantinople in 1866. He was an undergraduate in Oxford in the late 1860s, converted to Catholicism in 1868 at the age of twenty, and in the same year made a contribution to the building of St Barnabas. In the following year, with the aid of Burges, Bute decided to put up a chapel for a convent of the Sisters of the Good Shepherd outside his seat at Cardiff Castle. Though it is no longer in existence, Burges designed a domical roof for a baldacchino showing a Christ in Majesty at its centre surrounded by angels (fig. 134). Bute then turned his attention to Scotland, and in 1882, with the aid of Rowan Anderson, began 'a Byzantine Chapel at Troon'.[170] In 1883 St Patrick's Roman Catholic church was consecrated, and this was followed by a second church, St Sophia's in Galston (1885–6), loosely modelled on Hagia Sophia, Constantinople.[171]

132, 133 (top left and right) John Pollard Seddon,
St Catherine's, Hoarwithy, Herefordshire, c. 1874
134 (above) William Burges, panel from the baldacchino
of the Convent of the Good Shepherd,
Cardiff, 1869. National Museum of Wales, Cardiff

13 | The Arts and Crafts Movement

Towards the end of the 1880s Rowan Anderson was replaced as Bute's principal architect by one of his pupils, Robert Weir Schultz. This young Scot was working in Anderson's office until 1883 and, together with his patron, became one of the foremost Byzantinists of this period. In 1884 Schultz came to London to work for Norman Shaw, and his arrival corresponded with the moment when Byzantine art and architecture were beginning to have a significant collective appeal.

In 1887 Schultz won a Royal Academy Gold Medal and Travelling Scholarship. He first went to Venice, where he made careful drawings of the interior of San Marco,[172] and to Murano and Torcello. Then in 1889, on the advice of his colleague W.R. Lethaby, he went to Greece to study the remains of Byzantine architecture together with Sidney Barnsley, another young architect in Shaw's office.[173] It was in this year that Schultz seems to have met the 3rd Marquess of Bute, who was to play an important part in his life. Bute was so interested in Schultz's Greek drawings that he offered to finance further exploration in Greece. As a result, Schultz and Barnsley, with support from Bute, Edwin Freshfield (an archaeologist fascinated by Byzantine decoration) and the British School at Athens, set off once again for Greece. Their work, *The Monastery of St Luke of Stirsis in Phocis*, was not published until 1901 but their personal enthusiasm for Byzantine art and architecture was communicated to friends in their circle. Ernest Gimson, for example, who shared a desk with Ernest Barnsley (Sidney's brother) at Sedding's office, spent a week in 1889 revelling in the Byzantine sights of Torcello and Ravenna, and this visit left a permanent impression on his work.[174]

Perhaps the single most important figure behind this late nineteenth-century interest in Byzantium was William Morris. Its initial impulse came from Ruskin who, in *The Stones of Venice*, attached such importance to architectural integrity, honesty and the autonomy of the craftsman; but it was Morris who intensified the practical and pragmatic aspects of the message and shifted its political implications away from Ruskin's paternalism and towards egalitarian socialism. G.E. Street's work in 'brick and marble' had lent Ruskin's lyricism a practical edge, and this he communicated to Philip Webb, J.D. Sedding and Morris himself, all of whom were associated with Street's office. Despite Street's crucial role in encouraging this interest in a Byzantine Revival, it is Morris who may be called its father, since it was he who placed Byzantine art and architecture on a footing comparable with that of other major historical styles. Because Morris's ideas provided a nucleus around which the philosophy of Arts and Crafts consolidated, his interests and influence permeated the whole movement, extending as far as the poetry of W.B. Yeats.

For reasons probably connected with his interest in the 'Eastern Question' (see above, p. 13) and the threat of a Russo-Turkish war in the mid-1870s, Morris's attention was drawn to Hagia Sophia. In 1878 he asked a Greek friend, Aglaia Coronio, to send him photographs of the building, and he told his daughter that he had been 'reading a lot about the Byzantine Empire in Finlay's book', finding it 'interesting though somewhat dreary'.[175] In the same year he described Byzantium as 'rich and fruitful',[176] singling out Hagia Sophia as 'lovely and stately'[177] and the 'most beautiful' European building, after which 'the earth began to blossom with beautiful buildings.'[178] One of those buildings was, of course, San Marco, and in November 1879 he corresponded with Ruskin to protest against the damage that was being done to the building through its restoration. But Morris's understanding of Byzantine art and culture was much broader than Ruskin's, and in the 1880s the city of Constantinople, and Hagia Sophia, became central to Morris's thinking about the relationship between art and society. For Morris, Gothic art was the true art of the modern period, and Byzantine art was its earliest manifestation, 'new born' out of the decadence of Greece and Rome.[179] Morris's first extended account of Byzantium came in his 1882 lecture on the 'History of Pattern Designing'.[180] Here he illustrates the rise and fall of modern organic art by reference to three buildings: the palace of Diocletian at Split, St Peter's in Rome and Hagia Sophia. The first, he says, is encumbered by outworn classicism, and the second by 'pedantry and hopelessness', but in Hagia Sophia organic art 'has utterly thrown aside all pedantic encumbrances' and produced 'the most beautiful ... of the buildings raised in Europe before the nineteenth century'.[181] Hagia Sophia continued to be a measure for Morris of the greatness of Byzantine art; in 1889 in a paper entitled 'Gothic Architecture' he used it once again as an example of Byzantine 'freedom' breaking away from the deadly grip of classicism.[182] In this same year Morris recorded in his diary a visit to the Victoria and Albert Museum where he made a 'contrast between the bald ugliness of the Classical pieces and the great beauty of the Byzantine'. This he said, 'was a pleasing thing to me, who loathe so all Classical art and literature'.[183]

Morris's interest in Byzantine art may well have crystallized through his interest in Burne-Jones's 1881 commission for the work in St Paul's American Church in Rome. We have seen how Morris had helped Burne-Jones work out a scheme for his mosaic, and he saw this type of decoration as 'the crowning beauty of the most solemn buildings'.[184] It may have been invented by the Romans, he said, but the Byzantines had invested it with Eastern 'richness and mystery'. Both Morris and Burne-Jones developed the romantic idea that Byzantine society was one of social unity and equality. 'Who built Hagia Sophia?' he asks. The answer is 'men like you and me, handicraftsmen who left no names behind them'.[185] The essential characteristic of Byzantine art, he said in a lecture of 1881 ('The Art and Beauty of the Earth'), was that it was 'the work of collective rather than individual genius',[186] and just as it united architect and craftsman, it drew together East and West in a richly synthesizing process, joining Eastern love of freedom, mystery and intricate design with Western respect for discipline, structure and fact. 'It is the living child and fruitful mother of art, past and future.'[187]

Morris's dithyrambic, historically panoramic account of Byzantine architecture, which reaches its peak in 'Gothic Architecture', owes much to Ruskin's 'Nature of Gothic' in *The Stones of Venice*. But whereas Ruskin's version of Byzantium began and ended in Venice, Morris took the hint from later archaeological work and gave Byzantine architecture a global significance, drawing a cultural map with Byzantium at its centre. 'East and West,' he says, 'it overran the world wherever men built with history behind them. In the East it mingled with the traditions of the native populations, especially with Persia of the Sassanian period ... In the West it settled itself in the parts of Italy that Justinian had conquered, notably Ravenna, and thence came to Venice. From Italy, or perhaps even from Byzantium itself, it was carried into Germany and pre-Norman England, touching even Ireland and Scandinavia.'[188]

It is as if Morris has turned all the old attitudes to Byzantium on their heads. Gone is the talk of oppressive tyrants, inflexible religious hierarchies and creative stagnation, and in their place have appeared political and personal freedom, life, vitality and autonomy. Morris has mythologized Byzantium in positive economic, political, social and aesthetic terms. By 1884 his views were sufficiently widely accepted for five architects from Norman Shaw's office (led by W.R. Lethaby) to found the Art Workers' Guild under his auspices. In 1888 the Guild's public face, the Arts and Crafts Exhibition Society, held its first meeting in the New Gallery, London, and to celebrate its second show in 1889 Morris delivered his passionate account of Byzantium in 'Gothic Architecture'. (This was the same year, it may be remembered, that Lethaby urged Schultz to travel to Greece to study Byzantine architecture.) Morris considered this lecture sufficiently important to deliver it on another three occasions in London and to further groups in Liverpool and Glasgow. He finally published it in book form in 1893 and sold it at the Arts and Crafts Exhibition of that year.[189]

One of those who heard Morris speak on Byzantium was the young W.B. Yeats. He had first met the older man in Dublin, and during his time in London between 1887 and 1889 he was a regular visitor to Morris's house. In 1888 another note was struck in the revival of interest in Byzantium and once again Yeats was involved. This time it came from Oscar Wilde. In December Wilde read *The Decay of Lying* to an attentive and admiring Yeats who, in between visits to Morris, was spending time at Wilde's house in Tite Street. In *The Decay of Lying* one of Wilde's characters, Vivien, reads a paper that touches on the decorative arts. Wilde had already spoken extensively about the place of the decorative arts in Victorian society during his lecture tour of America in the early 1880s. At that time his examples and his attitudes were heavily dependent on Ruskin and Morris, and his stress lay firmly on the social importance of the 'lesser arts'. Now he changed tack and stressed the artificiality and anti-naturalist tendencies of Byzantine art. In *The Decay of Lying* Wilde (in the person of Vivien) claimed that the whole history of the decorative arts in Europe was 'the record of the struggle between Orientalism, with its frank rejection of imitation, its love of artistic convention, its dislike of the actual representation of any object in Nature, and our own imitative spirit'. His examples come from 'Byzantium, Sicily, and Spain', from which, he said, 'we have had beautiful and imaginative work in which the visible things of life are transmuted into artistic conventions'.[190] Wilde's shift away from Morris and Ruskin was a result of reading Whistler's 'Ten o'Clock Lecture' (reviewed by Wilde in 1885) which stressed the artificiality of art, and it also came from his reading of Huysmans's *Against Nature*, where the description of Gustave Moreau's paintings (see figs. 73, 74) had a 'staggering effect upon him'.[191]

One of the earliest architectural manifestations of the Arts and Crafts version of Byzantium appeared in the early 1890s with the work of Sidney Barnsley. Edwin Freshfield, who was already supporting Schultz, dipped into his pocket again when he and Sir Cosmo Bonsor commissioned Barnsley to design a Byzantine church for their parish of Lower Kingswood, Surrey (fig. 135). It was consecrated in July 1892, and as an architectural concept it was radically different from the interestingly eccentric Byzantine variations of Thomas Combe, William Poole and the

Marquess of Bute. Outside it is a rather squat brick building with a pitched roof; inside it is an archaeologist's jewel box modelled on the plan of St Irene in Constantinople. A short nave is separated from narrow side aisles by two bays of round arches, and at the end a larger triumphal arch encloses a shallow apse. The church is roofed with wooden barrel-vaulting painted by Barnsley himself. There are nine original Byzantine capitals brought back from Turkey by Edwin Freshfield. Two large ones incorporated in the nave arcade date from the fourth century and come from St John at Ephesus, as do several smaller examples of the sixth century. On the west wall above the doorway are two fourth-century capitals from St John Studion in Constantinople (rescued by Freshfield from their use for revolver practice), and two capitals from the Blachernae Palace. Constantinople also supplied an eleventh-century fragment of a frieze from the church of the Pantocrator, and further capitals from the Boddan Serail and a site near the Blachernae Palace. The walls are lined with a variety of coloured marbles including *cipollino*, *verde antico*, *breccia*, and even the royal Byzantine marble, porphyry. The apse walls and the semidome are covered with mosaics and dense with gold tesserae (fig. 136). The geometrical design around the apse derives from St Irene and from the monastery of St Luke in Phocis which Barnsley had studied so carefully. In keeping with the egalitarianism of the Arts and Crafts movement there is no Pantocrator, just a simple cross, and the tesserae were laid *in situ* to create that rugged Byzantine sparkle. Above the chancel steps hangs a cross copied from an original in San Marco, and until 1947 two enormous circular chandeliers in the manner of Hagia Sophia provided the only light.

135 (left) Sidney Barnsley, Hagia Sophia,
Lower Kingswood, Surrey, 1892
136 (right) Sidney Barnsley, Apse mosaic, 1892.
Hagia Sophia, Lower Kingswood, Surrey

Within the church two symbolic eggs are strategically placed: one is suspended over the font, the other over the chancel, the latter made of porcelain painted with angels and originating from Cairo. These mysterious objects point to another side of the Byzantine Revival whose ideals and impulses were rather different from those of the Arts and Crafts movement. Alongside the Arts and Crafts stress on honesty, integrity and common sense in Byzantine architecture and design was another group who adopted Byzantium for its mystery, its inscrutability and its Oriental irrationality. Broadly speaking, one approach was rational and empirical, the other imaginative and, in its furthest reaches, decadent. The imaginative, romantic attitude to Byzantium can be traced back to Ludwig I's insistence on reproducing the Cappella Palatina in Munich or Ruskin's love affair with San Marco; in its later manifestations it emerged in Wilde's stress on the essential artificiality of Byzantine art and Moreau's fascination with its kaleidoscopic visual excess. In Britain, the more rational side of the Byzantine Revival is linked to the name of Morris and the Arts and Crafts movement, and its most enduring monument is Bentley's Westminster Cathedral. Bentley's work, however, would have been impossible without the literary foundations laid down by contemporary writers on Byzantium, and it is those to which we now turn.

14 | W.R. Lethaby and Byzantine Scholarship

Both the empirical and the imaginative aspects of neo-Byzantinism came together in one man, William Richard Lethaby. Ironically, however, Lethaby had little faith in the revival of Byzantium. In his most important book on the subject, *The Church of Sancta Sophia, Constantinople* (1894), he warned that, though we may look to Byzantine methods and attitudes, 'the style cannot be copied by our attempting to imitate Byzantine builders.'[192] Hardly was the ink dry on Lethaby's account of Hagia Sophia when it inspired John Francis Bentley in the choice of the style for Westminster Cathedral. 'San Vitale at Ravenna and Lethaby's book', he said, 'told me all I wanted.'[193]

We have seen that Lethaby (with no first-hand knowledge himself of Byzantine art) had urged Schultz to make his trip to Greece. Yet Lethaby responded to Byzantine design as much for its potential for fantasy as for its practical possibilities. The fantastic in architecture had always appealed to him. A design for a cemetery chapel that he submitted to *Building News* in 1878 (fig. 137), with its sombre mixture of classical and Byzantine features, was enough to shock William Butterfield when Lethaby applied to join his office.[194] Instead he joined Norman Shaw and established a friendship with William Morris which paved the way for his easterly pilgrimage to Byzantium and Constantinople. Meanwhile he developed a lifelong admiration for the work of William Burges. It was, said Lethaby, 'play-acting … yet [Burges] was earnest and thorough, a real make-believer'.[195] It was Burges's 'strange and barbarously splendid' Tower House in Holland Park that most impressed him with its 'fusion of Eastern feeling'.[196]

Lethaby's first publication, *Architecture, Mysticism and Myth* (1891) is concerned with the irrational in architecture and building. It rode on the contemporary fashion for mythography, typology and mysticism, and was an attempt to understand architecture in terms of prevailing ideologies and as the expression of psychological symbols. In the book Lethaby draws on a wide range of styles from around the world, including Byzantine, to show how all architecture grew out of archetypes based on ritual. The names of Max Müller, Andrew Lang and E.B. Tylor are invoked to lend scholarly credibility to the idea and, using their work, Lethaby links architecture and architectural design to psychology, fantasy and dream. He speaks of the pleasures of 'dream edifices',[197] as he calls them, among which Byzantine buildings feature prominently. Hagia Sophia, 'the most splendid church Christendom has ever seen', was built as the material rival to the fantastic Solomon's temple.[198]

The appearance of *Architecture, Mysticism and Myth* corresponded with other divergent aspects of interest in Byzantium, the scholarly and the theatrical. The first is best represented by the work of John Bagnell Bury. Bury graduated from Trinity College, Dublin, as a philologist, but his interest in history came to dominate. Fluent in classical languages, Russian and Hungarian, he published the *History of the later Roman Empire* in 1889 at the age of twenty-eight. This was followed by many more studies of this period, including a monumental new edition of Gibbon published between 1896 and 1900. From the Chair of Modern History at Cambridge Bury effectively became the founder of British Byzantine studies.

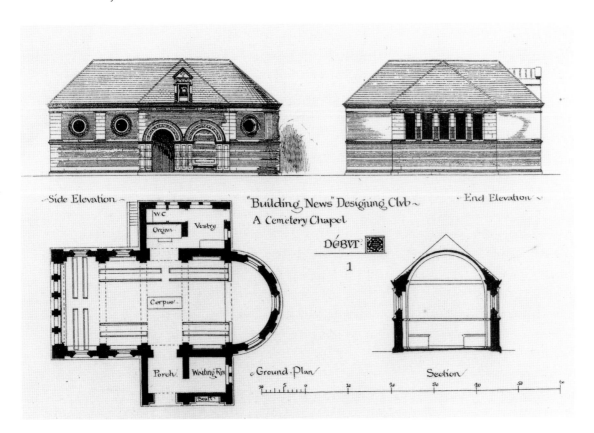

At the opposite end of the spectrum Byzantium caught the popular imagination. In December 1893 Bolossy Kiralfy opened *The Revels of the East* at Olympia in London. Over 2,000 artists were employed to represent life in an Oriental setting in some non-specific past. For this spectacle Kiralfy re-created the Golden Horn in Istanbul. He built shops and bazaars and used a huge group of workers to create underground cisterns. The architect Wilson Bennington was employed to create the subterranean forest of Byzantine pillars and, according to *The Times,* increased the 'weird and impressive effect' by the use of mirrors and coloured lights.[199] So extensive was this area that people could by ferried by Turks in caiques (fig. 138). Turkish women were employed elsewhere in a replica of the harem. Here they disported themselves suggestively in transparent veils for the delectation of the very large number of visitors. Over 30,000 people attended on the first day, many of them drawn by the 'Grand Ballet of the East' (fig. 139), in which 'ladies of the harem ride in gorgeous litters … Persian princes and Arabians of high rank are … attended by beautiful slaves', and to complete the mysterious theatricality there were 'priests clad in robes'.[200]

Robed Byzantine priests also featured in quite a different kind of spectacle, this time in Brighton. In 1895 Arthur Reginald Carew Cock had become vicar of the basilican church of St Bartholomew's. Cock was flamboyant, energetic and (as it happened) about to convert to Rome. He wanted a more vivid, colourful and dramatic interior for the church and he turned to J.D. Sedding's old office in London. Sedding had died in 1891 and the practice had been taken over by the remarkable figure of Henry Wilson, a close associate of Lethaby, who was greatly influenced by the imaginative, extravagant side of Lethaby's architectural character. Wilson also responded to Cock's demand for an arena for ritual of the most elaborate kind and his proposed Byzantine staging. A contemporary watercolour shows how Wilson intended to extend the church eastwards by three bays and introduce a round apse decorated with a giant mosaic Madonna, arms outstretched to welcome the blessed into paradise (fig. 141). This did not come about, but the mighty Byzantine round-arched baldacchino was built (fig. 140). It was raised twelve steps above the level of nave and

138 (left) 'The Hall of the Thousand and One Pillars' built by B. Kiralfy at Olympia, London, 1893. From the *Illustrated London News*, 11 November 1893
139 (right) 'Constantinople in London', from the *Illustrated London News*, 3 February 1884

140 (left) Henry Wilson, the baldacchino, 1899–1908.
St Bartholomew's, Brighton

141 (right) Henry Wilson, design for the extension of St
Bartholomew's, Brighton, *c.* 1898. Charcoal, gouache
and watercolour, 134 x 78 cm (52¼ x 30¼ in). Royal
Institute of British Architects, London

featured a glittering gold and mother-of-pearl vault over the altar. The square columns of the baldacchino stand on green and black bases, the capitals and the thin arches above decorated with interlaced vine patterns. Each side of the baldacchino is flanked by an immense Tuscan column of grey and white marble holding a candlestick. Above the altar is a high ledge supporting six more candlesticks in brass, below which stands a tabernacle with doors of beaten silver. Wilson's original crucifix has been moved to the Lady Altar and replaced by a larger and more theatrical version. The triumph of Wilson's design, however, is the octagonal pulpit clad in Irish green marble which stands on six piers of red African marble with white alabaster capitals and a plinth of black Tournai marble. The capitals, modelled on examples in Ravenna, are sensitively and delicately carved, and the pulpit is reached by a minute spiral staircase.

Wilson had worked out in practical terms some of the ideas about symbolism that Lethaby had expressed in *Architecture, Mysticism and Myth*. Lethaby's most influential book, *Sancta Sophia* (1894), is very different however. A monograph devoted to one building, it is largely a pragmatic work that focuses on its rational, logical and workmanlike qualities. In his friend the architect Harold Swainson he had found someone whose knowledge of ancient languages gave him access to original documents, and in March 1893 the two men set off to study the Byzantine buildings of Turkey. Their visit to Hagia Sophia took place in the strangest of circumstances. For reasons which are not absolutely clear, he and Swainson were unable to gain admission. An American lady named Margaret Crosby and her two daughters, Edith and Grace, were staying at the same hotel as Lethaby and Swainson, and were able to visit the mosque on the strength of Margaret's son's position as a judge in Alexandria. Lethaby and Swainson joined their party in clothes lent to them by the two daughters. From this cross-dressing visit came Lethaby's book *Sancta Sophia,* and also his marriage to Edith Crosby eight years later.

Lethaby's disguise in Hagia Sophia led to another kind of performance in the book itself – that of ventriloquism. The text approaches its subject obliquely by using the voices of others. First there is the scholarship in which the book is solidly grounded. This is dominated by Salzenberg's 'great work', *Ancient Christian Architecture in Constantinople*,[201] and is supplemented by other nineteenth-century writers such as John Mason Neale on the ecclesiology of the Eastern Church, and the French art historian Charles Bayet, whose *Byzantine Art* of 1883 (as we have seen) was one of the few books to deal extensively with Byzantine art. So it is that Lethaby draws on examples of Byzantine scholarship from many countries, but alongside them he includes the voluptuous sensuousness of Paul the Silentiary's famous encomium 'The Magnificence of Hagia Sophia', which is translated into English without comment.

Although Lethaby has no problem identifying Hagia Sophia with the Eastern mind, he counterbalances this impulse with a determination to see in the building the workings of reason rather than intuition. For him Hagia Sophia is 'the most interesting building on the world's surface' not because it offers architectural jouissance but because it is well-built, harmonious and splendidly proportioned. It is an emblem of integrity rather than decadence, the 'root of architecture … in sound common sense and pleasurable craftsmanship'.[202] He was fascinated by the workings of Byzantine guilds, the mutual dependency of Byzantine expertise in the building of this and other churches, the autonomy of the humble workman, and the rugged, spontaneous nature of their building techniques.

15 | Bentley and Westminster Cathedral

It is an odd quirk of fate that a man best known for his designs for needlework and church decoration should be chosen as the architect of Westminster Cathedral. Certainly, John Francis Bentley was an unlikely figure to have such greatness thrust upon him. Shy, retiring and solitary, he avoided all architectural competitions and waited passively for work to come to him. Between 1877 and 1898 he had built only four small Catholic churches and one Anglican one, together with some domestic buildings. When he entered Henry Clutton's office at the age of nineteen he had an interest in northern Italian architecture and fell under the spell of William Burges, who was working alongside Clutton. Clutton converted to Roman Catholicism, and in 1862 Bentley followed. In 1874 Gilbert Talbot, rector of the Church of the Assumption in Warwick Street, asked Bentley to remodel the church along Byzantine lines. Financial complications confined the proposed changes to an apse and a shrine (fig. 142). This, according to his daughter, was his first attempt in the style.[203]

All this was nothing compared to Westminster Cathedral. Both the physical and the symbolic scale of this structure were enormous. This was to be the largest Catholic church built in Britain since the Reformation. It was also the symbol of Catholicism reborn in Protestant Britain, a rallying point not only for Catholics in Britain, but an emblem of Catholic worship for the faithful throughout the British Empire. In 1892 Cardinal Vaughan determined to push forward with a project that had originally been set up in 1865 as a memorial to Cardinal Wiseman, and between 1892 and 1894 (when Bentley was appointed) some half-a-dozen architects were considered for the job. Bentley's daughter gives the impression that her father, retiring as ever, was nominated by Vaughan as the result of the universal approval of the architectural profession. The fact, however, is that eminent Catholic architects were in short supply.[204] As for the style of the new cathedral, Vaughan was in favour of 'the ancient Basilican or primitive form of Christian architecture'.[205]

Though Bentley agreed to take on a basilican project and to 'study the basilica in its own native haunts',[206] he was unsure at first about Vaughan's choice of style. Vaughan's reasons are familiar ones. First, it was capable of housing a large congregation, all of whom would be able to see and hear the 'great liturgies enacted'. Second, it was much cheaper than Gothic, and though the Catholic congregation was large, it was not rich. The third reason was that anything built in the Gothic style would suffer by comparison with the authenticity of nearby Westminster Abbey. The basilican mode also had the advantage of recolonizing the past. The Anglicans might have taken over Canterbury and Westminster, but in its allusions to an even more ancient and venerable past Westminster Cathedral would, in a sense, have pulled the historical rug from beneath their feet.

True to his word Bentley set off for Italy, but he was in a critical mood and, though he liked the simplicity of Sant'Ambrogio, he started out with a distaste for basilicas. The duomo of Florence was, he said, 'architecturally the worst large building [he had] ever seen', soon to be superseded in his estimation by St Peter's in Rome.[207] He moved on without pause to Assisi, Perugia, Ravenna (where he was deeply impressed by San Vitale), Bologna and Ferrara. But a 'minute

Britain Bentley and Westminster Cathedral

142 J.F Bentley, apse mosaic, 1874. Church of the
Assumption, Warwick Street, London

study' of San Marco and Torcello in Venice finally won him over to an early style, so that when he was prevented from continuing to Constantinople by a cholera epidemic he consoled himself with the fact that Lethaby's *Sancta Sophia* told him all he wished to know.

The result of his travels was a tantalizingly enigmatic building (see fig. 1). Lethaby suggested that it was based on 'Romanesque examples in the south-west of France and in Lombardy', and possibly the 'Byzantine church of St Irene, Constantinople';[208] Cardinal Vaughan added Palermo, Rome, Ravenna, Milan and Venice.[209] Bentley himself offered a number of accounts of the style, but in 1902, just before his death, said: 'It is early Christian Byzantine.' In his desire to discriminate between Byzantine and basilican, Bentley, unlike so many writers up to this date, actually set them in opposition to each other. 'You must understand', he insists, 'that Byzantine must not be confounded with what is generally and loosely called the Basilica style, as for instance the new church of Montmartre, in Paris, or the Romanesque style, which is common enough in Italy and Spain. The new Cathedral will, in style, be the same as that in which St Sophia at Constantinople is built. The nearest approach to it in Italy are the churches of St Mark's, Venice, and San Vitale, at Ravenna.'[210]

Although some of the clustered double arches and the delicate basketwork capitals (fig. 143) near the shrine of Our Lady of Westminster resemble both Hagia Sophia and San Vitale, the plan and the use of space at Westminster Cathedral are far more basilican than Byzantine.[211] Whereas the interior of Sacré-Coeur opens out into a vast, rising, light-filled space, and Sainte-Marie-Majeure in Marseilles offers a cavernous series of openings and arches culminating in the space of the sanctuary, Westminster's mysteriously crepuscular interior leads the eye from the shallow narthex to the high altar without interruption (fig. 145). The horizontality is increased by red and white marble banding which follows the eye-line, and by the fact that the whole upper part of the building, including the shallow domes, is lost in the darkness of dark coloured brick. Whereas everything in Hagia Sophia is designed to unsettle, disorientate and disturb, everything in Westminster Cathedral is designed to reassure, stabilize and consolidate. The massive exposed piers with the curtain wall dropped behind them and the logical geometrical division of space evident in the elevation all lend a sense of inevitability and security.

Partly because the structure of the cathedral was the vision of a single man it was swiftly put in place, and by 1903, a mere seven years after building began, it was largely complete.[212] The interior decoration, which involved large numbers of people, was quite a different matter. It produced a saga of changed opinions, discussions, debates and uncertainties which continued for at least another seventy years. The decoration was entirely a twentieth-century affair and presents a fascinating picture of that century trying to come to terms with a period which was remote in style and alien in culture. It is also a story of attempts to reconcile strongly conflicting attitudes and ideas. These were dominated by four main issues: first, there was the question of Bentley's intentions; second, the role of the decoration in relation to Catholic dogma; third, the aesthetics of the work were hugely controversial; and fourth, the authenticity of its Byzantinism was persistently called into question. Bentley had wanted the interior covered with mosaic but in the end this was done in a

143 (left) J.F. Bentley, Byzantine capitals in the Chapel of Our Lady of Westminster, Westminster Cathedral, London

rather piecemeal way. One of the most successful areas was the chapel of St Andrew, opened in 1915. Though it was controversial at the time, the cool sea-green effect of this design, with its maritime creatures swimming across the floor and golden fish-scales on the ceiling, is a consummate piece of Arts and Crafts work (fig. 144). The wall mosaics tell the story of Saint Andrew and his visits to Amalfi, Milan and Scotland and the translations of his relics to Constantinople (fig. 146), and were designed by Robert Weir Schultz in collaboration with the draughtsman George Jack and the mosaicist Gaetano Meo. With this chapel, commissioned by the 4th Marquess of Bute, Schultz succeeded in producing something close to true Ravennite work, as the critic Charles Townsend observed.[213]

Much later, in the 1950s, attention turned to the completion of the Chapel of the Blessed Sacrament. The Russian mosaicist Boris Anrep, who was then an old man living in Paris, was persuaded to present a design based on symbols of unity and the eloquence of the Word of God.[214] This late Post-Impressionist version of Byzantium, dominated not by the traditional gold background but by pink tesserae, was unveiled in 1962. The apsidal niches contain those mystical birds, the peacock (fig. 147) and the phoenix, and here Anrep has avoided all sentimentality in favour of a vigorous, decorative approach to the medium. Anrep's is just the most recent of many versions of neo-Byzantine design in Westminster Cathedral. He makes no attempt at nineteenth-century revivalism, nor does he really fit into the category of modernism. Roger Fry thought differently, however, and as we shall see, he saw in Anrep's earlier secular work a connection between the Byzantine style and the paintings of Cézanne and Matisse.

144 (left) St. Andrew's Chapel, Westminster Cathedral, (1915)
145 (right) J.F. Bentley, nave of Westminster Cathedral, 1895–1903

146 (above) R. W. Schultz, George Jack and Gaetano Meo, mosaic image of Constantinople in St Andrew's Chapel, Westminster Cathedral, 1915

147 (below) Boris Anrep, peacock mosaic from the Chapel of the Blessed Sacrament, Westminster Cathedral, 1956–62

16 | Bloomsbury and its Critics

In Chapter Two we saw how in France the Symbolists, Maurice Denis and Émile Bernard in particular, had developed a form of iconic modernism based loosely on Byzantine models. No similar theories had been developed in Britain, but the idea was germinating in the mind of Roger Fry. In the early years of the 1890s Fry was an aspiring artist in Paris, where he claimed to have learned 'all the latest theories of the Independents, the Symbolists, the members of the Society of the Rose-Croix, and of Sâr Péladan, the Wagnerian'.[215] At the same time he was preparing to write and lecture on art himself, and in 1891 made his first visit to Italy. He was both impressed and puzzled by the Byzantine art he found there. He visited Rome to 'get some idea of early Italian art as shown in the mosaics', and Palermo, where he found the 'amalgam of marble and mosaic' beyond description.[216] When he reached Ravenna he recognized his 'state of complete ignorance' about mosaic work.

In 1894, when he went to Italy again, Fry was intrigued by the mosaic of the Raising of Lazarus in the Cappella Palatina (fig. 148) which, he wrote in his notebook, was 'not much behind Giotto'.[217] Giotto and his Byzantine predecessors were very much on Fry's mind at this time because he had been invited to give some Cambridge University Extension lectures on the subject.[218] This was followed at the end of the decade by a request from Henry Newbolt to write an 'article of 8,000 words', entitled 'Art Before Giotto' and based on those earlier lectures, for the first volume of the *Monthly Review* in 1900.

The importance of 'Art Before Giotto' lies not in its scholarship but in its methodology. Fry makes no claim to original research. Instead he sets himself up as what he calls 'the middleman between the art-historian and the amateur',[219] adopting the role of an informed critic who offers his audience a stylistic reading of the changes which took place in Byzantine art. Although, like Maurice Denis, he suggests that 'the material of all art is symbolic',[220] his attitude to Byzantine art is entirely secular and he has almost nothing to say about its symbolic significance. Instead his strategies are formalist, and at his best he produces detailed and illuminating interpretations of changes in the representation of dress or physiognomy. In short, he aestheticizes Byzantine art in ways that were most unusual at the time. The empirical feel of his interpretation is intensified by his clear and enthusiastic response to his recent visits to Pompeii and Palermo, and also by his asides on modern art. Unlike the Symbolists of the early 1890s. Fry makes no direct link between Byzantium and modernism, but we can see that links were being set up in his mind, based upon his dislike of Impressionism and what he called 'the terrible … chaos of modern art'.[221]

Although the main focus of Fry's interests in this period was Italian Renaissance painting (in 1899 he had published his successful book on Bellini), he never lost his fascination with Byzantium.[222] If anything it was deepened by his reading of Jean Paul Richter and Alicia Cameron Taylor's *The Golden Age of Classic Christian Art* (1904). This monumental study – 'epoch making', as Berenson called it[223] – seems to have been catalytic in forging the link in Fry's mind between Byzantine and modern art. Fry's review of the book in the *Athenaeum* was highly complimentary and he mentions for the first time those authorities who for him were important in Byzantine studies.[224] He also offers a formal reading of some of the mosaics in terms of modern art. Invoking a comparison between the mosaics of Sta Maria Maggiore in Rome and a head in San Vitale, Ravenna (figs. 149, 150), Fry says that 'both … show an art dependent on outline, without modelling or

relief or true chiaroscuro.' This, he claimed, was 'an art … which is essentially modern, and in which the local visual impression of objects is symbolized.'[225] The images remained in Fry's mind, re-emerging several years later when he discovered the work of Cézanne.

In the first decade of the twentieth century Byzantine studies began to build up a serious corpus of work, and it is on that foundation that Fry was able to develop his own critical and scholarly systems. In Austria Jean Paul Richter had already published *The Mosaics of Ravenna* (1878).[226] In France, Charles Diehl's *Byzantine Studies* (1905)[227] was the culmination of nearly twenty years of research. In Germany Karl Krumbacher's periodical *Byzantinische Zeitschrift* disseminated recent work in the field, while in Russia V.G. Vasiljevskij and N.P. Kondakov inaugurated work on Byzantine archaeology and art history. In the latter part of the nineteenth century Americans too began to take an interest in the art of Byzantium, a trend that culminated in the uncovering of the mosaics of Hagia Sophia by Thomas Whittemore and the Byzantine Institute of America in the early 1930s.

In 1905 Fry travelled to America on business connected with the *Burlington Magazine,* and while he was there his interest in Byzantium was given added impetus by a visit to Boston and the Isabella Stewart Gardner Museum. There he met both Mrs Gardner herself and the deputy director of the Boston Museum of Fine Arts, Matthew Prichard, who was to play a significant backstage role in the twentieth-century reinvention of Byzantium. Prichard had been educated at New College, Oxford, and became the amanuensis to Edward Perry Warren, an expatriate Bostonian who lived in Lewes, Sussex. Prichard was learned, intelligent and eccentric, and during his time with the aesthete and collector Warren he

148 (top left) The Raising of Lazarus (detail), *c.*1150. Mosaic. Cappella Palatina, Palermo

149 (top right) Lot and his Followers (detail), 5th century. Mosaic. Sta Maria Maggiore, Rome

150 (above) Emperor Justinian (detail), *c.*548. Mosaic. San Vitale, Ravenna

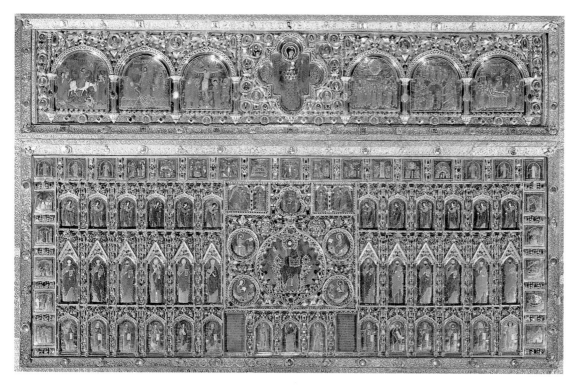

acquired a detailed knowledge of both the historical and technical aspects of classical art. During this period he was also instrumental in the business of valuing, buying and shipping art objects to Samuel Denis Warren, his employer's brother, who had been a trustee of the Isabella Stewart Gardner Museum since 1882. When S.D. Warren became president of the museum, Prichard was appointed deputy director in 1903. He was extremely well connected with a wide range of artists, dealers and museum personnel in America and Europe, but when Fry met him he was about to leave the museum and was seeking employment elsewhere.

Like Fry, Prichard had a well-developed interest in Byzantine art, and like Fry, he also had a burgeoning (but incomplete) understanding of current developments in France. On leaving Boston, Prichard spent two months in the summer of 1906 in Paris, 'absorbed in picture study',[228] during which time he met Fry once again. In 1909 Prichard underwent what his biographer calls 'a withdrawal'.[229] He rejected museums and museum life, with its materialism and treatment of art objects as symbols of personal status. He also turned against both classical and Renaissance principles of visual perception, which he felt had blighted the development of Western art. He left America, never to return, and plunged into continental Europe and the world of Byzantium. His decisive conversion to Byzantine art seems to have occurred in front of the Pala d'Oro in San Marco, two years before he left America. 'It was made', he wrote to Isabella Stewart Gardner from Italy, 'in the "dark ages" when people had foolish beliefs in angels … and I suppose I shall not ever see a more glorious page in my life-time' (fig. 151).[230] Fry was also in Venice in that same month, and may have been

151 Pala d'Oro, 796, remade 1342–5. Gold, enamel and gems, 212 × 334 cm (83½ × 131½ in). San Marco, Venice

stimulated by Prichard's enthusiasm to look once again at Byzantine work, for at around this time something triggered a connection in his mind that was to shape his whole attitude towards modern art.

The eighth annual exhibition of the International Society in London took place in January and February 1908, and included a small selection of works by Signac, Van Gogh, Cézanne, Gauguin and the first painting by Matisse to be shown outside France. In 1908 these artists were largely unknown in Britain and represented the cutting edge of the avant-garde. In trying to make sense of what was largely incomprehensible, an anonymous reviewer in the *Burlington Magazine* suggested that it was just the tired end of Impressionism.[231] Fry disagreed and defended the 'Neo-Impressionists', as he called them, by adopting a historical analogy which he had used first in his Cambridge lectures and in 'Art Before Giotto'. He saw a parallel between the work of the Impressionists (which he disliked) and the material realism of the work of the late Roman Empire. But now he added a new and important element – a further parallel between the work of the new group and the art of Byzantium. 'Impressionism', he said, 'has existed before, in the Roman art of the Empire, and it too was followed, as I believe inevitably, by a movement similar to that observable in the Neo-Impressionists – we may call it for convenience Byzantinism. In the mosaics of Sta Maria Maggiore … one can see something of this transformation from Impressionism in the original work to Byzantinism in subsequent restorations. It is probably a mistake to suppose, as is usually done, that Byzantinism was due to a loss of the technical ability to be realistic, consequent upon barbarian invasions. In the Eastern empire there was never any loss of technical skill; indeed, nothing could surpass the perfections of some Byzantine craftsmanship. Byzantinism was the necessary outcome of Impressionism, a necessary and inevitable reaction from it.'[232] 'MM Cézanne and Paul Gauguin', he wrote, are 'not really Impressionists at all. They are proto-Byzantines rather than neo-Impressionists.'[233] The label 'proto-Byzantines' did not stick, and by 1910 gave way to the more apposite 'Post-Impressionists';[234] but the idea endured, and it would not be long before both Fry and Prichard were developing further the connection between Byzantinism and modernism.

Prichard's fascination with Byzantium was more exclusive, fervent and fastidious than Fry's, and during this period he entered into a serious dialogue with Fry about the connections between Byzantine art and modern work. In the autumn of 1908, after his trip to Italy, Prichard went to live in Paris where he began a concerted study of Byzantine history and art. He also developed his interest in contemporary painting, and in January 1909 went with a friend to see some of Matisse's works. His first response was puzzlement, but by Easter Matisse, whose acquaintance Prichard now seems to have made, had become for him 'the greatest of the modern men'.[235] In November 1909 Prichard united his two preoccupations and made a direct connection between Byzantine and modern art. Whereas Fry had identified Cézanne and Gauguin as proto-Byzantines, for Prichard that role was played by Matisse. He told Isabella Gardner that he maintained his 'passion for the expression we find in Byzantine art', and how 'the symbolic expression of the East, of Byzantium' is to be found also in 'the modern French school of which Matisse is the artist most talked of'.[236]

Byzantine art was never far from Fry's mind, and it is perhaps not surprising that his involvement with the Bells seems to have stimulated an interest in Byzantium among the Bloomsbury Group. Already in 1906 Virginia Woolf had visited

Constantinople, and on her first morning had been struck by 'St Sophia, like a treble globe of bubbles frozen solid, floating out to meet us'. 'For it is fashioned', she continued in her diary, 'in the shape of some fine substance, thin as glass, blown in plump curves; save that it is also as substantial as a pyramid. Perhaps that may be its beauty …'[237] Four years later, in 1910, Duncan Grant and Maynard Keynes went to Greece and Constantinople, where they visited Hagia Sophia and the Kariye Camii, and in the spring of the following year they went to Sicily and North Africa. At the same time, in 1911, Clive and Vanessa Bell and Fry himself went to Constantinople.

On their return Vanessa Bell wrote to Fry saying: 'I'm trying to paint as if I were mosaicing not by painting in spots but by considering the picture as patches', which, she added, 'ought to give me something of the life one seems to get with mosaics'. The result of her attempts can be clearly seen in her *Byzantine Lady* of 1912 (fig. 152). Duncan Grant approved of this experiment and 'was very nice' about the pictures, saying that 'mosaic is the one thing to be done.'[238] In Sicily Grant had seen the twelfth-century mosaics at Monreale and soon after his return he was invited by Fry to offer designs for a series of murals at the Borough Polytechnic. Grant's contributions to 'London on Holiday' were *Bathing* (fig. 153) and *Football*. Contemporary critics had no doubt about the source of inspiration. The writer in the *Spectator*, for example, suggested that *Bathing* 'makes one want to swim – even in water like an early Christian mosaic', and Robert Ross, writing in the *Morning Post*, said that the water was very much like the 'strata and streaks such as you see in Christian Fifth Century mosaics at Rome or Ravenna'.[239]

Although Grant did not visit Ravenna until 1913, the influence of Byzantine linearity and decorative effects are clearly evident in *Byzantine Lady, Street Accident* and *The Queen of Sheba*. Byzantine art was also occupying Fry, since it formed the subject of a lecture at the Slade School of Art in 1911, where he spoke of the 'supernatural splendour and the ineffable glory of the divinity' of the figures in SS Cosma e Damiano, and the 'rendering [of] abstract types of divine supernatural beings' in Sant' Agnese and San Vitale.[240] He may well have been encouraged in this direction by Matthew Prichard whom he saw again in July 1911, just after his trip to Constantinople,[241] but similar tendencies can be seen in the writings of W.R. Lethaby and the archaeologist O.M. Dalton, whose work was known to Fry.[242]

152 Vanessa Bell, *Byzantine Lady*, 1912. Oil on canvas, 72.5 x 52 cm (28½ x 20½ in). UK Government Art Collection

So far the Byzantinizing impulse of these young artists had been fairly whimsical, but the arrival in their midst of Boris Anrep gave the interest a much more serious tone.

> Alone among living artists he has practically restored a lost art, and revived the tradition of the golden age of Christian art in this particular medium. Affected both by the early Byzantine traditions still surviving in Russia, together with the magnificent examples to be seen in Sta Maria Maggiore in Rome, and those of Ravenna and Palermo, he has succeeded in expressing modern conditions in terms which have too long been considered obsolete.[243]

This testimony to Anrep is by Augustus John who patronized him from the first. Anrep's early training was not as an artist but as a lawyer in his home town of St Petersburg, where he absorbed a native Byzantine tradition. According to one of his biographers he left Russia around 1907 and went with his first wife on a tour through France and Italy to Ravenna.[244] In 1908 he enrolled under J.P. Laurens at the Académie Julien, where he met Henry Lamb who introduced him into Bloomsbury. In 1910 Augustus John was so impressed by his designs for mosaic that he commissioned one for his house in Chelsea.[245] Anrep's approach to Byzantium, however, was exclusively mystical and symbolist. 'The innermost recesses of the Russian heart are filled with mystical passions,' he wrote in the introduction to the Russian section of the second Post-Impressionist exhibition of 1912. In 1913 John helped organize a one-man show for Anrep at the Chenil Gallery, for which Fry wrote the introduction, and in the following year he executed his first piece of work for Westminster Cathedral.

The period of greatest interest in Byzantine art, when Byzantinism and British modernism were most closely linked, corresponds precisely with that extraordinary moment of innovation and experimentation between 1908 and 1914 when so many established ideas were challenged or overthrown. In around 1912 Byzantinomania was at its height. Duncan Grant designed 'Byzantine' costumes for Granville Barker's *Macbeth*, and Roger Fry visited Ravenna again.[246] In the following year the *Daily Mirror* published an article on the Omega Workshops which clearly showed a reproduction of a mosaic head from Sant'Apollinare Nuovo hanging on the walls; and the signboard of the Workshops itself depicted what the one critic called 'an emaciated Byzantine youth'.[247] In 1914 Clive Bell's *Art* appeared and, whatever its shortcomings, it was long regarded as the textbook of Bloomsbury aesthetics. In it Bell popularized many of Fry's theories, including his stress on the centrality of Byzantine art for the West. Like Fry, Bell spoke of 'the thrilling design of Ravenna',[248] and offered Hagia Sophia as the supreme architectural expression of 'significant form'.[249]

153 Duncan Grant, *Bathing*, 1911. Oil on Canvas, 229 x 306.5 cm (90¼ x 120½ in). Tate, London

The fascination with Byzantium was not confined to the Bloomsbury Group, but extended to other modernists who did not share their values. T.E. Hulme, for example, the art critic of the *New Age*, was no friend of Bloomsbury. He despised their sentimental humanism, their conservative aesthetics and their élitism. Hulme admired the work of the French philosopher Henri Bergson, and in particular his attempt to find an alternative to nineteenth-century scientific determinism and his restatement of the doctrine of individual free will. In 1911 Hulme and Bergson both attended the fourth International Philosophical Congress in Bologna. During the conference the Italian government offered a tour to Ravenna. This experience was profoundly moving for Hulme, who had never before seen Byzantine mosaic, and between 1911 and 1913 he read the work of Wilhelm Worringer which confirmed for him the importance of Byzantine style in the history of culture. In his famous text *Abstraction and Empathy* (1908),[250] Worringer divided art into two tendencies: the need for empathy and the drive towards abstraction. In the first, empathetic phase, man, at ease with himself and his place in the world, creates vital, romantic, naturalistic art. The second phase, one of abstraction, 'is the outcome of a great inner unrest inspired in man by the phenomena of the outside world',[251] and results in a desire 'to create a certain abstract geometrical shape, which, being durable and permanent, shall be a refuge from the flux and impermanence of outside nature.'[252] Like Prichard, Hulme confessed a 'repugnance towards … all philosophy since the Renaissance' and he too was 'moved by Byzantine mosaic, not because it is quaint or exotic, but because it expresses an attitude I agree with.'[253] But whereas Prichard's enthusiasm for Byzantine work was developed around Bergson's intuitionism, Hulme's evolved in the context of Worringer's anti-humanism. For Hulme, Byzantium produced art which 'takes no delight in nature and no striving after vitality', and its forms are flat and geometric.[254]

From the time of his first exposure to the mosaics at Ravenna, Hulme perceived links between Byzantinism and modernism. Although he rejects most of Fry's ideas, he too uses the work of Cézanne, whom he sees as a proto-Byzantine, as a starting point. He describes the *Large Bathers* (fig. 155) as 'much more akin to the composition you find in the Byzantine mosaic [of the Empress Theodora] in Ravenna, than it is to anything which can be found in the art of the Renaissance'. In the Cézanne, 'the form is so strongly accentuated, so geometric in character, that it almost lifts the painting out of the sphere of "vital" art into that of abstract art.'[255] Referring to Duncan Grant and Vanessa Bell, Hulme dismissed the 'botched Byzantine' of Bloomsbury.[256] For him, the future lay in Picasso, Jacob Epstein, Wyndham Lewis and David Bomberg, and that future depended upon understanding the roots of their tendency to abstraction in Byzantine art (fig. 154). It was, he said, while standing before the mosaics in Ravenna that he came to understand 'how essential and necessary a geometrical character is in endeavouring to express a certain intensity.'[257]

Hulme died in 1917, but Fry continued to promote the connection between Byzantinism and modernism. In 1923, the same year that W.B. Yeats saw the neo-Byzantine work of Einar Forseth in Stockholm (fig. 4), Boris Anrep exhibited a series of mosaics called *Scenes in the Life of a Mayfair Lady* designed for the home of William and Lesley Jowitt. Fry was hugely enthusiastic about these and connected Anrep's work with Byzantine treatment of space and form: he described Anrep as 'able to treat a completely modern theme … with exactly the same sense of the monumental and resistant qualities of the medium as the Byzantine mosaicists displayed'.[258] For him, Anrep was a Byzantine in the way in which Cézanne, Gauguin and Matisse were Byzantines.

In Britain in the 1830s interest in Byzantine art and architecture had developed at the expense of the exclusive domination of the Gothic. It was presented as a purer and more primitive alternative to Gothic, and it remained in that outsider position thereafter. The centrality that Ruskin gave to the architecture and mosaics of San Marco in the 1850s was a form of passionate provocation. Though at first it was a *succès de scandale,* it rapidly won over artists and designers who were searching for fresh sources of inspiration. The mosaic revival, encouraged by royal patronage, drew attention to the peculiar beauty of Byzantine art, but the greatest force behind the Byzantine Revival in Britain was the Arts and Crafts movement. Several notable individuals with personal motives for wishing to build domes or basilicas developed the style in architecture, but its most colourful proponent was undoubtedly William Morris. Until now his name has been rather exclusively associated with medievalism, and not much has been made of the way in which he directed the attention of the Art Worker's Guild towards the East and Constantinople. Lethaby and Bentley at the end of the nineteenth century, and a host of lesser-known figures in the early twentieth, owe a debt to Morris's reinterpretation of the history of Western art and his stress on the importance of the role of Byzantium. Unlike France, Britain did not subscribe substantially to the idea of Byzantine decadence, but it was France and continental art which informed Roger Fry's reassessment of Byzantine art in formalist terms. The English tradition of Morris and the continental tradition of Fry were combined in W.B. Yeats, who in 'A Vision' and his Byzantium poems of the 1920s used the myths that had built up around Byzantium to celebrate artistic unity, visual plenitude and iconic formalism.

154 (left) Wyndham Lewis, *Indian Dance*, 1912.
Ink on paper, 27.2 x 29.2 cm (10¾ x 11½ in).
Tate, London
155 (left) Paul Cézanne, *Great Bathers, c.* 1906.
Oil on canvas. 208 x 249 cm (82 x 98¼ in).
Philadelphia Museum of Art, W.P. Wistach Collection

4 | North America

The American discovery of Byzantium was radically different from the European experience for one outstanding reason: Byzantium had played no part in the history, culture or heritage of America. America had not spent the eighteenth century distancing itself from Byzantine culture, nor had it seen a romantic resurgence of interest in the early nineteenth century.

In America there was no way in which Byzantine architecture could be used to link the present with a distant and romantic past, and in America the use of mosaic was never associated with saintliness or authoritarianism. Perhaps most importantly, the Byzantine style did not come to America laden with religious or theological associations. The connections between Byzantium and various forms of Catholicism, Anglo-Catholicism and Protestantism evaporated as the style crossed the Atlantic, so that Methodists, Jews and Episcopalians felt as easy worshipping in neo-Byzantine spaces as Roman Catholics. The early introduction of Romanesque into America had prepared the way for this aesthetic ecumenicism, but its real basis lay in the work of one of America's greatest nineteenth-century architects, Henry Hobhouse Richardson, who moulded Romanesque and Byzantine into a highly original American style. Richardson's influential achievement in making America feel comfortable with the round arch opened the way for Ralph Adams Cram and Bertram Goodhue to experiment with forms which were more purely Byzantine. Meanwhile, Louis Comfort Tiffany and John Singer Sargent, with their cosmopolitan, international outlook, felt free to plunder the East for sources of design. Tiffany in particular, using advanced techniques of production, turned to the Byzantine as just one style among others, and was the most adept in creating from it something peculiarly his own.

1 | Henry Hobhouse Richardson

The story of Byzantinism in America begins with Richardson's journey to Paris in 1859. As a student in exile during the American Civil War, Richardson spent six years in the city, first training at the Beaux-Arts in the atelier of Jules-Louis André and then working with Théodore Labrouste, brother of the more famous Henri. On his return to America in 1865 Richardson rapidly discovered a style peculiarly his own which was soon to be called 'Richardson Romanesque'. It served to change the whole direction of American architecture in the latter part of the nineteenth century and guide it out of the confusion and muddle into which it had fallen at around the time of the Civil War. But as Richardson's foremost student, James O'Gorman, points out, this style involved not only the 'Romanesque', but the 'Byzantine' and the 'Syrian' too, and it was this synthesis that Richardson used in his most important buildings of the 1880s.[1]

The Byzantine Revival in America was stylistically much further removed from originals in Constantinople or Ravenna than similar buildings in France or Britain. In America it was even more difficult to discriminate between the neo-Romanesque and neo-Byzantine styles. Moreover Richardson, like Tiffany later in the century, was no mere copyist; both men looked to the East and created something new and original out of what they found there. In fact, such is the brilliant assimilation of original models in Richardson's work that some commentators, such as Henry Russell Hitchcock, are reluctant to apply the terms Romanesque or Byzantine to it at all.[2] Yet in the broader American and French context Richardson's work can be placed only in a Romano-Byzantine framework, and that framework distinguishes it from the work of his American contemporaries.

Richardson was not the first to use Romanesque in America:[3] as early as 1844 Richard Upjohn had employed it in the Church of the Pilgrims in Brooklyn Heights,[4] and soon after this James Renwick, inspired by Robert Dale Owen (son of the social reformer Robert Owen), built the Smithsonian Institution in a Normano-Romanesque style (1846–52; fig. 157). Although it was against the competition rules, Renwick had in fact presented Dale Owen, chairman of the building committee, with both a Gothic design and the round-arched proposal that Owen finally selected. Justifying the decision in his book *Hints on Public Architecture* (1849), Owen said: 'I am not acquainted with any actual example, yet remaining from what has been variously called the Lombard, the Norman, the Romanesque and the Byzantine school, with which the Smithsonian building will not favorably compare.' He considered it 'the first edifice in the style of the twelfth century and of a character not ecclesiastical, ever erected in this country'.[5] Owen hoped that Romanesque – honest, democratic and cheap – might become the 'National Style of Architecture for America'.[6] Thomas Tefft's Union Station, Providence, Rhode Island (1848), was a splendidly Lombardic building like a Rhenish monastery, and during this period Richard Upjohn (best known as a Goth) was building Bowdoin College Chapel in Germanic Romanesque (1844–55) and Utica City Hall (1852–3) in a form of Ravennite *Rundbogenstil*. The Prague-born Leopold Eidlitz (who was later to work with Richardson on the New York State Capitol) was much influenced by the *Rundbogenstil* of Hübsch and Gärtner. Eidlitz had come to New York in 1843, worked briefly with Upjohn and then joined in partnership with the Bavarian Otto Blesch. In buildings like St George's Episcopal Church in New York (1846–8) they showed their devotion to Rhenish Romanesque and raised suspicions of 'popery' in the evangelical incumbent Stephen Higgison Tyng.[7] Similarly, the German émigré Paul Schulze built Appleton Chapel at Harvard in 1857 (destroyed in 1931) as a miniature version of the Ludwigskirche while Richardson was an undergraduate at the university.

Richardson had gone to Harvard from the Deep South in order to study engineering, but emerged as an architect – a change of direction for which we have no explanation. Following the example of Richard Morris Hunt (the first American trained at the Beaux-Arts and later founder of the American Institute of Architects), Richardson decided to go to Paris at a time when most architectural trainees went to Britain or Germany. He arrived when the Second Empire was firmly in place and urban planning – something unheard of in America – was under way with the enthusiastic support of Napoleon III. Richardson entered the Beaux-Arts (a considerable achievement for a foreigner) in 1860, and his period in Paris coincided with the rise of Baron Haussmann and the huge Second Empire building project. Some 20,000 houses were pulled down and 40,000 new ones built, squares and churches multiplied, and work had begun first on the Louvre and then the Opéra. We have already seen that this was a period when Romano-Byzantine work was hugely fashionable both in the history and in the practice of architecture. It was a period when Haussmann's great boulevards were turning Paris into what the Goncourt brothers, with unconscious irony, described as 'some future American Babylon',[8] and everywhere Richardson would have seen buildings going up in the new 'national'

157 James Renwick, Smithsonian Institution, Washington, D.C., 1856–42

Romanesque. In 1865 Julien Guadet won the Prix de Rome with a design for an Alpine Romanesque Hospice complete with a neo-Byzantine interior (fig. 63) and he was sufficiently close to Richardson to give him a signed copy of the work. Richardson was also familiar with the historical climate in which the French were developing a strong interest in the Byzantine origins of French architecture. What is particularly remarkable about his relationship with his historical sources, however, is that unlike almost every character discussed so far he saw almost nothing of the originals in his youth. Richardson's residence in Paris was dogged by financial difficulties. The Civil War in America was going against his family in New Orleans and his allowance was stopped. He was too poor to travel very far out of Paris, and it was not until his continental grand tour of 1882 that he first set eyes on Byzantine and Romanesque work in Italy and France. In the meantime he was obliged to rely on photographs and drawings. Although we do not always know when he bought them, he also had in his possession many of the books central to the Romano-Byzantine Revival, such as de Vogüe's *Central Syria* (1865), Texier and Pullen's *Byzantine Architecture* (1864), Dartien's *Study of Lombard Architecture* (1865) and Rohault de Fleury's *Monuments of Pisa* (1865).[9]

Richardson's return to America and New York in 1865 was a return to a country with no positive architectural direction. His own beginnings there were also hesitant, but his success in winning a competition for a new church in Brattle Square, Boston, in 1870 allowed him to find for the first time a style rooted in the lessons that he had learned in France. Richardson's memories of French work were reinvigorated just at this moment by the appearance of Charles F. McKim in his office. McKim, too, had had a Harvard education, followed by a brief period in Russell Sturgis's office in New York, and three years of intensive study at the Beaux-Arts. He came straight from Paris and was able to bring Richardson up to date with the developments there. In this newcomer, nine years younger than himself, Richardson found a fine and energetic draughtsman.

The Brattle church, in the words of Henry-Russell Hitchcock, suggests 'Second Empire Romanesque'. Though the detail is far from archaeological, he likens it to 'French Syrian-Romanesque work [such] as Vaudremer's St-Pierre-de-Montrouge'. St-Pierre, as we have seen (p. 85), echoed St Simeon Stylites in Syria, and had been started before Richardson left Paris.[10] Like St-Pierre, Brattle Square Church is an exercise in primitive simplicity. The tower has always been its most admired feature (fig. 158): a detached campanile, it is decorated with dramatically decisive trumpet-blowing angels by Frédéric Bartholdi, the sculptor of the Statue of Liberty, but echoes the structural simplicity of the church as a whole. Its success led directly to an invitation in 1872 to submit a design for Trinity Church, Boston, the work for which Richardson is best known. Other architects who were invited included William Potter and the well-known eclectic designer Richard Morris Hunt. Hunt's Byzantine design (fig. 159) was too great a departure from current notions of ecclesiastical architecture 'to have stood a fair chance of acceptance',[11]

158 Henry Hobhouse Richardson, tower of Brattle Square Church, Boston, 1870 according to the contemporary critic Montgomery Schuyler, and Richardson was selected as the architect for the project.[12]

The design which Richardson submitted for the Trinity Church competition was very different in appearance from the church that now stands in Copely Square. He originally planned a hemispherical dome above the crossing, surmounted by a squat tower, an octagonal lantern and a conical spire. The idea may well have been borrowed from an English church – St Paul's, Hooton, by James K. Colling – and combined with Richardson's knowledge of churches in the Auvergne.[13] But in the final design the tower was made much lower and wider, giving a more massive quality to the whole building. The great crossing tower was based on that of the cathedral at Salamanca[14] and was, said Richardson, 'a reminiscence, perhaps, of the domes of Venice and Constantinople'.[15]

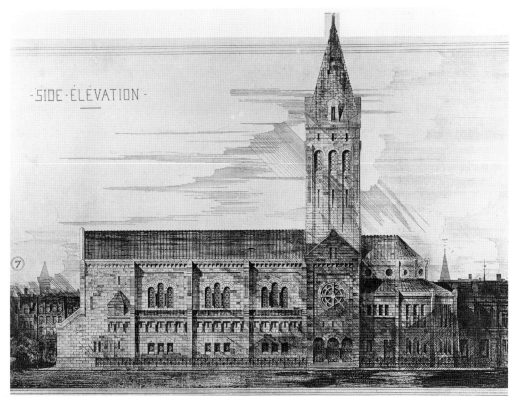

-SIDE·ÉLÉVATION·

That majestic sense of presence was increased by the famous and intricately carved porch (fig. 160). This was envisaged by Richardson, but not constructed until the 1890s when it replaced the simple round-arched west porch left at Richardson's death. Perhaps the most 'Byzantine' feature of the church is John La Farge's decorative interior. Hitchcock is surely correct in likening its strong use of colour to that of San Marco,[16] and the glowing effect that La Farge managed to achieve without the aid of mosaic is certainly remarkable (fig. 161). The interior is in the shape of a Greek cross with the tower crossing over the nave. This is held up by four large supports, part columns, part pillars, that are clustered so tightly that they appear almost flat like those in San Marco. The space is open, ostensibly to communicate the voice of the incumbent, Phillips Brookes, but it also gives the interior an unusual and strongly Byzantine quality. Indeed, so open is the interior of Trinity Church that it comes as a surprise that there is no dome. Instead, the high space under the tower is covered by a flat ceiling coffered and richly decorated. But it is the colour that is especially impressive. The effect is very warm, with dark terracotta, dark red, and the pillars outlined in dark blue and gold. The barrel vaulting over the apse shines with a copper colour, and the golden wall of the apse itself is embossed with a diaper effect. The upper levels are stencilled in repeated patterns and the barrel vaults of the transept are covered with what look like examples from the pages of Owen Jones's *Grammar of Ornament*. Richardson clearly had Byzantine work in mind when he demanded a 'rich effect of color in the interior', and he may also have had in mind Julien Guadet's polychromatic interior of the Swiss hospice, but the

159 Richard Morris Hunt, competition design for Trinity Church, Boston, 1872. Engraving from the *New York Sketch Book of Architecture*, 1879

idea of mosaic had to be shelved on account of its expense.[17] What differentiates this church from San Marco is that the ornamental work is almost entirely non-figurative. Of course an Episcopalian minister would have wished to avoid suspicions of 'popery', tolerating only the large, conventionalized figures which stand around the crossing. But the eye is so accustomed to an abundance of human figures, saints, martyrs, the Virgin or the Trinity in such a strongly coloured ecclesiastical interior that their absence leaves an emptiness.

Richardson's Byzantinizing tendencies were taken up again in the interior decoration of the New York State Capitol building in Albany of 1878 (fig. 162). The detail of the Senate Chamber is sumptuous. Above a row of settees and screens the walls are of unpolished pink Knoxville marble. On the north and south walls are square panels of golden Mexican onyx framed by yellow Siena marble. The east and west walls open into the great arches of the gallery in a manner slightly reminiscent of San Marco. These arches rest on heavy columns of highly polished red-brown granite, and have voussoirs of Siena marble selected for their variegated grains. The work, says Hitchcock, is suggestive of 'Byzantine luxury such as Richardson had only been able to imitate in paint with La Farge's help at Trinity',[18] and he goes on to draw attention to the Byzantine ornament in the fireplace at the Court of Appeals at Albany. Edward Freeman was particularly impressed by Richardson's work on the New York Capitol building, which he visited in 1882, and by the Byzantinesque arches in particular which were, he thought, 'worthy to stand at Ragusa'.[19] Because Richardson had never seen very much Romano-Byzantine work his contribution to its revival was original, personal and entirely un-archaeological; nevertheless, it is this style that dominates many of his most important works.

160 (left) Henry Hobhouse Richardson, porch
of Trinity Church, Boston, 1897
161 (right) Henry Hobhouse Richardson and John
La Farge, interior of Trinity Church, Boston, 1874–7

162 Henry Hobhouse Richardson, Senate Chamber,
New York State Capitol, Albany, NY, 1880–2

It was Richardson's European tour of 1882 which confirmed him in the view that some form of Romanesque was right for modern American architecture. In Britain he met William de Morgan and Burne-Jones at just the moment when Jones was beginning his mosaic work for Street's American Church in Rome. He also made a pilgrimage to the house of William Burges, whose architectural work he admired, though the house (which so resembled his own in its orientalizing tendencies) disappointed him. He got on extremely well with William Morris, whom he saw a couple of times, and no doubt discussed Morris's burgeoning interest in Byzantium. Architecturally, however, it was not England but southern France and Italy that most moved him. He 'fairly raved' over St-Trophîme in Arles, as a contemporary traveller from his American office put it.[20] The party moved on to Marseilles (did he see Vaudoyer's cathedral which was now well advanced, one wonders?), took a boat to Livorno and continued to Pisa, where the tower, cathedral and baptistery, which he had seen in Rohault de Fleury's *Monuments of Pisa* (1865), 'pleased him immensely'. This group of buildings, said Richardson, 'was the finest thing he had seen in Europe'.[21] Ravenna drove him into a fury of pleasure: 'Not waiting even for food, we were off sight-seeing … Mr Richardson's enthusiasm knew no bounds.' In Venice his excitement reached its peak, and 'the first thing after breakfast was always a visit to St Mark's.' It was at this time that he began to subscribe to a massive photographic and chromolithographic venture by Fernandino Ongania's publishing house. The volumes that made up *La Basilica di San Marco* (1881–95) were inspired by Ruskin's opposition to the 'restoration' of San Marco and attempted to reproduce, in every detail, the interior and exterior of the basilica. They appealed to connoisseurs of a high order, and Richardson's co-subscribers included Russell Sturgis and J. Pierpont Morgan in America, Henry Layard, Fairfax Murray and John Ruskin himself in England, Ludwig II of Bavaria, and Léonce Reynaud in France.

On his return to America Richardson's interest in Byzantine-influenced work in southern Europe continued, and he added not only Ongania's volumes to his collection but also the Architectural Association of London's *A Visit to the Domed Churches of Charente, France* (1884). By now, however, he was becoming seriously ill and he died in 1886. In a lifetime of work, Richardson had grounded American architecture within his broad understanding of ancient Mediterranean styles. At the time of his death his influence was considerable, and it continued to be felt not only in America but in other parts for the world well into the twentieth century. William A. Potter's Alexander Hall, Princeton, for example (1891–4; fig. 163), was praised by Montgomery Schuyler in 1891 for continuing the tradition briefly but powerfully initiated by Richardson. According to him, the result of Richardson's work was that 'the Provençal Romanesque has come to be more nearly the American style than any which preceded it.'[22] Schuyler also traced a line from Byzantium through San Marco to Provence, to Richardson and ultimately to contemporary American style.[23] In the same year, 1891, the Byzantinism of Richardson's style was discussed at the Royal Academy in London. In a lecture there George Aitchison (who had experimented himself with a Veneto-Byzantine office building in Mark Lane, London; see fig. 104) drew attention to the 'Byzantine air' that Richardson gave to his buildings and mentioned with approval 'the new Byzantine architecture of America'.[24]

2 | Ralph Adams Cram

One of Richardson's admirers, Ralph Adams Cram, is more closely associated with Gothic building than with Romanesque or Byzantine, but he gained much of his Eastern orientation from the work of Richardson. As he later remarked, 'Richardson burst upon an astonished world as a sort of saviour from on high … The "Brattle Street" church in Boston came first, closely followed by Trinity Church in Copley Square, and then the full tide was upon us. Town Halls, Court Houses, public libraries, college buildings, dwellings, railways stations and still more churches, poured forth in a steady and opulent stream, and we swallowed them all and clamoured for more.' Cram saw Richardson as a patriarchal, godlike figure whose effect he described in veiled sexual terms: 'Richardson was our first man, our Adam … here was the masculine element, potentially generative … bold, dominating, adventurous.' For Cram, the 'massive' and 'masculine' Trinity Church 'gave one the sort of thrill experienced on a seeing of any of the great churches of Europe – Byzantine, Norman, or Gothic', and 'for a space of time', he added, 'we were all Richardsonians.'[25]

In fact Cram's first appearance in print was a Richardsonian affair: in 1884 he wrote a letter to the *Boston Evening Transcript* protesting about a plan to build a house in front of Trinity Church. Cram was an aesthete. He admired the Pre-Raphaelites, especially Rossetti and Burne-Jones; he had read every word that Ruskin had written; he was fascinated by Gilbert and Sullivan's *Patience*, which he saw in Boston in 1882; and he might have met Oscar Wilde who visited Boston twice that year. His letter to the *Transcript* secured him the post of art correspondent and in 1884, at the age of only twenty-one, he wrote an article for the paper entitled 'A Consideration of Rubens' celebration of Color from Byzantium to Giorgione'. In 1886, the year that Richardson died, Cram made his first visit to Europe.[26] His pilgrimage was as much musical as architectural. Having heard performances of Wagner in Boston in the 1880s he had become 'a besotted Wagnerite' and, with Wagner as his 'idol'[27] and *Parsifal* his favourite work, he set off for Bayreuth where the opera had first been staged in 1882. He attended three performances which still made use of Paul von Joukowsky's Byzantine sets (see fig. 29). His early desire to visit Europe is recorded in his diaries of the 1880s, which also list all the rulers of Byzantium and coincide with the points when his interest in architecture came to dominate. Cram's brief experience of Venice was dreamlike, 'pure beauty … to a youth just escaped, for a moment, from nineteenth-century America'.[28] Designs for *Decorator and Furnisher* between 1885 and 1887 show him (in his own words) combining 'the vigor of the new [Richardsonian] Romanesque with the purity and formalism and lineal beauty of the Greek',[29] although by his own admission 'not one of us had … ever been in Southern France or Northern Spain, or even seen pictures of the churches that had been the young Richardson's inspiration.'[30]

In 1887, a year after his first trip, he returned to Italy and Rome where he was converted to Anglo-Catholicism at midnight mass on Christmas Eve in San Luigi dei Francesi. This was an emotionally traumatic period for him. Cram was homosexual or perhaps, as his biographer suggests, bisexual, but the circumstances surrounding his initiation into Byzantine architecture have strong gay overtones. Cram had gone to Rome in the role of tutor to the child of a married couple, and had entered reluctantly into what he considered to be their domestic dreariness. His meeting with, and attachment to, the architect Henry Randall was celebrated by the two men 'making careful drawings of the Cosmati and Opus Alexandrinum inlays and mosaics' in Sta Maria di Trastevere and other churches. In one of them they 'picked up two young naval officers' who told them about the sensuous pleasures of Sicily and 'how to get away from this awful climate'.[31] The 'awful climate' of Rome referred presumably as much to the heterosexual regulation of his domestic life as it did to the weather, while the pleasures of the south were not confined to architecture and mosaics. As Baron Wilhelm von Gloeden, the erotic photographer of young boys, was soon to discover, Sicily was more tolerant of unorthodox sexual mores than mainland Italy.[32] Neither Cram nor Randall had 'heard of Palermo, much less of Monreale, the Cappella Palatina, or the Martorana'; nevertheless, they took the officers' advice, promptly sailed for Sicily and stayed for three months in the 'delectable city of Palermo', revelling 'in a new world of inspiring art'.[33] The eclecticism of Byzantine mosaics, Arab inlays and Renaissance altars drove from Cram's head the purism of the Beaux-Arts and the schools in America and taught him a lesson that he said he 'never forgot'. His subsequent return to Venice 'settled the matter so far as an architectural career was concerned'. He saw Venice partly through the eyes of Ruskin and *The Stones of Venice*, which he had first read in 1876, and partly through his personal religio-erotic experience. Now San Marco seemed to him 'all sorts of things assembled and crystallized into a sort of apocalyptic unity in diversity'.[34]

Though Cram might well have picked up on the subliminally expressed eroticism of Ruskin's treatment of Venice, he could not have known that for Ruskin, too, the alternative aesthetics of Byzantium, with its mingling of the sensuous and the religious, was a flight from the puritanism of paternal rule. In Ruskin's case his passion for Venetian

164 (left) Ralph Adams Cram, competition design for St John the Divine, New York, 1889
165 (right) Bertram Goodhue, competition design for St John the Divine, New York, 1889
166 (opposite) George L. Heins and Grant La Farge, Winning design for St John the Divine, New York, 1889. Engravings in *American Architect and Building News*, 32, 9 May 1891

Byzantine was an attempt to assert himself against his father's set of aesthetic values. Ruskin's erotic attachment to the city confirmed him in his inability to conform to the demands of conventional hetero-sexuality. Cram's flight from Rome and his violent rejection of the attitudes of his employing family were in some ways similar. Like Ruskin before him and Prichard after him, he went to luxuriate in unfettered Byzantinism, first in the milder 'climate' of Sicily and then in the sterner but (given his attraction to Catholicism) religious atmosphere of San Marco. As with so many figures in this book, the rediscovery of Byzantium was also a discovery of the self, and though Cram was unable to say it directly, one suspects that his espousal of the architectural life after this trip to Italy was also a crucial moment in his coming to terms with his own homosexuality.

A balancing of architecture and eroticism was achieved when Bertram Grosvenor Goodhue entered Cram's newly formed Boston office in 1891. He was five years younger than Cram. Unlike Cram he came from a relatively poor background and had had no expensive education. In 1884, when he was fifteen and already possessed a clearly outstanding talent for architectural draughtsmanship, he was apprenticed to the firm of Renwick, Aspinall and Russell. (Renwick, it will be remembered, had been responsible for the Romanesque Smithsonian Institution back in 1852.) In 1889, the year before he met Cram, Goodhue entered a competition for the Episcopalian church of St John the Divine in New York (fig. 165). Cram also entered a design, which was eminently Richardsonian: massive, stern and somewhat forbidding (fig. 164). Goodhue's was less strongly influenced by Richardson's manner, and was in a freer Romano-Byzantine style capped with a prominent dome. Neither succeeded, however, and the Romanesque scheme of George L. Heins and Christopher Grant La Farge (John La Farge's son) was accepted instead (fig. 166).

Meanwhile Goodhue had won a competition for Dallas Cathedral (which was never built) and with this to his credit he offered himself to Cram and Wentworth in Boston. For many years Goodhue and Cram were complementary and inseparable. Cram, austere and intellectual, was the 'Roman' element in the partnership; Goodhue, spontaneous and fascinated with decoration, was the 'Byzantine' element. One contemporary, Charles Maginnis, contrasted 'the austere quality of his [Cram's] mind and the logical enterprise of his pencil' with the 'flamboyance' of Goodhue's skills, and Cram's biographer, Douglass Shand-Tucci, develops this into an explicit polarization between the 'male' and 'female' dispositions in the partnership.[35]

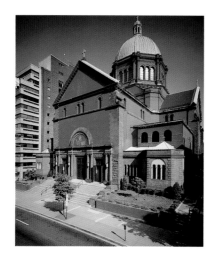

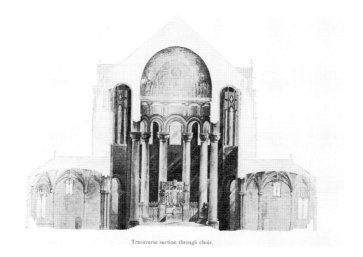

Transverse section through choir.

In the early years of the twentieth century the popularity of the Romano-Byzantine style was still running high. In 1893 La Farge had been commissioned to build St Matthew's Catholic Cathedral, Washington, D.C., in the Romano-Byzantine manner (fig. 167), and in Manhattan alone, at least six churches were being built in the same style. One of these was La Farge's St John the Divine. The planned interior was strongly Byzantine in its use of coloured marbles and mosaic, and ironically it resembled the very places that had strengthened Cram's resolve to become an architect in 1887: San Marco and the cathedral in Monreale. In 1907 La Farge wrote a defensive article in *Scribner's Magazine* in which he took great pains to stress the Gothic influence on St John's. But he failed to conceal his huge admiration for the cathedral at Monreale in 'the ancient wonderland of Sicily'. 'Like some marvellous chemical crystallization,' he wrote, 'this exquisite creation stands alone among the work of human hands';[36] and in his own drawings of the new cathedral that accompanied the piece the interior's Byzantine roots are evident (fig. 168). Yet when Cram took over as architect of the cathedral in 1911 he decided to Gothicize the remaining structure.

Although Cram admired Richardson, he had little time for the clichés of his followers which he described in 1907, as 'alien' and 'out of touch with our race and time, intrinsically aloof from our blood and impossible of ethnic adaptation'.[37] Yet Cram was no dogmatist and firmly believed in fitting architectural style to its purpose and location. This comes out most clearly in a university campus in Houston, Texas, which he was asked to design along with Goodhue in 1909. His brief was to create something for the flat and empty lands of the prairies. Edgar Odell Lovett, former Professor of Mathematics at Princeton, had been appointed as the first president of Rice University in 1907. In 1909 he interviewed various architects for the project, finally awarding the commission of the master plan and the design of four buildings to Cram, Goodhue and Ferguson. Cram had recently reshaped Princeton in Gothic, but in Houston the board of trustees dictated no style. Cram therefore tried to place himself in the position of imagining a past which had felt no Northern influences but had been developed out of the religious orders 'from the Cistercians to the Franciscans'.[38] Cram, who was very familiar with Mediterranean architecture, 'reassembled' elements from southern France and Italy, Byzantium, Sicily and Spain. Colour was used everywhere,

167 (left) Grant La Farge, St Matthew's Catholic Cathedral, Washington, D.C., 1893
168 (right) Grant La Farge, interior of St John the Divine, New York. Engraving in *Scribner's Magazine*, 41, April 1907

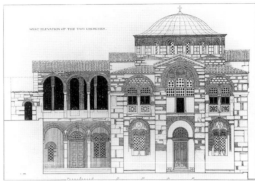

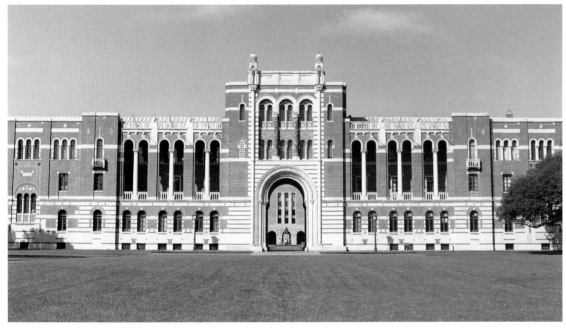

from the rose-and-dove-coloured marble from Oklahoma and red Texas granite to the many-coloured marbles from Greece, Italy and America, and a profusion of tiles.

The building known as Lovett Hall was finished first. It was based on a modified version of a strongly Byzantine design by Goodhue (fig. 169). The central domed cube, fronted with a large triumphal arch (fig. 171), has something of that twentieth-century basic Byzantine also found in Wagner's Am Steinhof (see fig. 35). According to William Ward Watkins, a draughtsman who prepared the presentation drawings of the general plan, one of the primary influences was Robert Weir Schultz and Sidney Barnsley's *The Monastery of St Luke of Stiris*, which had appeared in 1901 (fig. 170), together with the sort of ornament 'characteristic of Ravenna and of the earlier work of Venice'.[39]

169 (top left) Bertram Goodhue, preliminary design for the Administration Building (later Lovett Hall), Rice University, Houston, Texas, 1909. Engraving in *Architectural Record*, 29, January–June 1911

170 (top right) Robert Weir Schultz and Sidney Barnsley, Plate from *The Monastery of St Luke of Stiris, Phocis*, 1901

171 (above) Ralph Adams Cram and Bertram Goodhue, Lovett Hall, Rice University, Houston, Texas, 1912

3 | Louis Comfort Tiffany

In 1865, as the 27-year-old Richardson was leaving Paris to return to New York, the 17-year-old Louis Comfort Tiffany was setting sail from New York for Europe. He was shy but energetic and entrepreneurial, and his interest in Byzantine art was predominantly a stylistic one. Unlike his European counterparts earlier in the nineteenth century, he seems to have brought to it no religious, historical, social or ideological associations. The freight with which Europeans loaded Byzantine, Romanesque and Gothic seems to have had no meaning for him. Instead, the Byzantine was just one among many styles, albeit an important one, and it took its place alongside Japanese, Chinese, Persian and North African modes within his design repertoire. Like other Eastern styles it was exotic and offered the imagination an escape from the more conventional vocabulary adopted by late nineteenth-century Americans in their choice of silverware, glassware, furnishings and interiors, as well as in their choice of ecclesiastical ornaments, windows and wall decorations. Tiffany made a career and a fortune out of carefully calculated iconoclasm. This became, in its turn, an Art Nouveau orthodoxy, only to be savagely rejected by American modernism. Although Tiffany admired the creators of the British Arts and Crafts movement, he was determined to capitalize on a fashion that he and his fellow workers had created. In his later years, when both the need and desire for personal wealth diminished, he moved into a more idealistic mode, reinterpreting his aestheticism as a religion of beauty and setting up a foundation in his home, Laurelton Hall, for the education of artists and craft workers.

Tiffany was born rich and well connected. His father, Charles L. Tiffany, ran a hugely successful business in jewellery and silverware for which the refined metal was supplied by John C. Moore. John's son, Edward, had a strong predilection for Oriental objects and design. He collected vigorously and built up a substantial body of reference material which he made available to other Tiffany designers. His books included volumes on Japanese art and wallpaper, Persian art, photography of flowers from nature, Hokusai's *Manga*, Owen Jones's *The Grammar of Ornament* and Christopher Dresser's *Principles of Decorative Design*.[40] The young Tiffany, under Edward Moore's instruction, built up his own reference library and like him used it as a general source of inspiration.[41] Tiffany attended Eagleswood Military Academy and at the age of seventeen went on his first European tour through England, Ireland, France, Italy and Sicily. Samuel Bing, an old family friend and future promoter of the Art Nouveau movement, recorded that 'what impressed the young artist and filled his heart with a transport of emotion never felt before, was the sight of the Byzantine basilicas, with their dazzling mosaics', where Tiffany 'dreamed of Art for the Future'.[42]

In 1868 Tiffany returned to Paris to study for a year under Léon-Adolphe-Auguste Belly. So impressed was he by Belly's Orientalist paintings that in 1870 he went on a journey to Africa, Egypt, Tangier and Spain with a new-found friend, Samuel Colman. Tiffany's work in this period, as art historian Janet Zapata points out, is 'imbued with … atmospheric hues and Byzantine motifs'.[43]

172 Stanford White and Louis Comfort Tiffany,
Tiffany Mansion, New York, 1879

In the 1870s Tiffany and Colman began to think of ways to exploit their talents as colourists and in 1879 they set up Louis C. Tiffany and Associated Artists. Both Tiffany and Colman had been impressed by the British Arts and Crafts movement, but Tiffany in particular had no interest in its social or pedagogic idealism. He wanted Associated Artists to be 'a business … not a philanthropy or an amateur educational scheme. We are going after the money there is in art, but art is there all the same.'[44] Go for it he did, and within three years they were doing work in the White House, Washington, D.C. Tiffany's interest in Byzantium also coincided with his interest in glass. At first he had experimented at Thill's Glasshouse in Brooklyn, but by 1878 he had built a glasshouse of his own. Tiffany, of course, had no training or expertise in this difficult art, and he employed Andrea Boldini, who claimed to have come from the Murano factory of Salviati, to preside over the manufacture. Boldini, in spite of two disastrous fires, produced stained glass for windows and tesserae for mosaic on a regular basis,[45] so that by 1885 the Tiffany Glass Company was able to supply Tiffany with tesserae to create 'glowing fantasies', as Bing called them, in his own house.[46]

This was built on a plot on Madison Avenue and 72nd Street. In 1884 Louis Tiffany's wife had died and his father offered to pay for the building of a new home for his son and grandchildren. Stanford White, who had come recently from working with Richardson,[47] and Tiffany himself worked on the design[48] which was to be in the vanguard of taste, Richardson Romanesque. The raw, rugged, somewhat forbidding exterior, with its heavy rustication, was still unusual at this time (fig. 172). The outside was dominated by a 'massive arched entrance with its iron grill for a gate',[49] beyond which was an interior courtyard. The interior culminated in an exotic studio that combined many Eastern effects, including hanging Byzantine globes of glass. When Alma and Gustav Mahler visited the studio in 1908 they found themselves 'in a hall so vast it seemed boundless. Suspended in the dusk we saw luminous coloured glasses that shed a wondrous, flowery light. An organist was playing the prelude to *Parsifal*.'[50] The Wagnerian touch may have been a tribute to Mahler who was conducting Wagner in New York, but in this *Gesamtkunstwerk* sight and sound united to create a synaesthesia strongly reminiscent of the theatrical Byzantinism of Ludwig II at Neuschwanstein, whose forbidding Romanesque façade also concealed an elaborate and seductive interior. 'It was a dream,' said Alma Mahler: 'Arabian Nights in New York.'[51] One of the most prominent decorations was a mosaic placed in the drawing room. According to Tiffany, this 'floral design and a composition of peacocks by itself surpasses in richness of tones any single other ornament in the home'.[52] The design was Byzantine-inspired, and the peacock remained one of his favourite motifs throughout his life.

According to the scholar Robert Koch, Tiffany's interest in Byzantine design was strengthened in 1886 when he saw Sarah Bernhardt perform in Sardou's *Théodora* on the New York stage.[53] The Byzantine sets in particular impressed him and he incorporated some of these ideas into a stained-glass window for a New York church.[54] Tiffany's first opportunity to use Byzantine work extensively came through Samuel Colman in 1890. The hugely wealthy Louisine and Henry Osbourne Havemeyer, who were collectors on a titanic scale, wanted a suitable ambience in which to display their collections.[55] It is to their credit, however, that they did not wish to follow in the footsteps of many of

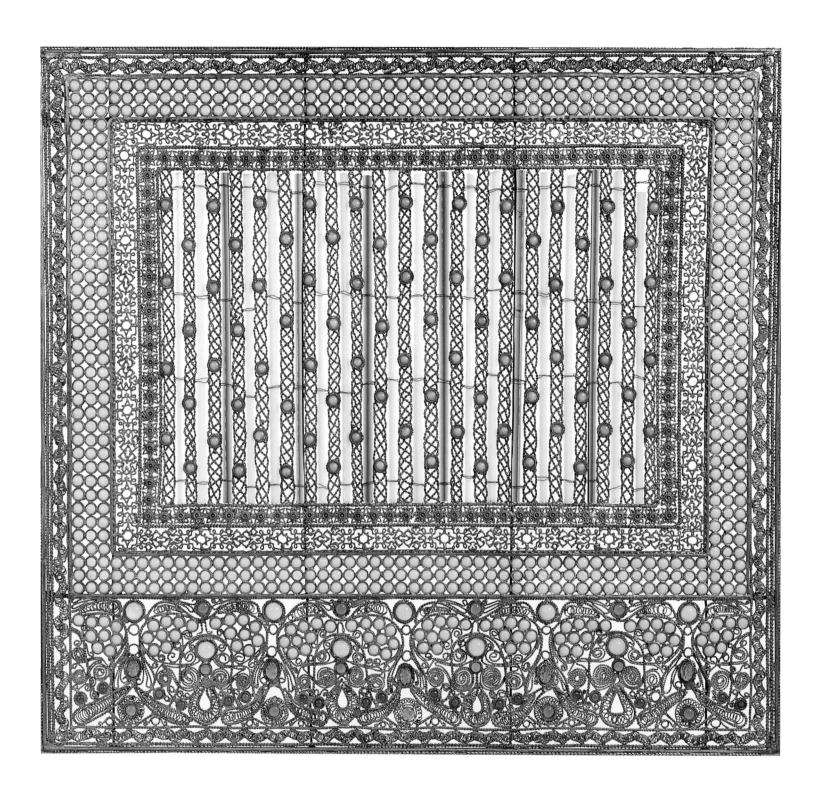

173 Louis Comfort Tiffany and Samuel Colman, fire screen from the entrance hall of the Havemeyer House, 1890–2. Gilt metal and favrile glass, 100.2 x 108.9 cm (39½ x 43 in). University of Michigan Museum of Art, Ann Arbor

their fellow millionaires by creating a replica of a French château or Italian palazzo. Instead they asked the architect Charles Haight to design a Richardsonian Romanesque house on the corner of Fifth Avenue and East 66th Street. Louisine wished to emulate the contrast between the weighty exterior and the delicate aesthetic interior that Tiffany had achieved in his own home, and in 1890 Tiffany and Colman were asked to design the interior. The Havemeyer residence was simultaneously a private house and a place for public receptions. It was intended that the Tiffany/Colman interior would blur the distinction between private and public, and possibly between sacred and profane, in what was to be a temple to art. The Byzantine style worked well in this respect. Without being specifically denominational, it communicated a sense of religious dignity and splendour to a domestic interior and effectively sanctified the materialism upon which that splendour was based.

The Byzantine inspiration might have been Louisine's. She had been hugely impressed by Ravenna and 'proud to have seen something of Byzantine art'[56] when she first visited it in around 1865 as a young girl. Her enthusiasm persisted, and she was delighted when Colman created for the Library (or Rembrandt Room) a ceiling out of the Japanese textiles that he and her husband had brought back from the Centennial Exhibition in Philadelphia in 1876. 'How shall I describe this ceiling?' she asked. 'It glows like the rich mosaic of the East, like Saint Sophia and the splendid tombs of Constantinople, like the Palatine Chapel of Palermo, the pride of Roger of Sicily. Like them our ceiling recalled the art of the East both in color and in design. The interwoven pattern of Byzantium prevailed, and when all was completed and fitted into several panels, the design was outlined by a heavy braid and it held the colors which were so beautifully distributed throughout.'[57] From the ceiling of the same room hung a pebble-and-glass Byzantine-inspired chandelier (fig. 174). Like much of Tiffany's later favrile glass, rich stones (beach pebbles in this case) were set within a bronze filigree framework, creating a Byzantinesque motif which was echoed again and again throughout the house. In the balustrade of the third-floor stairwell opalescent glass beads were wrapped in tendrils of gilt bronze, and a firescreen in the entrance hall was a much more rectilinear version of the same combination of metal and glass (fig. 173).

It was the entrance to the Havemeyer House that was the most 'Byzantine' in appearance, however (fig. 175). Here, to quote Bing once again, Tiffany 'discovered how to adopt the lofty character of Byzantine splendor to contemporary taste'.[58] The heavy doors which opened out into this secular basilican space were a variation on the bronze doors of San Giovanni in Laterano, with the original plaques replaced by coloured opalescent glass from Tiffany's furnaces (fig. 176). The first impression of the nineteenth-century visitor would have been one of ecclesiastical grandeur. The floor was covered with hundreds of thousands of small Hispano-Moresque tiles, and the walls glowed from floor to ceiling with mosaic. Since the house was destroyed in the 1940s we have only black-and-white photographs of these interiors, but Samuel Bing stressed the delicacy of the colour combinations when he wrote that Tiffany 'shifted the emphasis from oriental majesty to the soft harmonies appropriate to family living'. 'From the walls of the spacious entrance halls', he said, 'gleamed a rich variety of subtle shadings, sober,

174 Louis Comfort Tiffany and Samuel Colman, chandelier from the Library of the Havemeyer House, 1890–2. Bronze, favrile glass and beach stones. h. 177.8 cm (70 in). University of Michigan Museum of Art, Ann Arbor

chalky whites surmounted by polychrome friezes, diapered with the thousand details of woven cashmere.'[59] According to Louisine it was in Ravenna that 'Mr Tiffany found his inspiration for our white mosaic hall and the ten pillars at the entrance of our gallery', and she associated it with the Cappella Palatina in Palermo, which she considered 'the finest bit of mosaic work in Europe'.[60]

Cool, calm, tranquil and meditative, the entrance of the Havemeyer House has all the hallmarks of a Byzantine interior except, of course, that the design is almost entirely abstract and what imagery is used is secular. The abstraction of the interior's patterning reminds one of Islamic work: the frieze, for example, which encircled the hall, would have fitted well into the buildings of the Alhambra. But the focal point of the hall and its most dazzling item was the overmantle glass mosaic showing two peacocks framed by golden scrolls (fig. 177). The peacock was used extensively in Byzantine Christian art as a symbol of eternity. In the Havemeyer House Tiffany aestheticized it, but because the motif was located in a context which bore many other marks of Byzantium he was able to maintain its associations with Christianity and antiquity.

The Havemeyer interior brought Tiffany national renown as a designer of domestic interiors, but it was an ecclesiastical project that gave him truly international status. Ironically, however, it was a design not for a church but

175 (left) Louis Comfort Tiffany and Samuel Colman, entrance hall of the Havemeyer House, 1890–2
176 (right) Louis Comfort Tiffany and Samuel Colman, doors to the entrance hall of the Havemeyer House, 1890–1. Wood, copper, beach stones and favrile glass, each 245 × 91.5 cm (97 × 36 in). University of Michigan Museum of Art, Ann Arbor

177 Louis Comfort Tiffany and Samuel Colman,
peacock mosaic from the Havemeyer House,
1890–2. Favrile glass and plaster, 132.5 × 163.2 cm
(52½ × 64¼ in). University of Michigan Museum
of Art, Ann Arbor

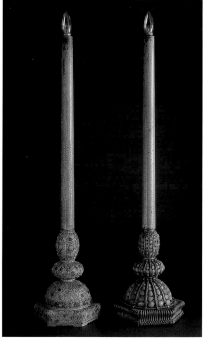

178 (left) Reconstruction of Louis Comfort Tiffany's chapel from the World's Columbian Exposition, Chicago, 1893. Charles Hosmer Morse Museum of American Art, Winter Park, Florida

179 (above right) Louis Comfort Tiffany, cross from the chapel from the World's Columbian Exposition, Chicago, 1893. Charles Hosmer Morse Museum of American Art, Winter Park, Florida

180 (below right) Louis Comfort Tiffany, two candlesticks set with glass jewels and quartz pebbles, 1893. Charles Hosmer Morse Museum of American Art, Winter Park, Florida

an advertisement. Tiffany's Byzantine chapel was one of the centrepieces in that showcase for American materialism, the World's Columbian Exposition held in Chicago in 1893. In Tiffany's remarkable display of mosaic virtuosity the peacock motif appeared once again. Tiffany himself explained the symbolism:

> For the reredos iridescent glass mosaic has been used, the design being a vine and a peacock, a bird which is found in late Roman and therefore Christian churches … and did in fact commend itself to the Hindus for two services it rendered: because it hailed the coming of the rains and because its clamour notified them of the presence of the dangerous big cats, the tiger and the leopard.[61]

Tiffany's first experiments in mosaic date back to 1879, when he used it in the Union League Club in New York. His success in the medium had been remarkable, but in 1893 he was anxious to counteract its glitzy theatricality ('well-nigh a million pieces of glass mosaic' had been used in the chapel, he told his readers) with an appeal to antiquity and primitive simplicity. In the late 1880s he had began to employ mosaic in earnest, often in ecclesiastical settings. In 1888, during the boom in church building, more than four thousand were under construction around the United States, and a 1910 account lists over thirty churches for which Tiffany Glass and Decorating Company (later Tiffany Studios) supplied materials and ornaments. It was into this market that the Columbian Chapel was intended to expand. The result was a complete chapel (fig. 178) that, according to a contemporary pamphlet, featured mosaics of Byzantine opulence in marble and glass for the floors, columns and the reredos with its peacock design.[62] At the chapel's centre was an altar on raised steps, decorated with a jewelled cross (fig. 179) with flared Byzantine ends and mounted with white topazes which, said the *Decorator and Furnisher*, were 'set so as to scintillate the light in every direction'.[63] On either side of the cross stood candlesticks set with glass jewels and quartz pebbles in gold filigree (fig. 180). As a recent critic has suggested, they are based on the work of early medieval goldsmiths and on Ottonian book covers and crucifixes.[64] The front of the altar was decorated with a jewelled wheel medallion and mosaic emblems of Saint Luke and Saint Matthew.

Surprisingly, Tiffany was highly attuned to the ecclesiastical symbolism of his work. 'A series of arches,' he wrote, 'with ornaments in relief overlaid with gold and set with jewel-like glass, represents the ciborium. The arches are supported upon mosaic-incrusted columns (fig. 181). There are inscriptions on the five steps which form the approach to the predella and three more steps which bring one to the altar … The upper three signify the Trinity, the lower the five wounds of Christ.'[65] There were also a lectern and a tabernacle in the chapel. The lectern was reproduced in the 1897 volume of the British journal *The Studio*, in which Cecilia Waern said that it was 'in pearly whites and gold, the cross inlaid in green Connemara marble and rosary beads, peacock blues prevail in the inlaid borders on the risers, dark marbles and rich deep blues in the background.'[66] The tabernacle, on the other hand, comprised a grille set with jade, amber, quartz pebbles and mussel and abalone shells, so splendid that the

181 Louis Comfort Tiffany, mosaic column, 1893. Favrile glass, mosaic and painted plaster. h. 337.8 cm (133¼ in). Metropolitan Museum of Art, New York

Jewelers' Circular featured it on the front cover of one of its later issues.[67] Tiffany's use of encrusted gems in the door of the tabernacle (fig. 182) is very reminiscent of objects in the treasury of San Marco (fig. 183). The mosaic-encrusted columns were returned to the Tiffany studio, and as late as 1926 were standing guard outside. A contemporary chromolithograph shows a hanging light fixture or 'electrolier' providing the light source. This was a fascinating amalgam of ancient and modern, composed of emerald-green turtle-back Byzantinesque glass tiles in the form of a three-dimensional cross and lit from inside by electric lights.

The chapel was a huge success. It is estimated that 1.4 million visitors came from all over the world, and there were many more who had seen it at a preview in the Tiffany offices in New York before it was sent to Chicago. The international response was extremely positive. Tiffany boasted that American glass-makers 'untrammelled by tradition were moved solely by the desire to produce a thing of beauty',[68] and many critics from abroad took up the theme of American freedom from worn-out traditions and methods. Julius Lessing, the director of the Berlin Kunstgewerbemuseum, was convinced that the Americans had struck out on a new path, and Wilhelm von Bode, director of the gallery of paintings in the Berlin Museum, claimed that he could see the seeds of a fruitful beginning for art in America. André Bouilhet, a goldsmith and member of the Union Centrale des Arts Décoratifs, praised the Tiffany chapel in an article for the *Revue des arts décoratifs*, saying that it conveyed 'the feeling of a new art [de l'art très nouveau] peculiar to the Americans'. It was Samuel Bing, however, who most strongly supported the idea of

182 (left) Louis Comfort Tiffany, tabernacle door, 1893. Jade, amber, quartz pebbles, and mussel and abalone shells. 38.7 x 29.8 cm (15¼ x 11¾ in). Charles Hosmer Morse Museum of American Art, Winter Park, Florida
183 (right) Reliquary of the True Cross, late 10th or early 11th century. Treasury of San Marco, Venice

Tiffany's 'art nouveau', and when he returned to Paris he opened a Salon de l'Art Nouveau to promote the work of Tiffany and others in France.[69] The newness of the Tiffany version of 'art nouveau' resided in its completeness of conception and its blending of a rich variety of elements into a single design concept. One of the few dissenting voices was that of Cecilia Waern, whose percipient observations anticipated attitudes to Tiffany's designs that were eventually to bring them into disfavour. 'Tiffany ecclesiastical work', she said, 'does not err on the side of baldness, as all will remember who saw the World's Fair chapel with its sumptuous wealth of Tiffany Byzantine in mosaic, scroll borders, gorgeous hanging lamps and marble inlays.' Many people, she added, might find the effect 'overripe and heavy' and 'much of it must perforce seem to purists barbaric, not to say barbarous, in taste.'[70] Although Cecilia Waern thought that Tiffany's symbolism was 'thoughtful, reverent, and –

eclectic',[71] there was no discussion in America of the religious implications of using the Byzantine style, and Episcopalians, Baptists and Jews all bought ecclesiastical objects from him.

Although Tiffany never produced such a comprehensive Byzantine scheme as the Columbian Chapel again, his subsequent work in interior design, jewellery, decorative ornament, lamps and mosaic returned again and again to this style. The lobby of the Osborne, a huge apartment block at 205 West 57th Street, was opened at about the same time as the Havemeyer House. It was designed by one of Tiffany's most active artists, the Swiss-born sculptor and painter Jacob Adolphus Holzer, as a Byzantine sanctuary and an escape from the bustle of city life (fig. 184). The walls and ceiling were covered with marbles, mother-of-pearl, iridescent glass, bas-relief sculpture and foil-backed mosaics in order to impress and subdue, with the result that this secular space was advertised as 'the most magnificently finished and decorated apartment house in the world'.[72] Holzer's work appeared again in 1892 in a Tiffany mosaic that decorated William Potter's Romanesque-style Alexander Hall at Princeton University. These were busy years for Tiffany. In 1893 the widow of Henry Field (brother of Marshall Field, the founder of the department store that still bears his name) commissioned him to design and execute a gallery for the Art Institute of Chicago. It was opened in 1894 and featured a mosaic floor, a mosaic fireplace and a frieze in metallic silver and bronze that ran round the whole gallery space. Marshall Field later commissioned an exuberant Byzantine ceiling for his famous Chicago store (fig. 156). In 1895 Tiffany provided an ambitious mosaic altar, a reredos and other fittings for Robert W. Gibson's rebuilt neo-Romanesque church of St Michael in New York, and thereafter the company supplied church interiors in a wide range of styles.

184 Jacob Adolphus Holzer, foyer of the Osborne, Central Park South, New York, c.1892

Smaller items were also constructed according to Byzantine patterns. In 1904 Tiffany produced a 'Byzantine' desk set, and in the following year designed an enamelled 'peacock' necklace (fig. 185). This was Tiffany's favourite exhibition piece.[73] The central pendant is a peacock mosaic composed of opals with gold walls between each piece. As Janet Zapata explains, this is constructed in much the same manner as cloisonné enamelling.[74] The underside of the peacock's tail is created by a black opal at the bottom, while an iron-stained matrix makes up the underside of the wings, striated to resemble feathers. The method, she adds, is 'characteristic of Byzantine work'.[75] Other pieces, too, carry a strong Byzantine imprint, and it is possible that Tiffany might have seen and been influenced by eleventh- and twelfth-century examples in J. Pierpont Morgan's collection in New York.

Towards the end of the first decade of the twentieth century the tide of taste began to turn against Tiffany. Although he was once America's foremost representative of Art Nouveau, a strong reaction set in against his historicism, his heavy decorative effects, his preference for colour above form, his hostility to classicism and his late nineteenth-century romanticism; and his shift from an avant-garde to a rearguard position took place in a very few years.

The later history of the once famous Byzantine chapel illustrates this rapid change of fortune. It returned to the Tiffany studios in New York when the Columbian Exposition closed, and in 1896 the millionairess Mrs Celia Whipple Wallace (Chicago's so-called 'Diamond Queen') bought it for the considerable sum of $40,000. She immediately offered it as a gift to the Cathedral of St John the Divine as a memorial to her son. Stylistically, the Tiffany chapel was in keeping with the original Romano-Byzantine design of the cathedral by Heins and La Farge. When both Heins and Tiffany's friend Bishop Potter died, La Farge (much to his dismay) was dismissed and R.A. Cram was asked to redesign the cathedral in the Gothic mode (see above, p. 198). But Tiffany was already going out of fashion when Cram took over as cathedral architect, and he rendered the chapel inaccessible by boarding up the crypt. Damp and decay set in, and in 1916 Tiffany applied to have it removed to a freestanding building at Laurelton Hall, his Long Island home, where it served as a memorial to Bishop Potter. At this point Tiffany himself began to withdraw from artistic modernism and from the world in general. He died in 1933, by which time both he and his work had become a matter of critical neglect and public indifference. In 1938 his Madison Avenue house was demolished, and in 1946 the trustees of his estate sold Laurelton Hall which was stripped of all that was removable, including the chapel. This was broken up and distributed around America, while the one remaining piece, the electrolier, was left to the mercy of vandals. In 1957 the house burned down.[76]

185 Louis Comfort Tiffany, 'Peacock' necklace, 1905. Gold, opals, amethysts, sapphires, rubies and emeralds. Charles Hosmer Morse Museum of American Art, Winter Park, Florida

4 | John Singer Sargent

In the same year that Tiffany's Columbian Chapel went on show in Chicago, John Singer Sargent signed a contract for a work in Boston which also had strong neo-Byzantine elements. He was persuaded by Charles McKim, the architect of the newly opened Boston Public Library, to decorate the long upper hall on the top floor. Sargent had first been approached by McKim during a visit in 1890 and he was very tempted by the idea of joining forces with Puvis de Chavannes, who had agreed to decorate the main stairway and whose mural work Sargent knew at the Panthéon. While considering the project Sargent travelled to Egypt, Athens and Constantinople. He painted a watercolour of Hagia Sophia from the Bosphorus and an interior view in oil from one of the galleries while he was inspecting the mosaics, but he later came to feel these mosaics were disappointing compared with other Byzantine work in Ravenna and Sicily. Originally the subject for the Boston project was to be taken from Spanish literature, but in the event Sargent chose 'The Triumph of Religion', inspired by the rationalist model of religious history suggested by Ernest Renan in his *History of the People of Israel* (1887–93). In his visual representation of the evolution of religious belief Sargent employed a number of different styles – Egyptian, Roman, Byzantine, Renaissance and Baroque – as equivalents for its various stages. In keeping with the humanist enterprise of the Public Library, Sargent followed Renan in adopting a positivist and detached view of the relationship between religion and civilization. The north wall represented the 'cruel, treacherous, false gods of the primitive peoples',[77] whereas the south wall carried the Christian 'Dogma of the Redemption' (fig. 186). The treatment of this wall, as one contemporary pointed out, is 'abstract and decorative in exactly the same way that the symbolic figures of a sixth-century mosaic would be'.[78] The frieze of angels, androgynous and with expressionless faces, owes something to the procession of saints that appear on the walls of Sant'Apollinare Nuovo, while beneath them runs a Latin inscription adapted from the cathedral at Cefalù which Sargent had revisited in 1897 and in 1901. Sargent, who had no time for organized religion, was using the Byzantine mode as an instrument of criticism. As a student in Paris in around 1874 he was fully aware of how Ultramontanism had employed the hieratic mode in the cause of Catholic propaganda (see above, pp. 61, 94). At that time hieratic distance had enforced authority and control; and at Boston Sargent was using hieraticism to create a critical distance between observer and subject, or to express what Sally Promey calls a kind of 'not believing'.[79] In Sargent's hands, at the beginning of the twentieth century, the relationship between Byzantinism and belief had come a long way from Hess's devout images in the Allerheiligen-Hofkirche and Flandrin's politically engaged murals in St-Germain-des-Prés. Like Tiffany, Sargent developed an American version of Byzantinism that was detached from religious or theological controversy. For both artists, too, the Byzantine was not powerfully loaded with political or social significance, but represented one among a wide range of styles involving both East and West.

186 John Singer Sargent, *The Dogma of Redemption* from the *Triumph of Religion* cycle, 1895–1916. Oil on canvas. South wall, Boston Public Library

5 | North America at the Turn of the Century

The last decade of the nineteenth century and the first decade of the twentieth produced some important, if unusual, examples of building in North America that combined Byzantine and Romanesque. One of the most outstanding was Louis Sullivan's Transportation Building at the World's Fair (or Columbian Exposition) in Chicago. This was a huge cathedral-like structure with numerous aisles containing every kind of conveyance from around the world, ranging from wagons and balloons to a model of the first railway to run between Manchester and Liverpool. This design went against the grain of the 'White City', the name by which the Exposition was known because it was built mainly in a severe Beaux-Arts style – clean, rational, centralized, classical and 'profane'. Instead, Sullivan's was a long rectangular construction, basilican in sectional form, with wide aisles flanking a central rectangular core that was illuminated by clerestory windows. Its clear allusion to Richardson and Romano-Byzantine building was confirmed by the grand entrance (fig. 187) consisting of a large, square block of richly detailed terracotta that framed a low-centred and deeply recessed arched doorway. This was named 'The Golden Doorway' on account of the reds, yellows and bronze of the coloured terracotta and the extensive use of gold leaf.[80] Just as Tiffany had carried off many medals from this Exposition, so Sullivan's Transportation Building (much to the embarrassment of local architects) was awarded the gold medal of merit by the French government.

As La Farge's St Matthew's Catholic Cathedral was nearing completion in Washington, D.C., the enigmatic choice of the Byzantine style for an Anglican church north of the border in Toronto was causing something of a stir. In 1907 the Building Committee of St Anne's decided to replace their small Gothic Revival church with a new one. A local architect, William Ford Howland, in conjunction with the Revd Lawrence Skey, drew up plans for a centralized building in the shape of a Greek cross, with a plain brick exterior and a central dome sixty feet high resting on pendentives. This was the first church in Canada to adopt the salient features of Byzantine architecture, yet paradoxically the congregation, which was working class, was composed mainly of Orangemen. Contemporaries described the interior (fig. 188) as 'most unconventional'. It has a curved apse decorated with a blue vine-scroll symbolizing the Eucharist, and is surrounded with Byzantine medallions similar to examples in San Vitale and Sant'Apollinare,

187 Louis Sullivan, 'The Golden Doorway', Transportation Building, World's Columbian Exposition, Chicago, 1893

Ravenna. The pendentives depict scenes from the life of Christ, and the dome (now gold and white) was originally painted red and contained Christian motifs. The programme of work was carried out by J.E.H. MacDonald who taught design at Ontario College of Art, and who said that he had used 'the flat treatment and strong simple colouring of the Byzantine style'.[81]

The application of the Byzantine style in North America is full of pecularities and, in contrast to its employment in Europe, it was often used with a creative indifference to historical authenticity. Why, for example, should Hornblower and Marshall choose a Romano-Byzantine fantasy for the snake pit at Washington National Zoological Park (1907), and why should the Methodist Episcopalian congregation of Asbury Park, New Jersey (1921; fig. 189) ask Smith and Warren to build a miniature version of Hagia Sophia and then call it 'Lombard Romanesque'?[82] With the Shrine of the Immaculate Conception in Washington, D.C. (1921) by Charles Maginnis, the choice of Byzantine to embody 'the highest ideals of Catholic art' is more comprehensible.[83] It seemed appropriate to choose a domed religious building in order to complement the dome on the political Capitol, and early drafts featured baroque or Renaissance models. This was modulated into a low, lanternless Byzantine dome in the final drafts, and a triumphal arch with a regular round-arched portico replaced the Greek propylaeum that appeared in the initial designs (fig. 190).

189 (left) Lucian E. Smith and Harry E. Warren,
First Methodist Espicopalian Church, Asbury Park,
New Jersey, 1921
190 (right) **Charles** Maginnis, National Shrine of the
Immaculate Conception, Washington, D.C., 1921

6 | Bertram Goodhue

This loose attachment to the past played an important part in the construction of one of the most splendid neo-Byzantine monuments in New York, the Church of St Bartholomew (fig. 191). The architect was Bertram Goodhue who, like Bentley (whom he admired), had hitherto specialized in Gothic Revival buildings. The commission for St Bartholomew's marked the divorce of the partners Cram and Goodhue, and Goodhue's first independent project. The choice of the Romano-Byzantine style was not, however, an act of creative independence on Goodhue's part but was dictated by several external factors. One of these was the design of the church that it replaced. The previous St Bartholomew's had been built in Romanesque by James Renwick in 1872. Another commitment to Romanesque took the form of a monument erected in 1902 by Alice Vanderbilt, a rich parishioner, in memory of her late husband Cornelius II. At her request Stanford White designed a large portal for the front of the church modelled closely on the twelfth-century façade of St-Gilles-du-Garde in the south of France (fig. 193). When plans for the new St Bartholomew's were drawn up in 1914 one of the conditions was that they should incorporate White's neo-Romanesque portal (fig. 192), and the building was described at this stage as unequivocally 'Romanesque'. This fitted well with the ideals of the incumbent Episcopalian minister, Leighton Parks. While he preferred Gothic aesthetically, Parks favoured Romanesque or Byzantine ideologically and theologically. For him Gothic was reminiscent of medieval Catholicism, and Parks was strongly anti-Catholic. In the earlier style he perceived what he thought was something more open, democratic, advanced and more American. For Parks the round arch suggested a Roman concern for brotherhood and community as opposed to the singular Gothic spire soaring towards heaven, an idea that goes back to Dale Owen's *Hints on Public Architecture* of 1849.[84] Goodhue's reponse to all of this was one of happy acceptance. In spite of the fact that he had been so closely associated with the Anglo-Catholic fervour of Cram, he had a distaste for organized religion and for Catholicism in particular. He also claimed that he

was uncommitted to Gothic architecture. Goodhue was unarchaeological, unscholarly and had no strong grasp, or perhaps no desire for a strong grasp, of the differences between Romanesque and Byzantine. He had a sensuous attitude to form in architecture, and in a letter he wrote in 1919 he combined two ideas that previously had been used so suggestively in the context of similar architectural fantasies. St Bartholomew's, he wrote, 'will look more like *Arabian Nights* or the last act of *Parsifal* than any Christian Church'.[85]

Goodhue's pleasure in St Bartholomew's appears to have been Eastern, and he seems to have relished the sensuousness of the materials and shapes irrespective of their precise historical precedents. He greatly admired the synthesis of motifs from southwestern France, Lombardy and Constantinople that he found in Westminster Cathedral when he visited it in 1913, thus echoing the way in which Lethaby had stressed these same influences in Bentley's work. Unlike Richardsonian Romanesque, there is a delicacy and lightness of touch in Goodhue's work; but like Richardson, Goodhue had never seen the historical models upon which his design was based. Despite not having seen them himself, in 1914 Goodhue suggested that Parks visit churches in northern Italy from which he felt St Bartholomew's derived. Most strongly he urged Parks to go to San Marco in Venice, 'the church whose plan undoubtedly inspired Périgueux and, as undoubtedly, the one I am now working on for you'.[86]

In her outstanding study of St Bartholomew's, Christine Smith shows clearly the building's debt to San Marco in terms of both plan and elevation. 'Resemblances,' she writes, 'are not only of general contour and proportional relations among the spatial parts, but also include specific structural qualities.'[87] Goodhue, of course, knew Ruskin's account of San Marco, and he had read Lethaby on its essential Greekness.[88] He must have picked up on Cram's youthful enthusiasm and had closely studied the designs of La Farge for St John the Divine. He was also acquainted with Charles Eliot Norton, a close friend of Ruskin,[89] who by this time was well known for his writing on San Marco in the Ruskinian *Church Building in the Middle Ages* (1880).

Although St Bartholomew's is a much smaller building than San Marco, it was intended, like its Venetian original, to be a highly assertive one. Goodhue planned for a substantially taller tower and dome than were actually built, so that the church would have risen proudly above Park Avenue rather than sitting rather comfortably and squatly at the feet of its gigantic neighbours as it does now. Furthermore, he wished for a much more central and Byzantinesque design. The exigencies of expense and the need to seat large numbers forced him to eliminate the tower and to extend the nave. This, in turn, produced a less exotic and more basilican building. Nevertheless, the interior, which is high and narrow, preserves something of that cavernous Byzantine quality. The space inside is strongly focused on the area under the dome (fig. 194). The transepts are merely vestigial and the side aisles are reduced to narrow arched corridors almost like tunnels. As we have seen elsewhere in buildings that echo Romano-Byzantine design, there is a strong contrast between outer and inner. Outside, Goodhue has built in crisp, boxy shapes capped with a single round dome; inside, columns cluster tightly together rising gracefully up to the rounded, voluptuous barrel-vaulted roofs. There is a strong contrast

194 Bertram Goodhue, interior of St Bartholomew's, New York, 1914–19

between the assertiveness of the exterior and the sensuality of the interior. One can see a similar binarism at work in Ludwig II's Neuschwanstein, in Richardson's Trinity Church, even in the Tiffany mansion, and one wonders if there is here, too, some unconscious desire to offer a 'masculine' persona to the world while preserving the hidden, 'feminine' interior of the private life. In the case of St Bartholomew's this contrast is strengthened by the decorative design which enhanced the church's Byzantine orientation. In 1924 Goodhue died and Parks left the church. Very little of the decoration was then in place and it was left to a new rector, Robert Norwood, to oversee its completion. Alvin Kretch, head of the Arts Committee, decided that in order to 'make St Bartholomew's Church in the City of New York a unique example of twentieth-century expression of Byzantine architecture in America', mosaic and wall decoration were imperative.[90] The decoration that resulted – the restrained honey-coloured marble in ochre and pale brown, the columns in blue, red and yellow marble that cluster around the apse, and the mosaic by Hildreth Meiere (fig. 195), who had travelled in Italy – all served to intensify the Byzantine feel of the church.[91] This was a period when the photographic documentation of Byzantine art was increasing. In 1926, for example, Hayford Pierce and Royall Tylor, Matthew Prichard's friend, published a huge compendium of coins, sculpture, plate, cups and mosaics in *Byzantine Art*. But apart from the Ravennite Transfiguration in the apse semidome, Meiere's work tends towards stylization. In the mosaics of the five interior domes depicting the six days of creation, Protestant words take priority over Roman images, and her use of birds and animals, especially the peacock, suggests something of that creative, Post-Impressionist response to the formalism of Byzantine art that Roger Fry had advocated (fig. 196). The apse and the narthex were dedicated in 1930 and they set the seal on the identity of the style of this church. It became known as 'Byzantine' and has remained so ever since.[92]

Not far from St Bartholomew's, on Park Avenue, is an even more curious exercise in the Byzantine mode. This is Christ Church, on the corner of 60th Street, for which the foundation stone was laid in 1931 just as Goodhue's church was being completed. Christ Church was a late project of Cram's and one in which he seemed to have

changed his mind about many of his earlier ideas. Gothic was no longer suitable, he felt, because 'there is something in this style that indicates domination, both spiritual and material', so he decided to 'go back to the first style that was evolved to express the Christian religion, long antedating the Gothic Catholic West'. 'A Byzantine basis', he added, 'is what we should use; and, instead of making futile efforts at domination by size, let us try to get something that will possess distinction in a jewel sort of way.'[93] He compared his work to 'the smaller churches of Palermo' and hoped that, when finished, the decoration of the interior would resemble work at Ravenna and Torcello. It is not recorded whether Cram persuaded the Methodists to adopt this style or vice-versa. Was Cram, perhaps, paying homage to his dead friend Goodhue? Or was there some rivalry between the Methodist and Episcopalian congregations? Like St Bartholomew's, Christ Church was built by a wealthy group to whom expense was no object. Christ Church is smaller than St Bartholomew's but it is perhaps even more finely polished and suave. The canopy over a Romanesque portal on Park Avenue leads into a narthex whose walls are clad in marble and whose ceiling is rich with gold mosaic. Inside, the high narrow nave is roofed with tunnel-vaulting of geometric glass mosaic in blue, gold, and red, 'after the fashion of the tomb of

196 (above) Hildreth Meiere, peacock mosaic, *c.*1930. St Bartholomew's, New York

Galla Placidia in Ravenna' (fig. 197).[94] In the nave four large columns in dark purple Levanto marble alternate with piers in *rosato d'or*. These are inset with French *fleur de pêche*. An adjoining chapel is also rich in marbles but has none of the figurative mosaics that feature in the main church. The mosaic scheme is dominated by the figure of Christ Enthroned in the semidome of the apse, 'much as in the case in the cathedral of Torcello, except that there the great figure is of the Blessed Virgin in blue'.[95] Beneath him are the four evangelists and to the left and right on the triumphal arch are the figures of John the Baptist and Moses. The Virgin is, of course, absent. The designs for these and the various medallions under the arches were supplied by Cram and Ferguson under the artistic direction of Alexander Hoyle. They were put in place by Bruno De Paoli, who worked for a firm in Long Island, and the tesserae were imported from Italy.

Both St Bartholomew's and Christ Church are essentially revival projects. They are much crisper, cleaner and less cluttered than their originals, but they made no attempt to take into account the modern movement which was well established by the 1920s. Perhaps, then, the final word in this story should lie with Bertram Goodhue's Nebraska State Capitol, Lincoln. This was his last important building. It was begun in 1920 and finished in 1932, long after the architect's death. It is one of the few buildings to incorporate Byzantine elements and yet attempt an accommodation with Modernism (fig. 198). The Capitol stands high, rising some four hundred feet over the plains of Nebraska, and covers four acres of land. It is essentially 'stretched Byzantine', in which the central tower has been pulled upwards using the steel girders of skyscraper building. In the triumphal arch with its buttresses and square portal there are clear echoes of St Bartholomew's, and in the domed octagon one can envisage the way in which Goodhue would have crowned his earlier church if he had had free rein. It was suggested by one of his draughtsmen that Goodhue was much impressed with Eliel Saarinen's recently completed Helsinki Railway Station (1906–16; fig. 199).[96] The comparison is a compelling one as both are entirely secular, but unlike Saarinen's building the Nebraska State Capitol is charged in both its general plan and its decoration with symbols

197 (opposite) Ralph Adams Cram, apse mosaic. Christ Church, Park Avenue, New York, *c.* 1939
198 (left) Bertram Goodhue, State Capitol Building, Lincoln, Nebraska, 1920–32
199 (right) Eliel Saarinen, Helsinki Railway Station, 1906–16

that emphasize its place within a wider geographical and political context. In a sense, Goodhue has created a building whose impulses derive from idealism and humanism, and in doing so he drew upon the architectural styles of both Christian and pagan religious groups.

What is implicit in the exterior becomes explicit in the interior. The decorative scheme was planned by Hartley Burr Alexander. Hildreth Meiere was again employed by Goodhue for the mosaics, and Augustus Vincent Tack for the murals. The wonderfully humanist and egalitarian mural in the basilican Governor's Suite is a reworking of the conventional Byzantine apse mosaic (fig. 200). Traditionally males take precedence in an apse space, but here a female Trinity represents Understanding, Justice and Mercy, and is surrounded by eight Virtues. The presence of females in important secular roles at Nebraska points to a new spirit in Byzantinism, and picks up on another prominent neo-Byzantine figure in another state building, namely Einar Forseth's controversial 'Queen of the Mälaren' for his wall mosaic in the Town Hall, Stockholm (see fig. 4). On the side walls around the Governor's room in Nebraska, 'Three Great Freedoms' are represented by groups of figures whose origins are to be found on the walls of the churches of Ravenna, and who were so frequently reinterpreted by artists like Flandrin and Puvis de Chavannes in the nineteenth century. It is, however, in the design and decoration of the vestibule, foyer and rotunda that the Capitol is at its most Byzantine. Goodhue left Meiere a magnificent basilican structure with narthex, domes, pendentives and floors to decorate (fig. 201). Much of the scheme is connected with the agricultural life of Nebraska, 'Reaping' in the south-east pendentive of the vestibule dome being characteristic. The medallions in the narthex represent 'Traditions of the Past', 'Life of the Present' and 'Ideals of the Future', but the climax is reached in the dome mosaic where winged and helmeted female figures represent the eight guiding Virtues of the State (fig. 202). They stand hand-in-hand in a variation of the saints of a Ravennite mosaic, with their attributions inscribed on the pedestal below, and solar iconography is substituted for Christian symbolism in the form of the sunburst which emanates from the centre of the dome.

200 Augustus Vincent Tack, *Justice, Mercy and Understanding*, 1923–8. Oil on linen. Governor's Suite, State Capitol Building, Lincoln, Nebraska

201 Hildreth Meiere, mosaic decoration, dome of the
vestibule, 1932. State Capitol Building, Lincoln,
Nebraska
Mosaic in the dome of the rotunda, State Capitol
Building, Lincoln, Nebraska
202 Hildreth Meiere, *Virtues of the State.*
Mosaic decoration, dome of the rotunda, State Capitol
Building, Lincoln, Nebraska

Conclusion   The Byzantine Revival, like the Gothic Revival, developed out of a nineteenth-century romantic impulse to return to a period that offered the fulfilment of ideals and ambitions that could not easily be realized in the present. The Gothic Revival was more widespread than its Byzantine equivalent and was supported by a powerful mythology and a corresponding literature. In contrast, the Byzantine Revival was confined largely to the arts of architecture, painting and mosaic, and had fewer similarities with native traditions. Nevertheless its neglect is surprising, and I hope that this study has shown what a rich, exotic and complex movement it was.

Interest in Byzantium was something of an outsider cult, often developed by individuals who were unorthodox or felt that they were living on the margins of their own society. The Byzantine world existed on the edge of a culture that was dominated by Greece, Rome and the Middle Ages. Neither fully Oriental nor fully Western, Christian and yet open to Muslim influence, it played no central role in the West's myth about its own origins. As the nineteenth century progressed, however, it became more and more a source of fresh attitudes and values for architects, patrons, artists and writers. The roots of this revival lie in a European interest in what we now call the Romanesque. The earlier fascination with Gothic and its magnificently elaborate decorative systems had given rise to curiosity about its predecessors. The universal pursuit of the origins of the pointed arch among architectural writers in the first part of the nineteenth century inevitably led them to investigate the deployment of the simpler, more massive round arch. Saxon, Norman, Romanesque, Ottonian and all the other variants of round-arched buildings slowly came into historical focus and all of them appeared to contemporaries to have more in common with Byzantium than with Gothic. It was Germany that gave the revived form of this style a name: *Rundbogenstil*. This was developed by Heinrich Hübsch and adopted by many architects in the second quarter of the nineteenth century, not so much as an attempt at archaeological accuracy but as an endeavour to echo something of the native German traditions of building. *Rundbogenstil* was neither Byzantine nor Romanesque, but a generalized form of both. Its principal characteristic was that, in its unadorned simplicity, it was not Gothic. German experiments with round-arched building seemed very avant-garde in the mid-nineteenth century, and their influence spread across Europe and into America where, in the hands of such creative talents as H.H. Richardson, it looked as if *Rundbogenstil* or Romanesque might become established as the principal American style. Furthermore, its simple dignity was an attractive foil to the dominance of nineteenth-century Gothic, and provided a significant trigger for the development of a more focused interest in the domed buildings of Byzantium.

Unlike neo-Gothic, which was adopted by the many, neo-Byzantine was the province of the few, and for this reason its revival was often fed by local ideological, political or psychological needs. The attraction of Byzantium often lay in its potential for theatricality and display. The Anglo-Catholic Church in Britain and the Catholic Church in both Britain and France recognized how the splendour and antiquity of Byzantium could be used to guarantee, by association, the legitimacy of ecclesiastical authority. The cathedral in Marseilles, Sacré-Coeur in Paris and Westminster Cathedral in London, for example, are bold architectural statements whose semiotics refer to the historical traditions of the Church and to its contemporary temporal and spiritual power. This theatricality also appealed to a number of individuals as a kind of 'erotics of the eye', and Byzantium provided a vehicle of expression for sensuousness in some and sensuality in others. In Germany, the rebellious cultural and sexual non-conformity of Ludwig I was connected with his desire for a lavish and exotic architecture that would make Munich stand out among European cities. His grandson Ludwig II was also drawn to Byzantium, but for different reasons: it provided him with a richly-coloured world into which he could escape from the pressures of monarchy and where his homosexuality could be given free expression in legends of chivalry and heroic knighthood. In Britain, Ruskin's championship of San Marco was a conscious act of rebellion against the architectural establishment; his love of its Eastern colour and texture, however, was expressed in terms that were replete with sensuous pleasure and an almost erotic delight. Ruskin's passion for Byzantium was taken up and developed in practical terms by architects like Scott, politicized by Morris and romanticized by Burne-Jones. In France, an overtly sensuous response was first established by Théophile Gautier, for whom San Marco was a stepping stone to the Byzantine East, and elaborated by Gustave Moreau who drew upon myths of Byzantine decadence and depravity to provide a setting for his series of pictures featuring Salome. The other side of the coin was the use of Byzantine mosaic as an emblem of saintliness and disembodied spiritual purity. From Ingres onwards the Church in France employed the hieratic quality of Byzantine design to reinforce a sense of stability and to create images of moral rectitude within a strict hierarchy of values. At the end of the century Catholic artists turned to this same stiff, ascetic, iconic style as an emblem of spirituality in reaction to the materialism of scientific realism.

Throughout the nineteenth century there was a tension between the authoritarian view of Byzantium and the egalitarian view, between the purity of Byzantine's associations with primitive Christianity (particularly in Rome) and the decadence of Byzantine life embodied in figures like Theodora, between architectural forms that were austere and 'manly', and colourful decorative elements that were sensuous and 'feminine'. In spite of Morris's romantic notions of social unity, the best neo-Byzantine works were never arrived at by any democratic process. Ludwig I's Allerheiligen-Hofkirche was a personal whim, constructed in the face of great opposition; similarly Ludwig II's building projects were the product of royal fiat, not discussion. St Paul's Cathedral received its mosaics only through the autocratic energies of Canon Gregory and the monomania of William Blake Richmond, while figures like the 3rd Marquess of Bute or Thomas Combe were able to adopt this eccentric style solely because they pushed on alone. Even the fabric of Westminster Cathedral was the creation of one man's imagination. By contrast the interior decoration of the cathedral is one of the few attempts at design by majority decision. Its Byzantine patchwork is the product of numerous committees, patrons, designers, art historians and clerics. It manages to combine nineteenth-century revivalism, Arts and Crafts skills and ideals, twentieth-century primitivism and, in some of the last Anrep mosaics, hints of twentieth-century modernism. The result is both striking and beautiful but it remains a collection of fragments. This is entirely appropriate, however, for the Byzantine moment had passed and in the ecclesiastical and aesthetic Babel that followed no one could agree what was 'Byzantine' and how best to conform to Bentley's wishes. Consequently, the unfinished cathedral is as much an emblem of aesthetic uncertainty as it is of economic deficiency.

It is remarkable how different, though no less vigorous, was the American Byzantine Revival from its counterpart in Europe. America was largely relieved of the burden of history, and though theological issues occasionally played a part in the choice of style, as at St Bartholomew's, New York, rarely were denominational questions central to decision-making. It was strange to Europeans that Methodists, rather than Episcopalians or Catholics, should build Christ Church – the most beautifully manicured neo-Byzantine church in New York – or that the most elaborate Byzantine chapel in mosaic and gold was constructed by Tiffany not for religious purposes but as an advertisement for the skills of his firm. It would be wrong to suggest that Americans chose Byzantine at random, but the conditions of choice were different, and many Europeans noticed how free from ancient prejudice was Richardson's creative employment of French form and how unrestrained was Tiffany's use of a whole range of Eastern styles. The difference between Sargent's use of Byzantine motifs and the way in which he saw them used by the Catholic Church in France sums this up rather well. In the hands of Orsel or Picot the figures from Byzantine art are models of hierarchy and control; in Sargent's hands they are objects of critical commentary and represent just one phase in the unfolding evolution of religious belief.

I am aware that, like Westminster Cathedral, this study, too, remains in a sense unfinished; it is a first word rather than a last. I have examined some, though by no means all, of the manifestations of the Byzantine Revival in the West. There remain large geographical and cultural areas where the return to Byzantium was as powerful, perhaps more so, but where the conditions were very different. I have said nothing about late nineteenth-century Russia, Serbia, Romania or Greece because here Byzantium was experienced as a survival rather than a revival, and these countries experienced a flowering of nationalistic art and architectural forms that were essentially vernacular. Nothing has been said here, either, about the choice of Byzantine style for synagogues. In this same period – from the early nineteenth to the middle of the twentieth century – the Byzantine style was one of the most popular choices for synagogue design across Europe and North America. Once again, the story is a rich and fascinating one, but beyond the scope of this book. In spite of the missing threads, however, I hope that this study has brought out the unexpected patterns, the strange alliances and affiliations, the neglected but spectacular monuments and, above all, the fascinating underground life that made up the Byzantine Revival.

Bibliography

A

'Anglicanus', 'Modern Romanesque', *Ecclesiologist*, 2 (1842–3), pp. 161–3.

A.W., 'Byzantine Decorative Colouring', *The Builder*, 20 (1862), p. 230.

Agincourt, J.-B. L.G. Seroux d', *Histoire de l'art par les monumens depuis sa décadence au IVe siècle jusqu'à son renouvellement au XVIe* (6 vols, Paris, 1823).

Albright, Daniel (ed.), *W.B. Yeats: The Poems* (London, 1990).

Architect, An, *Something on Ruskinism* (1851).

Architectural Association, *A Visit to the Domed Churches of Charente, France* (London, 1884).

Artaud de Montor, Alexis François, *Considérations sur l'état de la peinture en Italie dans les quatres siècles qui ont précédé celui de Raphael* (Paris, 1808, 1812).

Ashbee, C.R. et al, *Survey of London* (London, 1900–).

Aurier, G.-Albert, *Oeuvres posthumes* (Paris, 1892).

B

Bach, Herbert, Dietrich Mack and Egon Voss (eds), *Wagner: A Documentary History* (London, 1975).

Baker, Paul R., *Stanny: The Guilded Life of Stanford White* (New York, 1989).

Barclay, David, *Frederick William IV and the Prussian Monarch 1840–1861* (Oxford, 1995).

Barker, Nicolas, *Bibliotheca Lindesiana* (London, 1977).

Bassett, Arthur Tilney, *S. Barnabas' Oxford: a Record of Fifty Years* (London, 1919).

Baxter, Sylvester, 'The National Shrine of the Immaculate Conception', *Architectural Record*, 52 (1922), pp. 3–15.

Bayet, Charles, *L'Art byzantin* (Paris, 1883).

Bell, Clive, *Art* (London, 1914).

Beresford Hope, Alexander, 'On the Present State of Ecclesiological Science in England', *Ecclesiologist*, 7 (1847), pp. 85–91.

Bergdoll, Barry, '"The Synthesis of all I have seen": the Architecture of Edmond Duthoit (1837–89)', in Robin Middleton (ed.), *The Beaux-Arts and Nineteenth-Century French Architecture* (London, 1982, 1994).

————, *Léon Vaudoyer: Historicism in the Age of Industry* (Cambridge, Mass.,1994).

Bernard, Émile, 'Paul Cézanne', *Hommes d'aujourdhui*, no. 387 (1982), p. 2.

Betjeman, John, 'St. Barnabas, Oxford', in *Collected Poems* (London, 1980), p. 115.

Bing, Samuel, *Artistic America, Tiffany Glass and Art Nouveau* [1895], reprinted with introduction by Robert Koch (Cambridge, Mass., 1970).

Blau, Eve, *Ruskinian Gothic: the Architecture of Dean and Woodward 1845–1861* (Cambridge, 1982).

Blomfield, Arthur W., *A Description of St. Barnabas' Church, Oxford* (1871).

Boinet, Adémée, *Les Églises parisiennes* (3 vols, Paris, 1958–64).

Bolitho, Hector (ed.), *The Prince Consort and his Brother* (London, 1933).

Bolton, Arthur T., 'Richard Phené Spiers: Architect and Archaeologist', *Architectural Review*, 40 (1916), pp. 96–100.

Borsook, Eve, *Messages in Mosaic* (London, 1990).

Brooks, Michael, *John Ruskin and Victorian Architecture* (London, 1989).

Brownlee, David B., 'The First High Victorians: British Architectural Theory in the 1840s', *Architectura*, 15 (1985), pp. 33–46.

————, '*Neugriechisch/Néo Grec*: The German Vocabulary of French Romantic Architecture', *Journal of the Society of Architectural Historians*, 50 (1991), pp. 18–21.

Bruton, E.G., 'The Recent Discovery of Wall-Paintings in the Apse of Checkendon Church', *Proceedings of the Oxford Architectural and Historical Society*, n.s. 2 (1864–71), pp. 75–8.

Bullen, J.B. (ed.), *Post-Impressionists in England: The Critical Reception* (London, 1988).

————, 'A Clash of Discourses: the Reception of Venetian Painting in England 1750–1850', *Word and Image*, 8 (1992), pp. 109–23.

————, 'Ruskin, Gautier, and the Feminization of Venice', in Dinah Birch and Francis O'Gorman (eds), *Ruskin and Gender* (London, 2002), pp. 64–86.

————, 'Sara Losh, Architect, Romantic, Mythologist', *Burlington Magazine*, 143 (2001), pp. 676–84.

Bunsen, Carl Christian, *Die Basilikzen des christlichen Roms nach ihrem Zusammenhange mit Idee und Geschichte der Kirchenbaukunst* (Munich, 1823–43).

Bunsen, Frances, *Memoirs of Baron Bunsen* (2 vols, London, 1868).

Burges, William, 'Architectural Experiences at Constantinople', *Building News*, 12 February 1858, pp. 163–7.

————, 'Florence', *Ecclesiologist*, n.s. 19 (1861), pp. 155–61.

Burne-Jones, Georgiana, *Memorials of Edward Burne-Jones* (2 vols, London, 1912).

Bury, J.P.T., *France 1914–1940* (London, 1949, 1989).

Büsch, Otto (ed.), *Friedrich Wilhelm IV in seiner Zeit: Beiträge eines Colloquiums* (Berlin, 1987).

C

Chennevières, Philippe de, *Les Décorations du Panthéon* (Paris, 1885).

Collins, Judith, *The Omega Workshops* (London, 1983).

Concina, Ennio, *A History of Venetian Architecture*, translated by Judith Landry (Cambridge, 1998).

Cormack, Robin and Elizabeth Jeffreys, *Through the Looking Glass: Byzantium through British Eyes* (Aldershot, 2000).

Cornell, Elias, *Stockholm Town Hall* (Stockholm, 1965).

Corti, E.C., *Ludwig of Bavaria*, translated by E.B.G. Stamper (London, 1938).

Couchaud, André, *Choix d'églises byzantines de la Grèce* (Paris, 1841).

Cram, Ralph Adams, *The Gothic Quest* (London, 1907).

————, *My Life in Architecture* (Boston, 1936).

Crinson, Mark, *Empire Building: Orientalism and Victorian Architecture* (London, 1996).

Crook, J. Mordaunt, *William Burges and the High Victorian Dream* (London, 1981).

Csengeri, Karen (ed.), *The Collected Writings of T.E. Hulme* (Oxford, 1994).

Curzon, Robert, *Visits to Monasteries in the Levant* (1849), p. 111.

D

Dartein, Fernand de, *Étude sur l'architecture lombarde et sur les origines d'architecture romano-byzantine* (Paris, 1865).

Day, Lewis F., 'Modern Mosaic in England', *Architectural Record*, 2 (1892), pp. 79–88.

De l'Hôpital, Winefride, *Westminster Cathedral and its Architect* (2 vols, London, 1919).

Dean, Catherine, *Klimt* (London, 1996).

Denis, Maurice, *Théories, 1890–1910* (Paris, 1896, 4th edn, 1920).

Dickens, Charles, *Pictures from Italy*, ed. David Parroissen (London, 1989).

Didron, Adolphe and Paul Durand, *Manuel d'iconographie chrétienne greque et latine traduite du manuscrit byzantine, 'Le Guide de la Peinture'* (Paris, 1845).

Diehl, Charles, *Théodora, impératrice de Byzance* (Paris, 1904).

Donaldson, T.L., 'On a Certain Class of Gallo-Byzantine Churches in and near Perigueux in France', *The Builder*, 11 (1853), pp. 68–6.

Doughty, Oswald and J.R. Wahl (eds), *Letters of Dante Gabriel Rossetti* (4 vols, Oxford, 1967–).

Doyle, Peter, *Westminster Cathedral 1895–1995* (London, 1995).

Driskel, Michael Paul, 'Icon and Narrative in the Art of Ingres', *Arts Magazine*, 56 (1981), pp. 100–7.

————, 'Painting, Piety, and Politics in 1848: Hippolyte Flandrin's Emblem of Equality at Nîmes', *Art Bulletin*, 66 (1984), pp. 270–85.

————, *Representing Belief: Religion, Art, and Society in Nineteenth-Century* (Philadelphia, 1992).

E

Eggert, Klaus, *Die Hauptwerke Friedrich von Gaerters* (Munich, 1963).

Ellmann, Richard, *Oscar Wilde* (London, 1987).

F

Fairbrother, Trevor, *John Singer Sargent* (New York, 1994).

Farleigh, John (ed.), *Fifteen Craftsmen on Their Craft* (London, 1945).

Faude, Wilson H., 'Associated Artists and the American Renaissance in the Decorative Arts', *Winterthur Portfolio*, 10 (1875), pp. 101–30.

Fergusson, J.D., *Illustrated Handbook of Architecture* (2 vols, London, 1855).

Field, Cynthia R., Richard E. Stamm and Heather P. Ewing, *The Castle: An Illustrated History of the Smithsonian Building* (Washington DC, 1993).

Finlay, George, *History of the Byzantine Empire* (2 vols, London, 1853).

Flandrin, Marthe, *Les Frères Flandrin: trois jeunes peintres aux XIXe siècle: leur correspondence: le journal inédit d'Hippolyte Flandrin* (Olonne sur Mer, 1984).

Floyd, Margaret Hudson, *H.H. Richardson: A Genius for Architecture* (Boston, 1997).

Fortoul, Hippolyte, *De l'art en Allemagne* (Paris, 1841–2).

Fossati, Caspard and Louis Haghe, *Aya Sofia Constantinople as recently restored by order of H.M. the Sultan Abdul Medud* (London, 1852).

Foucart, Bruno, 'l'Église de Saint-Paul a Nîmes', *Connaissance des arts*, 394 (1984), pp. 61–6.

Fox, Stephen, *The General Plan of the William M. Rice Institute and its Architectural Development* (Houston, 1980).

Frayne, John P. and Johnson Colton (eds), *Uncollected Prose by W.B. Yeats* (2 vols, London and Basingstoke, 1975).

Freeman, Edward, *A History of Architecture* (1849).

Frelinghuysen, Alice Cooney, 'Louis Comfort Tiffany at the Metropolitan Museum of Art', *Metropolitan Museum of Art Bulletin*, 56 (1998), pp. 4–100.

Fry, Roger, 'Art Before Giotto', *Monthly Review*, 1 (1900), pp. 126–51.

————, 'The Last Phase of Impressionism', *Burlington Magazine*, 12 (1908), pp. 374–6.

————, 'Modern Mosaic and Mr Boris Anrep', *Burlington Magazine*, 42 (1923), pp. 272–7.

G

Gage, John (ed.), *Goethe on Art* (London, 1980).

Gailhabaud, Jules, *Monuments anciens et modernes* (4 vols, Paris, 1850).

Gerspach, Éduard, *La Mosaïque* (Paris, 1881).

Gibbon, Edward, *The History of the Decline and Fall of the Roman Empire*, ed. David Womersely (3 vols, London, 1776–88, 1994).

Gollwitzer, Heinz, *Ludwig I von Bayern. Konigtum im Vormärz. Eine politische Biographie* (Munich, 1986).

Gombrich, E.H., 'The Values of the Byzantine Tradition: A Documentary History of Goethe's Response to the Boisserée Collection', in Gabriel P. Weisberg, Ante Bultman Lembe and Elizabeth Holt (eds), *The Documented Image: Visions in Art History* (New York, 1987), pp. 291–308.

Görres, J., *Lohengrin* (Heidelberg, 1813).

Graf, Otto Antonia, *Otto Wagner. 7: Baukunst des Eros 1900–1918* (Vienna, 1985–2000).

Greenstead, Mary, *Gimson and the Barnsleys* (London, 1980, 1991).

Guichard, Léon (ed.), *Lettres à Judith Gautier par*

Richard Wagner et Cosima Wagner (Paris, 1964).

Gutensohn, J.G. and J.M. Knapp, *Denkmale der christlichen Religion, oder Sammlung der ältesten christlichen Kirchen oder Basiliken Roms* (Tübingen–Stuttgart, 1822–7).

H

Hafertepe, Kenneth, *America's Castle* (Washington DC, 1984).

Haltrich, Günther-Alexander, *Leo von Klenze, die Allerheiligenhofkirche in München* (Munich, 1983).

Harris, Neil, 'Louis Comfort Tiffany: the Search for Influence', in Alastair Duncan, Martin Eidelberg and Neil Harris (eds), *The Masterworks of L.C. Tiffany* (London, 1989), pp. 13–56.

Harvey, David, *Consciousness and Urban Experience* (Oxford, 1985).

Havemeyer, Louisine Waldron, *Sixteen to Sixty: Memoirs of a Collector* (New York, 1961).

Hawes, Elizabeth, *New York, New York: How the Apartment Home Transformed Life in the City 1869–1930* (New York, 1993).

Hefner-Alteneck, J.H. von, *Trachten des christlichen Mittelalters* (3 vols, Frankfurt and Darmstadt, 1840–54).

Hegel, Georg Wilhelm Friedrich, *The Philosophy of History*, translated by J. Sibree (New York, 1956).

Heinz, Gollwitzer, *Ludwig I von Bayern. Konigtum im Vormärz. Eine politische Biographie* (Munich, 1986).

Hitchcock, Henry-Russell, *The Architecture of H.H. Richardson and his Times* (Hamden, Connecticut, 1936, 1961).

_____, *Architecture: Nineteenth and Twentieth Centuries* (Harmondsworth, 1958).

Hobhouse, John Cam, *A Journey through Albania … to Constantinople* (2 vols, London, 1913).

Hope, Thomas, *A Historical Essay on Architecture* (2 vols, London, 1835).

Howard, Deborah, *The Architectural History of Venice* (London, 1989, 1987).

Howitt, Ann Mary, *An Art Student in Munich* (London, 1853).

J

Jeffares, Norman, *A New Commentary on the Poems of W.B. Yeats* (London, 1984).

John, Augustus, 'Five Modern Artists', *Vogue*, 3 October 1928, p. 104.

K

Kaplan, Julius, *The Art of Gustave Moreau: Theory, Style, and Content* (Ann Arbor, 1982).

Kelvin, Norman (ed.), *The Collected Letters of William Morris* (4 vols, New Jersey, 1984).

Koch, Robert, 'A Tiffany-Byzantine Inkwell', *Brooklyn Museum Bulletin*, 21 (1960), pp. 2–5.

Krause, Johann Heinrich, *Die Byzantiner des Mittelalters* (Halle, 1869).

Kugler, Franz, *Handbook of the History of Painting from the Age of Constantine the Great to the Present Time,*

translated by Margaret Hutton, ed. Charles Lock Eastlake (2 vols, London, 1841).

L

La Farge, C. Grant, 'The Cathedral of St John the Divine (New York)', *Scribner's Magazine*, 41 (1907), pp. 385–400.

Lane, Barbara Miller, *National Romanticism and Modern Architecture in Germany and the Scandinavian Countries* (Cambridge, 2000).

Larouche, Claude, *Paul Abadie, architecte 1812–1884* (Paris, 1988).

Layard, Henry, 'Architecture', *Quarterly Review*, 106 (1859), pp. 285–330.

Leaska, Mitchell A. (ed.), *A Passionate Apprentice: the Early Journals, 1897–1909, of Virginia Woolf* (London, 1990).

Lecky, William E.H., *History of the Rise and Influence of the Spirit of Rationalism in Europe* (London, 1865, 1910).

Lethaby, William Richard and Harold Swainson, *The Church of Sancta Sophia, Constantinople: A Study of Byzantine Building* (London, 1894).

Lethaby, William Richard, 'Westminster Cathedral', *Architectural Review*, 11 (1902), pp. 2–19.

_____, 'Richard Phené Spiers', *Journal of the Royal Institute of British Architects*, 23 (1916), pp. 334–6.

_____, *Philip Webb and His Work* (London, 1935).

Lindsay, Alexander William, *Letters on Egypt, Edom, and the Holy Land* (London, 1838, 2nd edn, 1858).

_____, *Sketches of the History of Christian Art* (3 vols, London, 1847).

M

Mackail, John William, *The life of William Morris.* (London, 1899).

Mahler, Alma, *And the Bridge is Love* (London, 1959).

Mango, Cyril, *Materials for the Study of the Mosaics of St Sophia at Istanbul* (Washington, DC, 1962).

Marchand, Leslie A. (ed.), *Byron's Letters and Journals* (11 vols, London, 1973–81).

Martin, Theodore, *The Life of His Royal Highness the Prince Consort* (5 vols, London, 1880).

Mason, Edmund J., *The Wye Valley: from River Mouth to Hereford* (1987).

Mathieu, Pierre-Louis (ed.), *L'Assembleur de rêves. Écrits complets de Gustave Moreau* (Paris, 1984).

Mcalindon, T., 'The Idea of Byzantium in William Morris and W.B. Yeats', *Modern Philology*, 64 (1966–7), pp. 307–19.

Mccomb, A.K. (ed.), *The Selected Letters of Bernard Berenson* (London, 1965).

McIntosh, Christopher, *The Swan King: Ludwig II of Bavaria* (London, 1982).

McKay, Marilyn, 'St Anne's Anglican Church, Toronto: Byzantium versus Modernity', *Journal of Canadian Art History*, 18 (1997), pp. 6–27.

McKean, Hugh F., *The Lost Treasures of Louis Comfort Tiffany* (New York, 1980).

McReady, Eric Scott, *The Nebraska State Capitol: its Design, Background, and Influence* (Unpublished PhD, University of Delaware, 1973).

Melchiori, Giorgio, *The Whole Mystery of Art* (1960).

Mercey, Frédérique, 'L'Art moderne en Allemagne', *Revue des deux mondes*, 4th series (January 1842), pp. 521–39.

Merimée, Prosper, 'Essai sur l'architecture religieuse du moyen âge', *Annuaire historique pour 1838* (Paris, 1837), pp. 283–327.

Middleton, Robin, 'The Rationalist Interpretation of Classicism of Leonce Reynaud and Viollet-le-Duc', *AA Files*, no. 11 (1986), pp. 29–48.

Moller, George, *An Essay on the Origin and Progress of Gothic Architecture Traced in and Deduced from the Ancient Edifices of Germany…from the Eighth to the Sixteenth Centuries* (London, 1824).

Montalembert, Charles de, *Du vandalisme et du Catholicisme dans l'art* (Paris, 1839).

Morris, May, (ed.), *The Collected Works of William Morris* (23 vols, London, 1910–15).

_____, *William Morris: Artist, Writer, Socialist* (New York, 1936, 1966).

Murray, Isobel (ed.), *Oscar Wilde* (Oxford, 1989).

N

Natter, Tobias G. and Gerbert Frodl, *Klimt's Women* (New Haven, 2000).

O

O'Dwyer, Frederick, *The Architecture of Deane and Woodward* (Cork, 1997).

O'Gorman, James, *H.H. Richardson: Architectural Forms for an American Society* (Chicago, 1987).

Ottewill, David, 'Robert Weir Schultz (1860–1951): An Arts and Crafts Architect', *Architectural History*, 22 (1979), pp. 88–115.

Owen, Robert Dale, *Hints on Public Architecture* (New York, 1849, 1978).

Ozanam, Frédéric, *La Civilisation au cinquième siècle* (2 vols, Paris, 1855).

P

Palgrave, Francis, *Handbook for Travellers in Northern Italy* (London, 1842).

Pardoe, Julia, *The City of the Sultan* (3 vols, London, 1838).

_____, *The Beauties of the Bosphorus* (London, 1874).

Parker, John Henry, *Mosaic Pictures in Rome and Ravenna* (Oxford and London, 1866).

_____, 'Mosaics', *Gentleman's Magazine*, 11 (1861), pp. 223–36; pp. 343–50; pp. 463–7.

Partsch, Susanna, *Klimt: Life and Work* (London, 1999).

Petit, J.L., *Remarks on Church Architecture* (London, 1841).

_____, 'Remarks on Byzantine Architecture', *Building News*, 12 March 1858, pp. 277–9.

Pevsner, Nikolaus, *The Buildings of England: Herefordshire* (Harmondsworth, 1963).

Plomer, William (ed.), *Kilvert's Diary* (London, 1999).

Promey, Salley, *Painting Religion in Public: John Singer Sargent's Triumph of Religion at the Boston Public Library* (Princeton, New Jersey, 1999).

R

Rensselaer, Mariana Griswold van, *Henry Hobhouse Richardson and his Works* (New York, 1888, 1969).

Révoil, Henri, *l'Architecture romane du midi de la France* (3 vols, Paris, 1867–73).

Richardson, H.H., 'Description of the Church', in *Consecration Services of Trinity Church* (Boston, 1877), pp. 55–70.

Rio, Alexis François, *De la poésie chrétienne* (Paris, 1836).

Robert, Cyprien, *Essai d'une philosophie de l'art* (Paris, 1836).

Rosslyn, Wendy, 'A propos of Anna Akhmatova: Boris Vasilyevich Anrep', *New Zealand Slavonic Journal*, 1 (1980), pp. 25–34.

Rubens, Godfrey, *William Richard Lethaby* (London and New York, 1986).

S

Said, Edward W., *Orientalism* (Harmondsworth, 1978, 1995).

Salles, Jules, *Notice sur l'église Saint-Paul* (Nîmes, 1849).

Salviati, Antonio, *On Mosaics: A Paper Read before the Leeds Philosophical and Literary Society, 21 February* (London, 1865).

Salzenberg, W., *Alt-christliche Baudenkmale von Constantinopel von V bis XII Jahrhundert auf Befehl seiner Majestät des Königs* (Berlin, 1854).

Sand, George, *Lettres d'un voyageur*, translated by Sacha Robinovitch and Patricia Thomson (Harmondsworth, 1987).

Schaefer, Herwin, 'Tiffany's Fame in Europe', *The Art Bulletin*, 44 (1962), pp. 309–28.

Schuyler, Montgomery, 'The Romanesque Revival in New York', *Architectural Record* (1891), pp. 8–36.

_____, *American Architecture*, ed. William H. Jordy and Ralph Coe (2 vols, Harvard, Mass., 1961).

Scott, George Gilbert, 'Byzantine and Gothic', *The Builder*, 20 (1862), p. 250.

_____, *Personal and Professional Recollections* (London, 1879).

Sécret, Jean, *Périgord Roman* (Yonne, 1968).

Shand-Tucci, Douglass, *Boston Bohemia: Ralph Adams Cram: Life and Architecture* (Boston, Mass., 1995).

Shapiro, Harold I. (ed.), *Ruskin in Italy: Letters to his Parents, 1845* (Oxford, 1972).

Sladen, Teresa, 'The Mosaics', in Chris Brooks (ed.), *The Albert Memorial* (New Haven and London, 2000), pp. 286–307.

Notes

Smith, Christine, *St. Bartholomew's in the City of New York* (New York, 1988).

_____, *The Mosaics of St Bartholomew's Church* (New York, 2000).

Smith, Lucien E. and Harry E. Warren, 'The First Methodist Episcopal Church of Ashbury Park, N.J.', *Architectural Record*, 50 (1921), pp. 472–80.

Sox, David H., *Bachelors of Art: Edward Perry Warren and the Lewes House Brotherhood* (London, 1991).

Spangenberg, Marcus, *The Throne Room in Schloss Neuschwanstein*, translated by Katherine Vanovitch (Munich, 1999).

Spiers, Richard Phené, 'The Influence of Byzantine Art in Italy (1893)', *Architecture East and West* (London, 1905), pp. 109–52.

Spirit, Jane, 'Emerging Views of Byzantium: Germs of the Modern and Its Paradoxes', *English Language in Transition*, 38 (1995), pp. 156–67.

Stallworthy, Jon, *Between the Lines: Yeats's Poetry in the Making* (Oxford, 1963).

Stamp, Gavin and Colin Amery, *Victorian Buildings of London 1837–1887* (London, 1980).

Stamp, Gavin, *Robert Weir Schultz: Architect: and his Work for the Marquess of Bute* (Mount Stuart, Ayrshire, 1981).

Street, George Edmund, *Brick and Marble Architecture in the Middle Ages* (London, 1855).

Sutton, Denys (ed.), *Letters of Roger Fry* (London, 1972).

T

Taine, Hippolyte, *Voyage en Italie* (Paris, 1866).

Texier, Charles and Richard Popplewell Pullen, *L'Architecture byzantine, ou recueil de monuments des premiers temps du Christianisme en Orient* (London and Paris, 1864).

Thompson, Paul, *William Butterfield* (London, 1971).

Tiffany, Louis Comfort and Charles DeKay, *The Art Work of Louis C. Tiffany* (New York, 1914).

Tite, Sir William, 'Memorial Chapel of St. James at Gerard's Cross', in *An Address [to] The Royal Institute of British Architects* (London, 1859), p. 37.

Titmarsh, M.A. and [W.M. Thackeray], *Notes of a Journey from Cornhill to Cairo* (London, 1846).

Toplis, Ian, *The Foreign Office: An Architectural History* (London and New York, 1987).

Twombly, Robert, *Louis Sullivan: His Life and Work* (Chicago, 1986).

U

Uckermann, René Patris d', *Ernest Hébert 1817–1908* (Paris, 1982).

V

Vergo, Peter, *Art in Vienna* (London, 1993).

Viollet-le-Duc, Eugène-Emmanuel, 'Architecture', in Barry Bergdoll (ed.), *The Foundations of Architecture: Selections from the 'Dictionnaire raisonné de l'architecture française du XIe au XVIe siècle'*, translated by Kenneth D. Whitehead (New York, 1990), pp. 31–101.

Vitet, Ludwig, 'De l'architecture Lombarde', *Revue française*, 15 (1830), pp. 151–73.

_____, 'L'Architecture byzantine en France', *Journal des savants* (1853), pp. 5–16; pp. 80–93; pp. 261–79.

Vulliamy, Justin, *Boris Anrep, 1883–1969* (London, 1973).

W

Waern, Cecilia, 'The Industrial Arts of America: The Tiffany Glass and Decorative Co', *The Studio*, 11 (1897), pp. 156–65.

Waring, J.B., *Masterpieces of Industrial Art and Sculpture at the International Exhibition 1862* (3 vols, London, 1863).

_____, *A Record of My Artistic Life* (1873), in association with Digby Wyatt.

Waterfield, Gordon, *Layard of Nineveh* (London, 1963).

Webb, Benjamin, *Continental Ecclesiology, or Church Notes in Belgium, Germany, and Italy* (London, 1848).

Wharton, Annabel, 'Westminster Cathedral: Medieval Architectures and Religious Difference', *Journal of Medieval and Early Modern Studies*, 26 (1996), pp. 525–57.

Whewell, William, *Architectural Notes on German Churches* (London, 1830).

Whitehill, Walter Muir, 'Some Correspondence of Matthew Stewart Prichard and Isabella Stewart Gardner', *Fenway Court: Art Review of the Isabella Stewart Gardner Museum*, 6 (1997), pp. 14–29.

Whitford, Frank, *Klimt* (1990).

Wiseman, Nicholas, 'Christian Art', *Dublin Review*, 22 (1847), pp. 486–515.

_____, 'Italian Guides and Tourists', *Dublin Review*, 6 (1839), pp. 1–30.

Wornum, R.N., 'The Exhibition as a Lesson in Taste', *Art Journal Catalogue* (London, 1851), pp. i★★★–xxii★★★.

Worringer, Wilhelm, *Abstraction and Empathy: a Contribution to the Psychology of Style* (London, 1953).

Wyatt, Matthew Digby and J.B. Waring, *The Byzantine and Romanesque Court in the Crystal Palace* (London, 1854).

Wyatt, Matthew Digby, 'On Pictorial Mosaic as an Architectural Embellishment', *The Builder*, 20 (1862), pp. 199–201 and 218–20.

Y

Yeats, W.B., *The Bounty of Sweden* (Dublin, 1925).

_____, *The Collected Poems of W.B. Yeats* (London and Basingstoke, 1933, 1973).

_____, *A Vision* (London and Basingstoke, 1937, 1978).

Z

Zapata, Janet, *The Jewelry and Enamels of Louis Comfort Tiffany* (London, 1993).

Foreword

1   This is a fascinating chapter in nineteenth-century history and I have touched on it elsewhere. See J.B. Bullen, 'Sara Losh, Architect, Romantic, Mythologist', *Burlington Magazine*, 143 (2001), pp. 676–84.

Introduction

1   *The Collected Poems of W.B. Yeats* (1973), p. 217.
2   The remark was deleted from the 1908 version of the story 'The Tables of the Law' and is quoted in Albright (1990), p. 630.
3   According to Jeffares (1984), pp. 211–12, he read W.G. Holmes, *The Age of Justinian and Theodora* (1905), Mrs A. Strong, *Apotheosis and After Life* (1915) and O.M. Dalton, *Byzantine Art and Archaeology* (1911).
4   Melchiori (1960), pp. 214ff., points out the importance of Yeats's visit to Sweden though he has not picked up on all the details.
5   Yeats (1925), pp. 28–9.
6   Cornell (1965), p. 17, suggests Monreale and Palermo. Miller Lane (2000), pp. 196–7, also points out the Byzantine elements in the design.
7   Stallworthy (1963), pp. 95–6. Stallworthy, however, makes nothing of the significance of the appearance of this Stockholm journey in the early draft.
8   He wrote in a contemporary letter that he bought a copy of Gibbon's *Decline and Fall of the Roman Empire* and some art books. Among these must have been Josef Strygowski's *Origins of Christian Church Art* (1923), since he consistently uses Strygowski as an authority in *A Vision*.
9   Yeats (1978), p. 279.
10 Yeats (1978), pp. 279–80.
11 Frayne and Colton Johnson (1975), 2, p. 478.

Chapter 1

1   The autobiography of Sulpiz Boisserée is quoted here from Gombrich (1987), p. 293. I am very much indebted to this chapter for information about the Boisserée brothers.
2   Quoted Gombrich (1987), p. 296.
3   Gage (1980), p. 133.
4   Gage (1980), p. 134.
5   Gage (1980), p. 137.
6   For this, see Brownlee (1991).
7   Friedrich Schlegel, *The Philosophy of History*, trans. James Robertson (London, 1846), p. 374.
8   Gollwitzer (1986), p. 745.
9   Thirty-six of his multiple affairs are recorded in the 'Gallery of Beauties' in the Nymphenburg.
10 Corti (1938), p. 156.
11 Ibid.
12 Corti suggests (p. 167) that there were as many as 87 German-speaking artists in Rome at about this time.
13 *Die Basiliken des christlichen Roms*.
14 Ludwig I to Leo von Klenze, 11 February 1818. Quoted Haltrich (1983), p. 3.
15 Corti (1938), p. 182.
16 Howitt (1853), i, 6.
17 Howitt (1853), i, 6–7.
18 *De l'art allemande*.
19 Fortoul (1841–2), i, 405ff.
20 Fortoul (1841–2), i, 106.
21 Fortoul (1841–2), ii, 118. Enthusiasm for Hess's archaism was more qualified in another important account of contemporary German art, Athanase Raczynski's *Histoire de l'art moderne en Allemagne* (*History of Modern Art in Germany*; 1836–41).
22 Mercey (1842), p. 525.
23 Mercey (1842), p. 532.
24 Howitt (1853), i, 9.
25 The term is quoted by Gerd-H Zuchold, 'Friedrich Wilhelm IV und die Byzanzrezeption in der preussischen Baukunst', in Büsch (1987), p. 221.
26 *Histoire de l'empire de Constantinople, Histoire de Constantinople, Histoire du Bas Empire*.
27 These are now in the Schloß Glienicke, Potsdam.
28 David Barclay, 'Medievalism and Monarchy in Nineteenth-Century German: Ludwig I and Frederick William IV', a conference paper kindly shown me by Professor Barclay.
29 Barclay (1995), p. 25.
30 Zuchold, op. cit., p. 224.
31 *Alt-christliche Baudenkmale von Constantinopel*.
32 Mango (1962), p. 8. This is the most substantial source of material on the restoration of Hagia Sophia in 1847–9.
33 Adalbert de Beaumont, 'Cérémonie d'inauguration de la mosquée de Sainte-Sophie de Constantinople, restaurée par Messieurs Fossati', *Revue orientale et algérienne*, 1 (1852), 160–175. p. 171.
34 The original caption is in an archive in Bellinzona and is quoted in Mango (1962), p. 14n.
35 Mango (1962), p. 19n.
36 In the event, Salzenberg's drawings were incomplete, inaccurate, but extremely beautiful, and since Fossati never published his own version in many cases Salzenberg's are the only extant record of the interior decorations. The reason for this is simple. In 1931 the Byzantine Institute, Inc, was given permission to uncover the mosaics once again and in 1953, by order of Atatürk, Hagia Sophia was transformed into a museum. Thomas Whittemore and several other archaeologists followed in Fossati's footsteps, slowly revealing the whole mosaic decoration. But, oddly, more than half of the mosaics recorded by the earlier investigators are no longer visible. Professor Cyril Mango believes that some may still be hidden from view under plaster and many may have been destroyed in the redecoration which followed an earthquake in 1894.
37 *Constantinopolis und der Bosporus*.
38 *Die Byzantiner des Mittelalters*.
39 *Le Palais Impérial de Constantinople*.
40 'In fernem Land, unnahbar euren Schritten, liegt eine Burg, die Montsalvat genannt; ein lichter Tempel stehet dort inmitten, so kostbar, als out Erden nichts bekannt; drin ein Gefäss von wundertät'gem Segen wird dort als höchstes Heiligtum bewacht: Es ward, dass sein der Menschen reinste pflegen, Herab von einer Engelschar gebracht …' Richard Wagner, *Lohengrin*, Act III, Scene ii.
41 Cosima von Bulow's Brown Book, quoted in Ulrich Müller and Peter Wapnewski, *Wagner Handbook* (Cambridge, Mass., 1992), p. 85.
42 Wagner quoted in McIntosh (1982), p. 55.
43 Spangenberg (1999), p. 18.

44 Görres, it will be remembered, was invited to Munich in 1825 by Ludwig I to establish the Chair of History. He was one of the most influential figures promoting the idea of a Catholic German state.

45 J Görres, *Lohengrin* (Heidelberg, 1813), pp. xx–xxii.

46 During the nineteenth century there was an extended debate about the symbolism and style of this building. One of the early editors, Sulpiz Boisserée, was convinced that it was Gothic; Bereseford-Hope in Britain offered the Byzantine Church of the Holy Sepulchre at Jerusalem as a model, and others in the 1870s, including F. Zarnke, identified it as Byzantine or Romanesque.

47 Ludwig II quoted in Spangenberg (1999), pp. 20–5.

48 Wagner quoted in McIntosh (1982), p. 45.

49 Wagner in McIntosh (1982), p. 45.

50 Spangenberg (1999), p. 26.

51 Dollmann quoted in Spangenberg (1999), p. 25.

52 Spangenberg (1999), p. 27.

53 Ibid.

54 Guichard (1964), p. 62. Letter 13, dated 9 November 1877.

55 Quoted in McIntosh (1982), p. 97.

56 Quoted in McIntosh (1992), p. 99.

57 Entry for 7 June 1886, quoted in McIntosh (1982), p. 159.

58 'Das Sehnen, das furchtbare Sehnen, das alle Sinne mir fasst und zwingt!/ O! – Qual der Liebe! –/ Wie alles schauert, bebt und zuckt in sündigem Verlangen! … Es starrt der Blick dumpf auf das Heilsgefass –/ Das heil'ge Blut erglüht/ … Erlöser! Heiland! Herr der Huld!/ Wie büss ich, Sünder, meine Schuld?' Wagner, *Parsifal*, Act II, Scene i.

59 With the exception of Landgravine Elizabeth of Thuringia and Queen Clotilde of France.

60 By 1898 Von Joukowsky was employed by the Tsar to decorate a monument to the Emperor Alexander II in Moscow. The mosaics were by the Salviati company. See 'Advertisments' in *A Guide to Westminster Cathedral* (London, 1902).

61 Wagner, '"Parsifal" at Bayreuth, 1882', *Richard Wagner's Prose Works*, trans. W. Ashton Ellis (1892), vi, 301–2.

62 Bach (1975), p. 249. Cosima's diary entry for 20 August 1880.

63 S. Baring Gould, *Wagner's Parsifal at Baireuth* [sic] (1892), p. 11.

64 On Wagner's historicism see H.F. Mallgrave's introduction to Otto Wagner, *Modern Architecture* (Santa Monica, 1988), pp. 30–1.

65 See Graf (1985–2000), pp. 2314ff. Critics have pointed out there are also influences from Palladio, the Roman Pantheon and Schinkel's Nikolaikirche in Potsdam. See Akos Moravánsky, *Competing Visions: Aesthetic Invention and Social Imagination in Central European Architecture 1867–1918* (Cambridge, Mass., 1998), p. 166, and Edwin Heathcote, 'Otto Wagner: Church of St Leopold am Steinhof, Vienna 1905–07', *Church Building*, 62 (2000), pp. 14–15.

66 Hitchcock (1958), p. 470.

67 Vergo (1993), p. 81.

68 Lenz, quoted in Whitford (1990), p. 86. Klimt

sent a postcard to his mother showing the interior of San Vitale.

69 Vergo (1993), p. 82.

70 Tobias G. Natter, 'Portrait of Adele Bloch-Bauer I', in Natter and Frodl (2000), p. 115.

71 A useful account of the house and frieze is given in Susanna Partsch, *Klimt: Life and Work* (London, 1999), pp. 218–28.

72 Loos quoted in Dean (1996), p. 36.

Chapter 2

1 Vitet (1830), p. 155.

2 *Histoire générale de la civilisation en Europe*.

3 *Récit des temps mérovingiens*.

4 Merimée (1837), p. 315.

5 *Essai sur les églises romanes et Romano-Byzantines du département de Puy-de-Dôme* and *Cours d'antiquités monumentales*.

6 *Les Monumens de la France*.

7 [Vaudoyer and Lenoir], 'Études d'architecture en France', *Magasin pittoresque*, 7 (1839), p. 334 n.

8 *L'Architecture byzantine en France*.

9 Verneilh was not the first to write about St-Front. In 1821 the antiquarian Joseph-Théophile de Mourcin aided Henri Taillefer in the publication of *Antiquités de Vésonne*, but he locates the church in neither local nor oriental traditions.

10 Vitet (1853).

11 Viollet-le-Duc (1990), p. 60.

12 Viollet-le-Duc (1990), p. 62.

13 Jean Secret is one of these, although he points out that without the technology to hold old masonry and stonework in place Abadie had no choice but to replace seriously decayed areas. Abadie had either to rebuild or allow the structure to collapse. Secret (1968), entry 28.

14 Abadie in 1851, quoted in Larouche (1988), p. 130, n. 1872. The artist Charles Lameire developed a project to clothe the 'nudity' of St-Front, which generated considerable debate.

15 Driskel (1981), pp. 100–7, and Driskel (1992), p. 104.

16 Artaud de Montor (1812), pp. 28–9.

17 *Le Bien et Le Mal*.

18 Montalembert (1839), p. 179 n.

19 Théophile Gautier, 'La Chapelle de la Vierge à Notre-Dame-de-Lorette', *Moniteur universel*, 15 April 1854. Quoted in Driskel (1992), p. 119.

20 *Architecture antique de la Sicile*.

21 *L'Architecture moderne de la Sicile*.

22 J. Hittorff and L. Zanth, 'Appendice sur les mosaïques de la Sicile', *Architecture moderne de la Sicile ou recueil des plus beaux monumens religieux et des edifices … de la Sicile* (Paris, 1835), p. 24.

23 Driskel (1992), p. 145.

24 *Histoire de l'art par les monumens*.

25 Agincourt (1823), 29.

26 Taine (1866), 2, p. 270.

27 *De la poésie chrétienne*.

28 Rio (1836), p. 10.

29 *Lettres d'un voyageur*.

30 Sand (1987), p. 110.

31 Robert (1836), p. 63.

32 Ozanam (1855), quoted in Driskel (1992), p. 153.

33 Albert Lenoir, 'Études Historiques sur les principaux caractères de l'architecture en France et en Italie, depuis le IVe siècle de notre ère jusqu'au XIIIe' (1834), quoted in Bergdoll (1994),

pp. 122–3.

34 In vol. 1, 1840.

35 Fortoul to his parents in 1840, quoted in Bergdoll (1994), p. 127.

36 Fourtel quoted in Middleton (1986), p. 42.

37 Mazenod quoted in Bergdoll (1994), p. 212.

38 Bergdoll (1994), p. 230.

39 Bergdoll (1994), p. 233.

40 Espérandieu to Charles Blanc, quoted in Bergdoll (1994), p. 237.

41 *Essai sur les églises romanes et romano-bysantines du département du Puy-de-Dôme*.

42 *Choix d'églises byzantines de la Grèce*.

43 Couchaud (1841), p. 1.

44 The full title of this was: *Aya Sofia, Constantinople, as recently restored by order of H.M. the Sultan Abdul Medjid* (London, 1852).

45 *Système de la Mediterranée*.

46 Bergdoll (1994), p. 254.

47 Ibid.

48 *L'Architecture arabe*.

49 *Architecture romane du midi de la France*.

50 Quoted in Foucart (1984), p. 64.

51 Flandrin (1984), p. 114.

52 Rossetti, *Letters* (1965), I, 66.

53 Driskel (1984), p. 277. My information about Flandrin's murals at Nîmes is substantially derived from this article.

54 Salles (1849), p. 30.

55 Salles (1849), p. 28.

56 Questel quoted in Driskel (1992), p. 148.

57 Driskel (1992), p. 148.

58 Klotz writing in 1841, quoted in Driskel (1992), p. 150.

59 *Moines caloyers décorant une chapelle du couvent d'Iviron sur le mont Athos Basilican*.

60 Théophile Gautier, 'Exposition de 1847', *La Presse*, April 1847, n.p.

61 Papety also published a long account of late Byzantine culture in the *Revue des deux mondes* and *Magasin pittoresque*. His Pre-Raphaelite interest in Byzantine work included the West as well as the East, since in 1850, just before his death, the *Revue Archéologique* used two careful studies of Justinian and Theodora to illustrate an article on San Vitale in Ravenna. See 'Mosaïque de l'église St-Vital de Ravenne', *Manuel archéologique*, 7 (1850), pp. 351–3. Papety's coloured illustrations appeared opposite pp. 352–3.

62 Didron and Durand (1845), p. xxxi.

63 Didron and Durand (1845), p. 7 n.

64 Viollet-le-Duc to Verneilh in 1853, quoted in Bergdoll (1994), p. 224.

65 *L'Architecture byzantine*.

66 Texier and Pullen (1864), p. v.

67 *Étude sur l'architecture lombarde et sur les origines d'architecture Romano-Byzantine*.

68 Dartein (1865), p. 5.

69 *Monuments de Pise au Moyen Age*.

70 Revoil (1867–73), I, 2. For Révoil, see Jorge Coli, 'Henri Révoil et les mosaïques néo-byzantines', *Monuments historiques*, 125 (1983), pp. 63–6.

71 Hitchcock (1958), p. 205, n. 17.

72 *Mémoire sur une mission au Mont Athos*.

73 *L'Art byzantin*.

74 De Quincy quoted in Boinet (1964), 3, p. 285n.

75 Boinet (1964), 3, p. 299.

76 Hébert's journal, quoted in d'Uckermann (1982),

pp. 157–8.

77 There had once been a mosaic factory in Paris under the direction of one Belloni who had come from the pontifical factory in the Vatican. This establishment lasted until 1831, and produced some mosaics floors for the Louvre. Interest in mosaic was reawakened, however, by Garnier's opera house. In the 1860s it was decided to try mosaic in the foyer, on the ceiling of the loggia, and seven medallions on the outside. The mosaicists were Salviati and Facchina, then busy in London where the mosaic revival was in full swing.

78 The encounter with Pius IX is recorded in Chennevières (1885), pp. 124–6.

79 Éduard Gerspach, *La Mosaïque* (Paris, 1881), p. 231. This book appeared two years before Charles Bayet's *L'Art byzantin* in the same series, called 'Bibliotèque de l'enseignement des beaux-arts'.

80 Chennevières (1885), p. 131.

81 Driskel (1991), p. 159.

82 Hébert quoted in Chennevières (1885), p. 121.

83 Puvis de Chavannes's first Geneviève cycle was finished in 1877.

84 Ménard quoted in Petrie (1997), p. 54.

85 Chennevières quoted in Petrie (1997), pp. 94–5.

86 Harvey (1985), p. 223.

87 Georges Rohault de Fleury was the architect who wrote on Pisa. Both he and his father Charles were devoted Catholics and edited a huge compilation of material in eight volumes entitled *La Messe: études archéologiques* (Paris, 1883–9).

88 Harvey (1985), p. 233.

89 Quoted in Harvey (1985), p. 239.

90 These and other details can be found in Larouche (1988).

91 Larouche (1988), p. 224.

92 For more on this see J.B. Bullen, 'Ruskin, Gautier and the Feminization of Venice', in *Ruskin and Gender*, ed. Dinah Birch and Francis O'Gorman (London, 2002), pp.64–86.

93 Ironically, the same palazzo in which the erstwhile lover of Judith Gautier, Richard Wagner, died in 1883.

94 Henry James, *Italian Hours* (Harmondsworth, 1992), p. 14.

95 Gautier (1852), p. 125.

96 Gautier (1852), pp. 122–3. The idea probably comes from Victor Hugo, who in *Notre Dame de Paris* (1831) claimed to be able to read the history of Paris in the stones of the church.

97 Gautier (1852), pp. 120–1.

98 Gautier (1852), p. 117.

99 Gautier (1852), p. 124.

100 Gautier (1852), pp. 119–120.

101 *Salomé dansant devant Hérod*.

102 *À Rebours*.

103 Huysmans (1971), p. 63.

104 Kaplan (1982), pp. 62–3.

105 Mathieu (1984), p. 153.

106 Kaplan (1982), p. 14.

107 Moreau quoted in Kaplan (1982), p. 6.

108 Moreau quoted in Kaplan (1982), p. 7.

109 Moreau quoted in Kaplan (1982), p. 19.

110 Moreau quoted in Kaplan (1982), p. 58.

111 Huysmans (1884), pp. 65–6.

112 Gibbon (1994), 2, p. 567.

113 Anon., 'Sardou's "Theodora"', *New York Times*, 27 December 1884.

114 *L'Impératrice du Bas-Empire*.

115 *Théodora, impératrice de Byzance*.

116 Diehl (1904), p. 5.

117 Bernard (1892), p. 2. Driskel (1992), p. 239, points out that the words 'hieratic' and 'iconic' were shibboleths of Symbolist criticism in this period.

118 Arier (1892), p. 216.

119 Denis, 'Notes sur la peinture religieuse' (1920), p. 37.

120 Denis, 'Définition de néo-traditionnisme' (1920), p. 10.

121 'Notes sur la peinture religieuse'.

122 Denis (1920), p. 8.

123 Denis (1920), pp. 33–4.

124 Driskel (1920), p. 236.

Chapter 3

1 A good example occurs in a letter written by the eminent architect George Moller to Thomas Donaldson, president of the Institute of British Architects, in 1838, in which he describes how one of his nephews had 'discovered Byzantine churches with painted wooden ceilings in the north of Germany' (British Architectural Library, RIBA: LC/2/1/2).

2 Bullen (2001), pp. 676–84.

3 In 1826 Thomas Bowdler published a version 'with the omission of all passages of an irreligious or immoral tendency'. Editions by Guizot (1828) and Milman (1840) attempted to correct Gibbon's anti-Christian bias, and in the 1890s the eminent British Byzantinist J.B. Bury brought the text up-to-date in the light of more recent scholarship.

4 Gibbon (1994), pp. 595–6.

5 Pardoe (1838), 2, p. 45.

6 Pardoe (1838), 2, pp. 52–3.

7 Pardoe (1874), p. 63.

8 Titmarsh (1846), p. 98.

9 This had first been shown at the Strand in 1829.

10 Notably Moller (1824) and Whewell (1830).

11 Hope (1835), 1, p. 124.

12 Hope (1835), 1, p. 143.

13 These were supplemented by less successful colour engravings by the young Owen Jones, including rather peculiar images of Justinian and Theodora in Ravenna and other mosaics from Sta Pudenziana (fourth century) and Sta Prassede (ninth century) in Rome. Rather surprisingly they were much admired at the time as 'brilliant specimens of lithochromatography, and exemplify the perfection to which this beautiful art has been brought by Mr Owen Jones'. 'Fine Arts', *Athenaeum*, 8 April 1843, p. 345.

14 *Ecclesiologist*, 10 (1850), p. 122.

15 'Anglicanus' (1842–3), p. 161.

16 Anon., 'Romanesque and Catholick Architecture', *Ecclesiologist*, 2 (1842), pp. 5–16. The view that 'GOTHICK IS THE ONLY CHRISTIAN ARCHITECTURE' was endorsed by its insertion into the third edition of the Camden Society's Bible for new churches, *A Few Words to Church-Builders* (Cambridge, 1844), p. 5.

17 Rio (1836), p. 10.

18 [Wiseman] (1847), p. 493.

19 Kugler (1841), 1, p. 18.

20 Kugler (1841), 1, p. 22.

21 He was one of the commissioners for the Fine Arts Commission and future president of the Royal Academy (1850).

22 Kugler (1841), 1, p. 24 n.

23 Kugler (1851), 1, pp. 52–3, 75.

24 Lindsay (1847), 1, p. 66.

25 Lindsay (1847), 1, p. 59.

26 Alexander Lindsay quoted in Barker (1977), pp. 52–3.

27 *Voyage de l'Arabie Pétrée*.

28 Lindsay (1858), pp. 187–9.

29 Barker (1977), p. 106.

30 'Lectures on Art and Poetry', Ruskin (1903–12), 12, p. 174. Lindsay's theory accounted for the progress of civilization through a persistent struggle between sense, intellect, and spirit. The idea was developed in a preliminary essay, *Progression by Antagonism* (London, 1846), which was to be published as a preface to *Sketches*. During the 'childhood of Europe', he wrote, 'the Eastern or Byzantine Empire' was 'the living link between Hindoo and Medo-Persian Europe – the mother of Christian art, and the trustee and guardian of the Greek language and literature during the nonage of the Teutonic race' (Lindsay (1846), p. 70). Lindsay's view of Byzantine work was Hegelian. When the early Romano-Christian tradition was overrun by Teutons, the hieratic Byzantine style developed in Constantinople and in turn instructed the Teutons.

31 Crinson (1996), p. 79.

32 There was, to quote David Brownlee, 'less zealotry and more philosophy at Oxford'. Brownlee (1985), p. 14.

33 Proceedings of the Oxford Society for the Propogation of Gothic Architecture, Hilary Term, 1845, pp. 4–10.

34 Proceedings, Easter and Trinity Terms, 1846, pp. 19–31; Beresford Hope (1847), p. 90.

35 Freeman (1849), p. 164–5.

36 Freeman (1849), p. 169.

37 Freeman (1849), p. 171.

38 Freeman (1849), pp. 172–3.

39 Freeman (1849), p. 175.

40 Wiseman (1839), p. 21.

41 [Palgrave] (1842), pp. 342–3.

42 Dickens (1989), pp. 121–3.

43 Webb (1848), pp. 142–4.

44 Webb (1848), pp. 268–9.

45 Ruskin (1903–12), 3, p. 518.

46 Shapiro (1972), p. 206. Letter dated 18 September 1845.

47 Shapiro (1972), p. 236.

48 Ruskin (1903–12), 8, p. 190.

49 Ruskin (1903–12), 8, p. 206.

50 Ruskin (1903–12), 8, p.120.

51 Ruskin (1903–12), 10, p. 83.

52 Ruskin's acknowledged sources on Byzantine art are few and include Lord Lindsay's *Sketches*, Robert Willis's *Remarks on the Architecture of the Middle Ages* and Richard Curzon's *Visits to Monasteries in the Levant* of 1849, which he said was the 'most delightful book of travels [he] ever opened' (Ruskin (1903–12), 9, p. 35 n.). He also read Albert Lenoir's article in Jules Gailhabaud's four-volume *Ancient and Modern Monuments of*

1850, which pointed out that San Marco might have been much influenced by the so-called church of the Theotokos in Constantinople. In an appendix to the first volume of *Modern Painters* Ruskin illustrated a piece of inlay work on the Palazzo Trevisan which, he said, was 'almost exactly copied from the church of Theotocos at Constantinople, and correspondent with others in St Mark's'. (Ruskin (1903–12), 9, p. 425). The so-called 'church of the Theotocos' or Kilise Camii no longer holds this position; scholars now look to the sixth-century Apostoleion which was destroyed in the fifteenth century.

53 Ruskin (1903–12), 10, p. 20.

54 Ruskin (1903–12), 10, p. 27. He mentions the Madonna in *The Seven Lamps of Architecture*.

55 Ruskin (1903–12), 10, p. 29.

56 Ruskin (1903–12), 10, p. 19.

57 Ruskin (1903–12), 10, p. 65.

58 Ruskin (1903–12), 10, p. 66.

59 Ruskin (1903–12), 10, p. 64.

60 Ruskin (1903–12), 10, pp. 80–1.

61 Ruskin (1903–12), 10, pp. 82–3.

62 Ruskin (1903–12), 10, pp. 84–6.

63 Ruskin (1903–12), 10, p. 88.

64 Ruskin (1903–12), 10, p. 120.

65 Ruskin (1903–12), 9, p. 183.

66 Ruskin (1903–12), 10, p. 132.

67 See Bullen (1992), pp. 109–23.

68 Ruskin (1903–12), 9, p. 15.

69 Said (1995), p. 57.

70 Ruskin (1903–12), 10, p. 98. Ruskin often uses the word 'masculinity' in connection with architecture, which for him has a range of interestingly related meanings. It is a quality of 'self-command' in the face of violence and extravagance (4, p. 139); it is connected with use rather than pleasure, and is associated with the restrained and the unaffected (12, p. 84 and 9, p. 457); within the realm of architecture it signifies honesty and may be rudely expressive (8, p. 69 and 8, p. 215); the large simple buttresses at Beauvais are 'masculine', and battlements designed for war are more masculine than decorative ones; Butterfield's recent church of All Saints, Margaret Street, is 'masculine' and direct in its forms, and the capitals in the Scuola di San Rocco are 'less corrupt and more masculine' than one would normally find on a Renaissance building (9, p. 206, 11, p. 229, and 9, p. 471); in literature Shelley is 'contemplative' but Scott is 'masculine'; and though his work was wanton and irregular, he emerged in a more 'masculine' mode (4, p. 297, and 13, p. 408).

71 Ruskin (1903–12), 10, p. 176.

72 Ruskin (1903–12), 10, p. 177.

73 I have explored elsewhere how Ruskin's account of Venice is linked to his own sexual psychopathology. See Bullen (2002), pp. 64–86.

74 *The Times*, for example, a paper that rarely reviewed books on art and architecture, was moved by the uncompromising tone of the book. The reviewer, probably the young George Meredith, drew attention to Ruskin's stress on the importance of Byzantine architecture in the moral history of Venice. 'The Byzantine style is evidently the especial object of Mr Ruskin's

affection,' he said. The reason for this, Meredith suggested, was that Ruskin was 'a passionate lover of colour, he cannot but feel partiality for the only architecture which admits of perfect and permanent chromatic decoration.' 'Mr Ruskin', he continued, 'believes the spirit of the early Venetians to have been essentially, deeply, even sternly religious, and he traces the expression of this spirit in the first buildings erected by the fugitives of Altinum. (*The Times*, 24 September 1853, p. 9).

75 Ruskin (1903–12), 8, p. 206.

76 Tite quoted in Brooks (1989), p. 152.

77 *The Builder* quoted in Ruskin (1903–12), 8, pp. xlii–xliv. The most extended attack came from an anonymous writer in a pamphlet signed 'An Architect'. The satirist was 'impressed … not with admiration of St Mark's, [but] with astonishment at Mr Ruskin's notions of loveliness'. Given that St Mark's is 'little better than a piece of architectural patchwork', he was amazed that Ruskin was 'unable to discern either grossly barbarous taste or any other defect in such a heterogeneous medley of monstrosities as the façade'. (An Architect (1851), pp. 44–5).

78 Street (1855), pp. 128–9.

79 Finlay (1853), p. 10.

80 Donaldson (1853), pp. 66–8.

81 Waring (1873), p. 212.

82 Wyatt and Waring (1854), p. 53.

83 Wyatt and Waring (1854), p. 35.

84 Wyatt and Waring (1854), p. 68.

85 Jones was friendly with César Daly, the editor of the Saint-Simonian *Revue générale de l'architecture*. From 1840 onwards Daly had been urging co-operation between architects, designers and industry, and believed in a modern style built upon a scientific understanding of the past.

86 Wyatt and Waring (1854), p. 7.

87 Fergusson (1855), 1, p. 943.

88 Fergusson (1855), 1, p. 962.

89 Petit (1858), p. 279.

90 Burges (1858), pp. 163–7.

91 Scott (1879), p. 192.

92 Scott (1879), pp. 158–9.

93 Camden Church has been demolished.

94 Toplis (1987), p. 112.

95 Scott (1879), p. 197 and Ashbee (1900–), 38, p. 179.

96 A.W. (1862), p. 230.

97 Scott (1862), p. 250. Scott seems to distinguish 'true Byzantine' from Romanesque, but his syntax is extremely confusing in this letter.

98 In the event William Burges was awarded the commission.

99 The inspiration came to him 'during a tour in Perigourd, among the half-Byzantine churches of south-western France', and the scheme that he mapped out was, he claimed, 'a completion of the idea of St Sophia: a central pendentive dome, surrounded by four semi-domes.' (Scott (1879), p. 279).

100 Blau (1982), pp. 31–2.

101 *Ecclesiologist* for 1845, quoted in Thompson (1982), p. 229.

102 Ibid.

103 Ruskin (1903–12), 7, p. 415 n.

104 Anon., 'Architecture of the Day', *The Builder*, 16

(1858), pp. 842–3.

105 Rossetti said that it was 'the most perfect piece of civil architecture of the new school' and added: 'I never cease to look at it with delight'; Ford Maddox Brown thought that it was 'the most exquisite piece of architecture I have seen in England'; and Thomas Woolner said that it was 'brilliant in effect and original'. Quoted in O'Dwyer (1997), pp. 314–15.

106 These include Prichard and Seddon's design for a general post office in Church Street, Cardiff (1857), Alfred Waterhouse in his Royal Insurance Buildings, Manchester, Henry Jarvi's New Warehouses, Southwark Bridge Road, and Frederick Jameson's Registered Land Company building, Cannon Street.

107 'The exterior', said the Literary Gazette, 'is undoubtedly Byzantine in character … [which] has probably been suggested by that modification of Byzantine found in the neighbourhood of Venice and Padua. Quoted in J. Gordon Harrison, Gerrards Cross and its Parish Church (Tonbridge, Kent, 1959, 1983), p. 7. The church was illustrated in The Builder, 17 (1859), p. 617.

108 Tite (1859), p. 37.

109 Layard (1859), p. 304.

110 Bolitho (1933), p. 85.

111 Bolitho (1933), p. 125.

112 Victoria's journal for 28 September 1860, quoted in Martin (1880), 5, p. 199.

113 Wyatt (1862), p. 219.

114 Salviati (1865), p. 33.

115 Wyatt (1862), p. 219.

116 Waring (1863), plate 97. This can also be seen in the illustration of the Russian Court in Cassells Illustrated Exhibitor of 1862 on p. 201.

117 The Times for 1862, quoted in Salviati (1865), p. 42n.

118 Parker (1861). He followed this with Mosaic Pictures in Rome and Ravenna (Oxford and London, 1866).

119 Wyatt (1862), p. 199.

120 Anon., 'On Ancient Mosaics found in Britain', The Builder, 20 (1862), p. 564.

121 Anon., 'Mosaic versus Frescoes for the Houses of Parliament', The Builder, 20 (1862), p. 565.

122 Parker (1861), p. 467.

123 Sladen (2000), p. 294.

124 According to Day (1892), p. 79.

125 Scott quoted in Sladen (2000), p. 289.

126 Waterfield (1963), p. 308.

127 The Builder, 17 (1859), p. 204.

128 Burges (1861), p. 158.

129 Crook (1981), pp. 154–69.

130 Crook (1981), p. 160.

131 The press took sides, with the Ecclesiologist, the Saturday Review, the Church Builder, the Art Journal and the Athenaeum all supporting Burges. The Builder was consistently hostile and was backed up by the Building News. The Times spoke for the outraged Protestant majority. See Crook (1981), p. 163.

132 The Builder, 22 (1874), pp. 407–8. William Lecky in his History … of Rationalism in Europe (1865) had recently and influentially described Byzantine art as 'vicious, conventional' and 'offensive to religious feeling' (Lecky (1910), pp. 234–5).

133 It adopted the title 'Royal' in 1866.

134 The Times, 15 June 1874, p. 10.

135 Mordaunt Crook's expression. See Crook (1981), p. 168.

136 Burne-Jones (1912), 2, p. 219.

137 Builder's Journal (1899), quoted by Crook (1981), p. 168.

138 Simon Reynolds, William Blake Richmond: An Artist's Life 1842–1921 (London, 1995), p. 240.

139 Quoted in Crook (1981), p. 168.

140 The Times, 22 May 1899, p. 6.

141 William Blake Richmond, 'New Mosaics at St Paul's Cathedral', Illustrated London News, 8 June 1895, p. 700.

142 The Times, 22 May 1899, p. 168.

143 It was probably the success of Keble College Chapel that prompted Beresford Hope to revive the St Paul's project in 1877.

144 Alexander J. Beresford Hope, 'Classical and Byzantine: St Paul's and Keble Chapel', Church Quarterly Review, 2 (1876), pp. 447–66. Beresford Hope, who died in 1887, was never to see the completion of St Paul's.

145 Beresford Hope (1876), p. 461.

146 Paul Thompson, William Butterfield (London, 1971), p. 460.

147 The Builder, 34 (1876), p. 495.

148 Beresford Hope (1876), pp. 461, 463.

149 Henry Bailey, An Argument for the Decoration of Churches, founded upon Holy Scripture, and on Reason (Worthing, c.1886), p. 30.

150 Richard Dorment, 'Burne-Jones's Roman Mosaics', Burlington Magazine, 120 (1978), pp. 73–82. I am much indebted to this careful study of the chronology of the mosaics.

151 G.E. Street, 'On Colour as Applied to Architecture', Associated Architectural Societies Reports and Papers, 3 (1854–5), p. 364.

152 Burne-Jones (1912), 2, pp. 37, 66.

153 Burne-Jones (1912), 2, p. 13.

154 Burne-Jones (1912), 2, p. 134.

155 Burne-Jones (1912), 2, p. 41.

156 Burne-Jones (1912), 2, p. 142.

157 Both Lewis Carroll and the Marquess of Bute also made small contributions.

158 Thomas Combe, letter to Holman Hunt, 19 November 1868, Bodleian Library: MS Eng. Lett. c. 296. According to his correspondence with Holman Hunt, Combe was in Venice in 1869. Blomfield claimed that the interior details had an affinity with 'the interior of San Clemente' (Blomfield (1871), p. 6), while contemporary reports described it as 'the only specimen of the oriental Byzantine work … in Oxford' (unidentified newspaper cutting, c.1871, in a book of material relating to St Barnabas; Bodleian G.A. Oxon. b. 154, p. 24). More recently John Betjeman referred to it as 'Byzantine St Barnabas'. Betjeman (1980), p. 115.

159 Blomfield (1871), p. 9.

160 Blomfield (1871), p. 12.

161 Bruton (1864–71), pp. 75–8.

162 Thomas Hardy, Jude the Obscure (1895), in The Works of Thomas Hardy in Prose and Verse (London, 1912), 3, p. 422.

163 Plomer (1999), p. 316. Entry for 25 May 1876.

164 Reproduced in Bassett (1919), opp. p. 66. Bute, it will be remembered, gave a donation of £10 to the endowment of St Barnabas.

165 Quoted in Stamp and Amery (1980), p. 129.

166 Building News, 44 (1883), p. 886.

167 The material on Poole is kept in his private diaries and correspondence in Hereford County Record Office (C95/B/4/Liii-).

168 According to Mason (1987), pp. 168–9.

169 Pevsner (1963), p. 192.

170 Unpublished letter quoted in Stamp (1981), p. 11.

171 This was much modified later and the dome was replaced with a spire.

172 These are in the Royal Institute of British Architects collection (CUT RAN II/N/10 (1-4)).

173 Shultz quoted in Ottewill (1979), p. 90. Ironically, Lethaby himself had never been further abroad than France.

174 For Gimson and Byzantium see Greenstead (1991), p. 32, and Farleigh (1945), p. 207. Gimson's drawing of Torcello is reproduced in Greenstead (1991), p. 8.

175 Kelvin (1984), 1, p. 463. Letter dated 18 March 1878.

176 Morris (1914), 22, p. 7.

177 Morris (1914), 22, p. 78.

178 Morris (1914), 22, p. 207–8.

179 Morris (1914), 22, p. 185.

180 It was first given as a lecture in 1879 and published in Hopes and Fears for Art in 1882.

181 Morris (1914), 22, p. 208.

182 'The first expression of this freedom is called Byzantine art, and there is nothing to object to in the name. For centuries Byzantium was the centre of it and its first great work … remains its greatest work. The style leaps into completion in this most lovely building.' Morris (1966), 1, pp. 273–4.

183 Morris quoted in Mackail (1899), p. 575.

184 Morris (1914), 22, p. 109.

185 Morris (1914), 22, pp. 6–7.

186 Morris (1914), 22, p. 159.

187 Morris (1914), 22, p. 159.

188 May Morris (1966), 2, pp. 274–5.

189 In Mcalindon (1966–7), pp. 307–19. He suggests that Lethaby's Medieval Art (1904) is powerfully influenced by Morris's ideas of Gothic/Byzantine.

190 Murray (1987), p. 225.

191 Ellmann (1987), p. 238.

192 Lethaby and Swainson (1894), p. vi.

193 De l'Hôpital (1919), 1, p. 35.

194 Rubens (1986), pp. 25, 32.

195 Lethaby (1935), pp. 72–3.

196 Lethaby (1935), p.254–5.

197 Lethaby (1892), p. 202.

198 Lethaby (1892), p. 205.

199 The Times, 27 December 1893, p. 8.

200 West London Observer, quoted in Spirit (1995), p. 158.

201 Lethaby and Swainson (1894), p. v.

202 Lethaby and Swainson (1894), p. vi.

203 De l'Hôpital (1919), p. 449.

204 Stamp (1981) suggests that the Marquess of Bute and the Duke of Norfolk favoured Robert Weir Shultz for the job, but Shultz refused to convert to Catholicism.

205 Catholic Times, August 1894, quoted in Wharton (1996), p. 530.

206 De l'Hôpital (1919), p. 23,

207 De l'Hôpital (1919), pp. 29, 32.

208 Lethaby (1902), p. 3.

209 Anon., Guide to Westminster Cathedral (London, 1902), p. 61.

210 Ibid., p. 33.

211 Annabel Wharton goes so far as to suggest that it was 'progressively defined in opposition to its Byzantine models' (Wharton (1996), p. 535).

212 It was in regular use by 1905 and consecrated in 1910.

213 Townsend quoted in Doyle (1995), p. 77.

214 He had first worked in the crypt of the cathedral in 1914 but had left to fight in World War I, returning in 1924 to execute a mosaic panel dedicated to Oliver Plunkett.

215 Sutton (1972), p. 8.

216 Sutton (1972), p. 137. Letter to G.L. Dickinson dated April 1891.

217 Roger Fry, 'Palermo Notebook', Archive Centre, King's College, Cambridge, 4/1/4. Hereafter as K[ing's] C[ollege] A[rchive].

218 These were entitled 'The Transition from Classical to Modern Art' and 'Changes to Neo-Christian Art'. Notes for them are in Roger Fry, 'Cambridge University Extension Lectures' (KCA, 1/65).

219 Sutton (1972), p. 126.

220 Fry (1900), p. 128.

221 Sutton (1972), p. 159.

222 His contribution to the 1901 Macmillan Guide to Italy was an entry on Italian art in which Byzantium was represented by a condensed version of 'Art Before Giotto' (Macmillan's Guides: Italy (1901), pp. xxxiv–lxxx), and in 1904 he referred to Blake as having recovered 'for a moment that pristine directness and grandeur of expression which puts him beside the great Byzantine designers' (Burlington Magazine, 4 (1904), pp. 267–98).

223 Berenson, letter to Richter dated 5 January 1905, quoted in Mccomb (1965), pp. 69–70.

224 Fry speaks of the Russian scholar D.B. Ainalof, whose Origines hellenistiques de l'art byzantin had appeared in 1900; the six-volume study by R. Garucci, Storia dell'arte cristiana ne' primi otto secoli della chiesa (Rome, 1873–81); and Giovanni Battista Rossi's three-volume La Roma sotterranea cristiana (Rome, 1864–77).

225 For Fry's review of Richter, see the Athenaeum, 11 February 1905, p. 184.

226 Die Mosaiken von Ravenna.

227 Études byzantines.

228 Isabella Stewart Gardner to Mrs Bernard Berenson. Letter dated 17 August 1906, quoted in Whitehill (1997), p. 16.

229 Sox (1991), p. 186.

230 Letter to Isabella Stewart Gardner dated 4 August 1907. Unpublished letters in the Isabella Stewart Gardner Museum, Boston, hereafter referred to as ISG.

231 Anon., 'The Last Phase of Impressionism', Burlington Magazine, 12 (1908), pp. 272–3. Reprinted in Bullen (1988), pp. 41–4.

232 Fry (1908), pp. 374–6. Reprinted in Bullen (1988), pp. 44–8.

233 Roger Fry, 'Epic' (KCA 1/76/2, p. 46).

234 Like the term 'proto-Byzantines', Fry seems to have formulated the name 'Post-Impressionists' on the spur of the moment.

235 Letter to Isabella Stewart Gardner, Easter Day

1909 (ISG).

236 Letter to Isabella Stewart Gardner dated 12 November 1909 (ISG).

237 Leaska (1990), p. 347. Virginia Woolf introduced the experience into the Turkish episode of *Orlando* in 1928.

238 Sutton (1972), p. 40. Letter dated June 1911.

239 *Spectator*, 11 November 1911, p. 795. I have been unable to identify the precise reference for Robert Ross's words in the cuttings collection of the Tate Gallery.

240 Roger Fry, 'Slade Lecture no 1 on Monumental Art' (KCA 1/88/1).

241 Letter to Isabella Stewart Gardner dated July 1911 (ISG).

242 Lethaby's 'Byzantine Art' in *Encylopaedia Brittanica* (1911) and Dalton's *Byzantine Art and Archaeology* (London, 1911) were reviewed sympathetically by Fry in the *Burlington Magazine*, 23 (1911), p. 358.

243 John (1928), p. 104.

244 Vulliamy (1973), n.p. Other details from Rossyln (1980), pp. 25–34.

245 This was not executed until the end of the World War I.

246 According to Fry's diary for 1912 (KCA).

247 Quoted in Collins (1983), p. 65.

248 Bell, *Art* (1914), quoted in Bullen (1987), p. 39.

249 Bell (1914), p. 8.

250 *Abstraktion und Einfühlung*.

251 Worringer (1953), p. 95.

252 Csengeri (1994), pp. 273–4.

253 Csengeri (1994), p. 257.

254 Csengeri (1994), p. 273.

255 Csengeri (1994), p. 281.

256 Csengeri (1994), p. 264.

257 Csengeri (1994), p. 271.

258 Fry (1923), p. 277.

Chapter 4

1 O'Gorman (1987), p. 40.

2 Hitchcock (1961), p. 184.

3 The most exhaustive contemporary account of this is to be found in Schuyler (1891), pp. 8–36.

4 Now Our Lady of Lebanon Roman Catholic Church.

5 Owen (1978), pp. 104, 109.

6 Owen (1978), p. 109. See also Field, Stamm and Ewing (1993), and Hafertepe (1984).

7 'Leopold Eidlitz', in Schuyler (1961), p. 142.

8 Goncourts quoted in Bury (1989), p. 112.

9 Hitchcock (1961), p. 101.

10 Hitchcock (1961), p. 111.

11 Schuyler, 'The Works of the Late Richard M. Hunt' (1895), in Schuyler (1961), pp.532–3.

12 An unexpected contemporary project for Trinity Church, Buffalo, was more authentic in its Romanesque detailing and in many ways more Byzantine in its orientation than Brattle Square. It had an interior with sheathed wooden barrel vaults and a shallow Byzantine dome on pendentives over the crossing.

13 Floyd (1997), pp. 44ff.

14 This was probably adapted by Stanford White from photographs sent to the pair by John La Farge or from an illustration in G.E. Street's *Some Account of Gothic Architecture in Spain* (1865), which Richardson possessed. Richardson himself was conscious of the Byzantinism of his design.

15 Richardson (1877), p. 68.

16 Hitchcock (1961), p. 142.

17 Rensselaer (1969), p. 62 n.

18 Hitchcock (1961), p. 194.

19 Rensselaer (1969), p. 77 n. 'No praise which Richardson ever received pleased him so much as this,' she claims.

20 The account of the European tour came from the pen of a 'Mr Jaques, a young friend', quoted by Rensselaer (1969), pp. 27ff.

21 Rensselaer (1969), p. 29.

22 Schuyler (1891), p. 15.

23 Ibid.

24 George Aitchison, 'Byzantine Architecture', *Architectural Record*, 1 (1891), p. 95. He also referred to William Weeden Babcock's 'eulogy' of this style in the United States.

25 Cram (1936), p. 33 and p. 31.

26 This was also the year that Ludwig II of Bavaria died.

27 Cram (1936), p. 8.

28 Cram (1936), p. 64.

29 See Shand-Tucci (1995), p. 84. Much of the information here about Cram is drawn from this remarkable study.

30 Cram (1936), p. 32.

31 Cram (1936), p. 60.

32 Von Gloeden went to Sicily in 1889.

33 Cram (1936), pp. 60–1.

34 Cram (1936), p. 66.

35 Maginnis quoted in Shand-Tucci (1995), pp. 288–9.

36 La Farge (1907), pp. 398–9.

37 Cram (1907), p. 153.

38 Cram (1936), p. 125.

39 Watkin quoted in Fox (1980), p. 20.

40 In 1877 Moore acquired items from the auction sale of Dresser's possessions that Dresser had collected in the Far East.

41 Zapata (1993), p. 21ff.

42 Bing (1970), pp. 195–7.

43 Zapata (1993), p. 26.

44 Faude (1875), p. 102.

45 Eventually, in 1893, Tiffany successfully employed Arthur J. Nash from Stourbridge in England to manage what was known as the Stourbridge Glass Company at Corona, Long Island.

46 Bing (1970), p. 138.

47 Baker (1989), pp. 17ff.

48 Tiffany's original sketch for this still exists.

49 Tiffany (1914), p. 57.

50 Werkel (1959), p. 49.

51 Ibid.

52 Tiffany (1914), p. 60.

53 Koch (1960), pp. 2–5.

54 These are now in an annexe of the Plymouth Church, Hillis Hall.

55 The Havemeyer family had been almost single-handedly responsible for the production of sugar for America, and the funds available from the 'Sugar King', as he was called, were more or less limitless.

56 Havemeyer (1961), p. 99.

57 Havemeyer (1961), p. 16.

58 Bing (1970), p. 141.

59 Ibid.

60 Havemeyer (1961), pp. 99–100.

61 Tiffany (1914), p. 49.

62 Quoted by Frelinghuysen (1998), p. 22.

63 Decorator and Furnisher, quoted in Zapata (1993), p. 34.

64 Schaefer (1962), p. 313.

65 Tiffany (1914), p. 49.

66 Waern (1897), p. 158.

67 Zapata (1993), p. 34.

68 Tiffany quoted in Harris (1989), p. 39.

69 Schaefer (1962), pp. 312ff.

70 Waern (1897), pp. 158, 162.

71 Waern (1897), p. 158.

72 According to Hawes (1993), pp. 105–6.

73 As reported by McKean (1980), p. 248.

74 Zapata (1993), p. 95.

75 In a correspondence with the author.

76 Many parts of the chapel, together with other items by Tiffany, were assembled by Hugh McKean who became President of Rollins College in Winter Park, Florida. His book, *The 'Lost' Treasures of Louis Comfort Tiffany* (1980), marks a renaissance in the designer's reputation.

77 Sargent Promey (1999), p. 58.

78 An anonymous critic of 1903, quoted in Fairbrother (1994), p. 90.

79 Promey (1999), p. 57.

80 *Handbook of the World's Columbian Exposition* (1893), quoted in Twombly (1986), p. 262.

81 McKay (1997), pp. 6–27. She quotes MacDonald on p. 7.

82 Smith and Warren (1921), p. 473.

83 Baxter (1922), p. 15.

84 In 1891 George Aitchison told the readers of *Architectural Record* that 'Byzantine architecture may be said to be pre-eminently Christian, just as Gothic may be called Roman Catholic Architecture.' Aitchison (1891), p. 85.

85 Goodhue quoted in Smith (1988), p. 211, n. 29. Much of my information about this church comes from Smith's scholarly study.

86 Goodhue to Parks, August 1914, quoted in Smith (1988), p. 104.

87 Smith (1988), p. 104.

88 'Murano, Torcello and St Mark's are Greek churches on Italian soil.' W.R. Lethaby, *Mediaeval Art from the Peace of the Church to the Eve of the Renaissance* (London, 1904), p. 97.

89 Goodhue may have been introduced to Norton by Cram at a dinner in 1893 to celebrate the Columbian Exposition. See Smith (1988), p. 121.

90 Kretch in 1928, quoted in Smith (1988), p. 70.

91 See Smith (2000).

92 A rather curious inversion of the labels attached to mid-nineteenth-century British churches like Christ Church, Streatham, and Wilton, which started life as 'Byzantine' and were later denominated 'Romanesque' as discrimination became sharper.

93 Cram (1936), p. 246.

94 Cram (1936), p. 247.

95 Ibid.

96 McCready (1973), p. 43.

Acknowledgements

To my long-suffering family and particularly Mollie who tolerated so many Byzantine churches

I am enormously grateful to librarians throughout Britain, Europe and North America who have provided material help with the writing of this book. I also owe a debt of gratitude to my colleagues at Reading University and to the A.H.R.B. who have supported me with research leave and teaching assistance. It is difficult to list all those to whom I am especially indebted but some individuals stand out. The encouragement is theirs; the mistakes and omissions are mine. I would, therefore, like to thank Mark Antliffe, Stephen Bann, David Barclay, J. Mordaunt Crook, Dinah Birch, Barry Bergdoll, Christopher Butler, Giovanni Ciani, Mark Crinson, Bernard Dod, Caroline Elam, Helen Evans, Christopher Green, John Harvey, Elizabeth James, Rémi Labrusse, Briony Llewellyn, Tim Mowl, Robert Nelson, Peter Nicholls, Ing-Marie Osterlund, Laura Scuriatti, Christine Stevenson, Douglass Shand-Tucci and Janet Zapata.

J.B. Bullen

Phaidon Press Limited
Regent's Wharf
All Saints Street
London N1 9PA

Phaidon Press Inc.
180 Varick Street
New York, NY 10014

www.phaidon.com

First published 2003
© 2003 Phaidon Press Limited

ISBN 0 7148 3957 4

A CIP catalogue record for this book is available from the British Library.

Designed by Lippa Pearce
Printed in Hong Kong

Frontispiece Eduard Ille, design for a Grail Hall based on Hagia Sophia, 1877. Watercolour, 52.4 x 39.5 cm (20¼ x 15½ in). Staatlicher Schlösser und Gärten, Munich

Jacket fig 131, © Angelo Hornak